D1338301

THE GOLDEN TREASURY

OF

SCOTTISH POETRY

THE
GOLDEN
TREASURY OF
SCOTTISH POETRY

SELECTED AND EDITED BY
HUGH MACDIARMID

EDINBURGH
CANONGATE PRESS
1993

First published in 1940 by Macmillan
This edition published in 1993 by
Canongate Press Ltd, 14 Frederick Street,
Edinburgh EH2 2HB.

Foreword copyright © Michael Grieve 1993

Acknowledgments for permission to use copyright poems are due to
The Hogarth Press for "The Stirrup-Cup", by Douglas Ainslie
from *Chosen Poems*; the estate of Marion Angus and Faber & Faber
Ltd for "Alas! Poor Queen" from *The Turn of the Day*; the
Clarendon Press, Oxford for "Hesiod" translated by A W Mair; the
estate of Helen B Cruickshank for "Shy Geordie" from *Up the
Noran Water*; the estate of Alexander Gray for "Scotland", "Lassie,
what mair wad you hae?" and "The Kings from the East"; the estate
of Violet Jacob for "Tam i' the Kirk"; the estate of A D Mackie for
"Molecatcher"; the estate of Will H Ogilvie for "The Blades of
Harden"; The David Rorie Society for "The Pawky Duke" by
David Rorie; the estate of Muriel Stuart and Jonathan Cape Ltd for
"The Seed Shop" from *Poems*; the estate of Rachel Annand Taylor
for "Ecstasy", and "The Princess of Scotland"; Carcanet Press Ltd
for poems by Hugh MacDiarmid; Michael Grieve for Hugh
MacDiarmid's translations of Alexander MacDonald's *Birlinn
Chlann-Raghnaill*, Duncan Ban MacIntyre's "The Praise of
Ben Dorain", and translations of poems by Iain Lom, William
Livingston and Donald Sinclair.

Every attempt has been made to contact copyright holders, but if any
material has been included for which permission has not been
sought, apologies are tendered in advance to proprietors and
publishers concerned.

The Publishers acknowledge subsidy from the Scottish Arts Council
towards the publication of this volume.

ISBN 086241 446 6

British Library Cataloguing in Publication Data
A catalogue entry is available on request
from the British Library

Printed and bound in Great Britain by Biddles Ltd

TO MY FRIEND
FRANCIS GEORGE SCOTT
THE COMPOSER

PIONEER AND PATHFINDER IN EVERY DEVELOPMENT OF
ANY VALUE IN SCOTTISH LITERATURE AND MUSIC DURING
THE PAST THIRTY YEARS, AND BY FAR THE MOST POTENT,
IF (THE WORD SHOULD PROBABLY BE THEREFORE) THE
LEAST ACKNOWLEDGED, INFLUENCE IN EVERY CULTURAL
CONNECTION IN SCOTLAND TODAY

FOREWORD

It was Douglas Sealey who observed that my father had "the faith of Joan of Arc, who would not look behind to see if anyone was following her."

The path Christopher Murray Grieve (Hugh MacDiarmid) chose to pioneer was a perilous one on the high frontiers, a trail of dizzying heights and cataclysmic drops as he advanced the cultural and political aims of the Scottish Renaissance, the movement he created from the quagmire of the kailyard.

It is, therefore, with pride and joy that I welcome this new edition of *The Golden Treasury*, a landmark collection produced in the continuing aftermath of personal tragedy, and published as the thunder of war rolled across Europe.

Despite the obvious temptation to take the easy way out, MacDiarmid's preface, which illuminates this wide-ranging anthology—including translations for the first time from Scotland's great Gaelic and Latin poets—makes no concessions to spoon-feeding ordinary folk.

His clearly held vision was that people should be encouraged to live to the "full reach of their potentialities."

For this reason he spent a lifetime fighting against ignorance and anti-intellectualism and "the incessant cry of stupid socialists and communists that nothing should be written save what is intelligible to the mass of the people, and that consequently there should be no learned allusions or high-brow difficulties in the work of writers.''

It was in 1935 that his incomparable energy—poet, critic, polemicist, socialist, nationalist, internationalist and the scourge of mediocrity—finally succumbed to the emotional and financial worries that followed the break-up of his first marriage and complete severance from the two children, Christine and Walter.

A couple of months later, despite this psychological collapse brought on by severe nervous exhaustion, he had returned to the Shetland island of Whalsay and started again on the work treadmill. It included *Scottish Eccentrics*, *What Lenin has meant to Scotland*, (later changed to *Red Scotland*), a book on *The Wolfe of Badenoch*, and *The Golden Treasury*. In addition, on the early death of his friend and literary collaborator, Lewis Grassic Gibbon (James Leslie Mitchell), he took over as editorial adviser for a series on *Meanings for Scotland*.

The various commissions and advances were often so small that the need to earn—even though we were living well below the poverty line—created a constant climate of financial crisis, and so he added to his burden by undertaking to deliver an additional two books, *The Islands of Scotland*, and *Scottish Doctors*.

It was from this maelstrom of hack work and great poetry, punctuated by flurries of journalism and brief speaking engagements in Scotland and England, that *The Golden Treasury* eventually emerged.

In it for the first time he printed a prose translation of "A Fisher's Apology", by Arthur Johnstone (1587–1641) which deals "in splendidly witty fashion" with the issue of the Sabbath and its observance—still a subject guaranteed to raise more than a few hackles. Included also is an extract, again in translation, from George Buchanan's masterly "Epithalamium for the Dauphin of France and Mary Queen of Scots", which he felt should be known to every Scots child.

He had "The Path of the Old Spells", written by his friend Donald Sinclair (Dómhnull Mac-na-Ceardaich), specially translated for inclusion; and there was Alexander MacDonald's (Alasdair MacMhaighstir Alasdair's) great sea-poem "The Birlinn of Clanranald" along with Duncan Ban MacIntyre's "The Praise of Ben Dorain"; and resurrected too were poets, some scarcely known and others sadly neglected.

Then there are the anonymous writers of some of Scotland's, and the world's, great ballads such as "Sir Patrick Spens", "The Twa Corbies", "The Bonnie Earl o' Moray" and "The Battle of Otterbourne" which sit alongside an extract from "The Kingis Quhair" by James I of Scotland, and William Dunbar's satirical flaying, "The Trelis of the Tua Mariit Wemen and the Wido".

The spread of poems, the preface peppered with ideas, and the accompanying notes combine to give a learned insight into the Scotland of independent mind.

A vital exercise for he knew—as we do to our ever-lasting shame—that Scotland is still held fast in the grip of a disease which causes a lack of will-power, and still has need of a "national awakening, a spiritual renaissance".

Fuelled by defiance and undaunted hope to the end, he despaired of Scotland's much-vaunted education with its systematic neglect, even today, of much that should be common knowledge to all in any self-respecting nation.

With a furious passion he believed in the great need, in Lenin's phrase, *to learn from the bottom up*.

> To learn of Scottish history, Scottish literature, and the ins and outs of Scottish life, the physical Scotland, and the Scotland of all its international contacts, ramifications and affiliations, the Scotland whose circumference is that of the whole world.

And to that end he encouraged a love and knowledge of a blossoming Scotland—a Scotland quite unlike the present where, under the English ascendancy, the Scots are still "so subjugated and befooled, so deceived and self-deceiving" that all too often the response to challenge is one of craven submission.

It was from Thomas Davidson, that wayward genius, that he culled what he described as the best definition of his own general attitude and purpose in life:

> I think the time has come for formulating into a religion and rule of life the results of the intellectual and moral attainments of the

last two thousand years. I cannot content myself with this miserable blind life that the majority of mankind is at present leading and I do not see any reason for it. Moreover, I do not see anything really worth doing but to show men the way to a better life. If our philosophy, our science, and our art do not contribute that, what are they worth?

And:

What I want to do is to help people to think for themselves, and to *think round the circle*, not in scraps or bits.

To think, that is one of the aims of this book which stands firm against the Anglo-Scottish perpetrators of mediocrity and cultural sterility.

Michael Grieve
September 1993

INTRODUCTION

The Rose of all the world is not for me.
I want for my part
Only the little white rose of Scotland
That smells sharp and sweet—and breaks the heart

I have sung elsewhere, and it is the choicest examples of the flowering of that rose in our poetry during more than half a millennium I have sought to collect in this anthology. But if I have been concerned with the little white rose of Scotland, I have also been concerned to ensure that its roots are given their proper scope. Those who have tried to root up one of the dwarf bushes of our white rose—on the Island of Eigg, say, where they grow profusely—know how astonishingly far these run. So it is with our poetry too. It cannot be confined to a little Anglo-Scottish margin. Recent Scottish poetry has been trying to reclaim a little of its lost territory. A study of *The Works of Morris and of Yeats in Relation to Early Saga Literature* appeared in 1937. Towards the end of his life Mr. Yeats returned to the Upanishads and commended these to the attention of our younger poets. That movement back to the ancient Gaelic classics and then North to Iceland and then East to Persia and India is the course the refluence of Gaelic genius must take. We in Scotland (a Gaelic country)—where our language problem has fitted us better than our Southern neighbours to understand and welcome the great work of Charles Doughty, and to note his remarkable knowledge and understanding of the ancient Britons—have appreciated in recent years that we must not only transcend the largely false divisions of Highland and Lowland, Scots and Scottish Gaelic. If, as it requires, our national genius is to refresh itself at its most ancient sources, we must realise that, as our Scottish scholar Colonel L. A. Waddell[1] has shown, the Edda is not, as has been imagined, a medley of disjointed Scandinavian mythological tales of gods, but one great coherent epic of historical human heroes and their exploits, based upon genuine hoary tradition, and an ancient British (*i.e.* Celtic), not Scandinavian, epic at that. At the present great turning-point in history, too, it is of major consequence to appreciate in all its implications the fact that the Edda " deals circumstantially with the greatest of all heroic epochs in the ancient world, namely, the struggle for the establishment of civilisation, with its blessings to humanity, over five thousand years ago ". This is the proper perspective of Scottish poetry, and if our national spirit today sorely needs to replenish itself at its most ancient sources, that is surely true of civilisation itself. And if someone quotes

> East is East, and West is West, and never the
>   twain shall meet,

[1] See *The British Edda*, by L. A. Waddell (London, 1930). Dr. Waddell's brilliant reconstruction is, of course, not in English but in Scots.

here, even more precisely than Mr. Yeats pointed
to it in his recourse to the ancient poems of India,
is the meeting-place, where we can lay hold of
the deepest root in human motivation. In *The
Chronicles of Eri*—which the *Dictionary of National
Biography* far too sweepingly (as Dr. L. Albert
proves in his latest edition of Roger O'Connor's
book, where he devotes an admirable essay to
the establishment of the essential historical vera-
city of these Chronicles) dismisses as " mainly
imaginative "—the great odyssey whose course we
must thus retrace, as Doughty's concern with the
English spirit dictated all his wanderings and took
him to Arabia Deserta, is shown as having begun
near Caucasian Georgia (where the story of
Tristan and Iseult had its origin), whence came
the migration westward that led to the establish-
ment of our Gaelic peoples. Years ago I wrote
that if the new Scottish literary movement which
began just after the Great War were to produce
major literature it could only do so by resuming
and renewing the traditions of our ancient Gaelic
heritage. That opened up great perspectives—but
here the greatest perspective before us, and the
key to all the others, is revealed, and it is un-
doubtedly for this that Yeats and Morris and
many other poets in the last half-century or so
have cast to the North and to the Far East. Our
Empire—the proper scope of the roots of the white
rose—is not the Bulpington of Blup's Varangian
vision of Canute's Empire (all the north of the
world) reaching from Massachusetts to Moscow,
but that vast Celtic Empire which, about the

fourth century B.C., claimed as its frontiers the Dniester in Russia (where the city of Carrodunum was constructed) in the East and the shores of Portugal in the West, from the ocean off Scotland in the North to the central part of Italy in the South, and even extended through the Balkans to Asia Minor, to the Galatians of St. Paul.

The difference—or one of the main differences—between this anthology and all previous anthologies of Scottish poetry—is that some little effort has been made to present an " all-in view " of Scottish poetry and in particular to give some little representation to its Gaelic and Latin elements. I have been able (with the assistance in regard to Gaelic of Mr. Somhairle Maclean, and in regard to Latin of Mr. George Elder Davie) to include translations of some of our principal Scottish Gaelic poems—like Alasdair MacMhaighstir Alasdair's " Birlinn of Clanranald " and Duncan Ban MacIntyre's " Praise of Ben Dorain ", and of some Latin poems by George Buchanan and Arthur Johnstone. I have been unable to cover the whole ground—unable, for example, to give any adequate choice of gems drawn from the great little-known panorama of that period in our history which Dr. Magnus Maclean in his *The Literature of the Highlands* conjures up when he says : " At the beginning of the nineteenth century quite an unprecedented number of Highland bards existed ; among others Duncan Ban MacIntyre, Ewen Maclachlan, Allan MacDougall, Alexander Mackinnon, John Maclean, Donald Macleod, Kenneth Mackenzie, James

Shaw, James Macgregor, John Macdonald, Donald
Macdonald, Angus Fletcher and Allan MacIntyre.
The splendid renaissance of the Forty-five had
thus culminated in the remarkable result that there
was scarcely a parish or a clachan throughout the
Highlands and Islands that had not its own poet.
And yet the noontide glory had already departed,
for of the great sons of the Muses, Macdonald,
Maccodrum, Macintyre, Roy Stuart, Macpherson,
Buchanan, Rob Donn and William Ross, only one
was still living—the venerable hunter-bard of
Glenorchy, who outlived his peers and died at
Edinburgh in 1812." Yet I have been able to
do a little to alleviate the painful and absurd
position Mr. William Power describes in his
Literature and Oatmeal (1935), the ablest and
most delightful book yet devoted to Scottish litera-
ture, when he says : " Gaelic has had a far bigger
and longer run in Scotland than Scots or English.
Teutonic speech is still a comparative upstart, and
its sweeping victory did not begin till well on in
the seventeenth century. A conscientious China-
man who contemplated a thesis on the literary
history of Scotland would have no doubt as to
his procedure : ' I will learn a little Gaelic, and
read all I can find about Gaelic literature, from
the oldest Irish poets down to Duncan Ban
MacIntyre ; and nearly a third of my thesis will
be on Gaelic literature '. He would be rather
mystified when he discovered that historians of
Scotland and its literature had known and cared
as much about Gaelic as about Chinese, and that
they had gone on the remarkable assumption that

the majority of the Scots were Anglo-Saxons and
that their literature began with Thomas the
Rhymer, in the reign of Alexander III." (" Per-
chance before the next century is far advanced,"
says Dr. T. F. G. Dexter in his fascinating
pamphlet, *Civilisation in Britain 2000 B.C.*, " the
history of Britain will be commenced, not at
55 B.C., the date of the Invasion of Julius Caesar,
but at about 2000 B.C., the approximate date of
the erection of Avebury. . . . We have a fairly
continuous history of Britain for nearly 2000
years—from the first invasion of Caesar to the
present day.   But there is another history of 2000
years' duration from the end of the Stone Age to
the first Roman Invasion, in other words, there is
as much history of Britain to learn as we already
know."   Since Dr. Dexter penned these sentences,
the insistence on that arbitrary official beginning
has been rendered much more difficult by the im-
plications of the discoveries made in the excavation
at Maiden Castle, and the " conspiracy of silence "
is likely to be abandoned—just as recent research
has led Scottish historians to cease to view with
the traditional unwarranted suspicion and contempt
the essential Irish Gaelic sources of our national
beginnings.   But 2000 years B.C. is a bagatelle ;
the Edda refers to exploits of about 3380–3350
B.C., and Dr. Albert's edition of *The Chronicles of
Eri* (1936) is well entitled *Six Thousand Years of
Gaelic Grandeur Unearthed*.)   Alas, the very great
difficulties of making or obtaining verse trans-
lations in English or in Scots of Gaelic poems,
which give any idea of the beauties of the originals,

have rendered it impossible for me to give in this anthology anything like a representative selection from the poets in question. There is a great field for Scottish Gaelic translators of the calibre of such Irish Gaelic translators as James Stephens, Professor Bergin, Frank O'Connor and Robin Flower ; and when such translators really get to work any anthology of Scottish poetry will speedily become a very different matter. It is not too much to say that if literary considerations alone determine the choice, two-thirds of any such anthology will be " from the Gaelic ", and every one of the poets named in the passage quoted above, and about forty others, will earn their proper place at last in the bead-roll of the best poets our country has produced.

Our Scottish Latin poets have fared no better at the hands of our anthologists and literary historians ; there are a round dozen more I would fain have represented here ; and the general position is well shown by the fact that I am able to print here for the first time a prose translation (I hope later to recast it into English verse) of one of the most delightful of Scottish Latin poems, " A Fisher's Apology ", by Arthur Johnstone (1587–1641). So far as I know no translation of it has hitherto appeared, yet it is a star piece of Scottish country life, and a poem that should certainly find place in any thoroughly representative anthology of Scottish poetry. Fresh and engaging as on the distant day it was written, it is in line with a well-established tradition of Scottish poetry in all its constituent tongues, and deals in splendidly witty fashion with that issue of Sabbath Observance which is still a very live topic in many quarters in Scotland.   It is surely amazing that a poem of such quality should be unknown to all but half a dozen or so people in the land to whose literature it belongs—again proving what gems " of purest ray serene the dark unfathomed caves " of Scottish literature are still capable of vouchsafing to the diligent researcher.   It is certainly no exaggeration to say that it is with Scottish literature as it is with an iceberg—only a small fraction of it is visible above the obliterating flood. It is too generally assumed that Scottish Latin poetry, being written in a " dead language ", must be dead too, and only a matter of arid academic exercises.   Nothing could be further from the mark.   This " Fisher's Apology ", for example, gives an exceptionally fine and comprehensive picture of Scottish rural life and mentality over three hundred years ago and is thus a valuable social and historical document.   It is a far more highly civilised work than all but a very small proportion of Scotland's subsequent verse production, and in light-running technical accomplishment, this fine bland roguish poem, so resourcefully and plausibly elaborated—such a pleasant and mischievous masterpiece of light verse—is practically unequalled in the whole range of our literature.   Not only so, but it is one more delectable example of the extent to which our poets and our clergy have always been at variance, and of that mock-serious poetic gibing at the Puritan régime which characterises so many of Scotland's best poems (no matter in what tongue) throughout the whole range of our literary history. George Buchanan (some of whose work no less a translator than Milton rendered into English verse) and Arthur Johnstone are among the greatest poets Scotland has produced—lovers of Scotland second to none, though they wrote in Latin, and second to none in their well-informed and highly cultivated concern with Scottish affairs—and it is high time they were generally recognised as such, and that their work was available in good translations in our schools and colleges, and to our reading public generally. The extract I give (in translation) from George Buchanan's " Epithalamium for the Dauphin of France and Mary Queen of Scots " should certainly be known by heart by every Scottish child. It proclaims in regard to Scotland the centuries-long unconquered possession of a cat-like vitality similar to the vigour, vitality, and strength of the common people of Spain, which survived Romans, Visigoths, Moors, Napoleon—that *improvisación ibérica*, an indefinable quality which astounded Wellington and Napoleon. Forty years ago Angel Ganivet, a brilliant Spanish writer who died by his own hand at the age of thirty-three, diagnosed the disease from which his country was suffering as ἀβουλία, or lack of will-power, and preached the need of a spiritual renaissance. All the best Scottish writers of the past two or three decades have been similarly concerned with the fact that Scotland is deep in the grip of the same disease and in like need of a national awakening.

B

About a dozen years ago a well-known Scottish
(or rather Orcadian) critic wrote : " No writer
can write great English who is not born an English
writer and in England : and born moreover in
some class in which the tradition of English is
pure, and, it seems to me, therefore, in some
other age than this ". The facts have not changed ;
I cannot see that any Scottish writer, writing in
English, has managed to write first-class work or
to contribute anything essential and indispensable
to the central tradition, the main stream, of
English literature. But the critic in question has
now changed his opinion,[1] and a few years ago
wrote a book in which he recommended his
countrymen to cast aside Scots altogether as a
" trash of nonsense " and reconcile themselves,
with what grace and gratitude they could, to the
paradoxical fact that their only chance of writing
literature of any worth is to write in English—a
strange recommendation, indeed, at a time when
we have not only the example of Charles Doughty
and the difficulties of vocabulary which have in-
creasingly beset all recent creative writers of any
consequence in English, but when the younger
English poets today " travel back some six cen-
turies to take lessons from Langland, and find in
his homely Anglo-Saxon verse a suitable form for.
their address to the plowman's modern counter-
part.   Not that the English labourer would
understand the idiom of Lewis or Auden, but
the vigorous rhythm and marked alliteration of
Piers Plowman appeals to these poets for its

[1] " Scott and Scotland ", by Edwin Muir (1936).

summoning qualities." With like motives, we Scottish poets must needs travel back in like fashion into Scots and Gaelic. Anglo-Saxon is not for us. (The revival of the literary use of Scots has gone hand in hand with Scottish nationalist political developments, and Mr. Muir might well have considered Mr. Edgell Rickword's point—that English has developed in keeping with English Imperialism, and may decline with it. Certainly in the Soviet Union minority languages have been encouraged not only alongside but even at the expense of Russian itself. This is a pointer in the right direction.) A recent writer points out that : " Ninety-two per cent of the Indian people are illiterate. . . . For Higher Education there is one college for every $10\frac{1}{2}$ millions of the population. . . . Literary education — *the literature of England, of course, not of India* ! — predominates over everything else." In the same way Dr. Douglas Hyde in his *Literary History of Ireland*, and many Scottish and Welsh critics, have complained that under the compulsory educational systems imposed on these countries the native literatures have been occluded and English given a virtual monopoly (as William Robertson, the Scottish historian, 1721–1793, foresaw and lamented would be the consequence of Scotland's union with England, instead of a rich synthesis of all the available elements). Professor Joad, for example, recently complained that so much time is devoted at Coleg Harlech to Welsh literature and characterised it as an imbecile waste of time, though he admitted that he knew little or nothing of Welsh

literature ! This is typical of what has happened
all along the line. It is pertinent to wonder to
what extent the fame of English literature is due
to such methods rather than to its real merits
relative to other literatures. Has not American
literature in recent years " found itself " by dis-
carding that over-influence of English literature
which was a hang-over from the colonial period
before the American War of Independence ?
There is a great deal more to the problem than
even this. Matthew Arnold wrote in the first essay
in the first *Essays in Criticism* : " It has long
seemed to me that the burst of creative activity in
our literature, through the first quarter of this
century, had about it in fact something pre-
mature ; and that from this cause its productions
are doomed, most of them, in spite of the sanguine
hopes which accompanied and do still accompany
them, to prove hardly more lasting than the pro-
ductions of far less splendid epochs. And this
prematureness comes from its having proceeded
without having its proper data, without sufficient
material to work with. In other words, the
English poetry of the first quarter of this century,
with plenty of energy, plenty of creative force, did
not know enough. This makes Byron so empty
of matter, Shelley so incoherent, Wordsworth even,
profound as he is, yet so wanting in completeness
and variety." In his *European Balladry* (1940),
Professor W. J. Entwistle gives, especially in his
chapter entitled " The Ascent of Ballads ", valuable
clues to what " the proper data " of perdurable
poetry have proved to be. In the course of a

comprehensive survey of those types of poetry from which the generally accepted glories of English literature are a — perhaps very ephemeral — departure, Professor Entwistle writes of the ballads and folk-songs that " have clung to life, sometimes during four to seven centuries, and that without any aid from courtly society, nor from the schools (who have adored the ancient classics and are now embalming the moderns), nor from official literature, contemptuous of such wild snatches ". Since Scottish poetry has not developed away from these great staples of poetry to anything like the same extent, it is at once a reassurance with regard to it and a warning with regard to English poetry to read the reminder Professor Entwistle gives on the basis of his vast and most thorough survey that the amazing survival and appeal " in widest commonalty spread " of these kinds of poetry is " a glory not often achieved by the great artistic poets and, when achieved, it is through some partial endowment of the generous ballad simplicity ". English poetry's development of a greater " variety of poetic forms " than Scottish poetry certainly wears a very different look in the light of such comprehensive evidence as Professor Entwistle assembles. The rôle English has played in relation to human consciousness throughout the world is well worth thorough reconsideration in view of such a tremendous body of evidence, drawn from neurology, brain physiology, psychiatry and other sciences, as is presented in Count Alfred Korzybski's *Science and Sanity : An Introduction to Non-Aristotelian*

Systems and General Semantics (1933). Again, it would be most illuminating and useful to analyse the content of all English poetry accepted as great in some such way as Professor Denis Saurat, in *La Littérature et l'occultisme* (Paris, 1929), tabulates the elements in the work of many of our greatest European poets, including Spenser, Milton, Blake, Shelley and Wordsworth. His table shows the extent to which they have been dependent, without direct recourse to or first-hand knowledge of them, upon certain dubious anti-Christian sources at variance with the ostensible course of that European civilisation of which they are accepted as among the major glories — a fixation largely responsible for the depotentization of human intelligence, and not unlike that early matriarchal control which, as Colonel Waddell shows, delayed the coming of civilisation for thousands of years, just as, in Count Korzybski's words, our "semantic blockages" perpetuate the state of general unsanity to-day.   Mr. Muir assumes that Scots may serve our emotions but that we cannot think in it. (Mr. Muir seems to give the word "thought" some peculiar private sense quite different from the sense in which it is commonly used.   Scots poetry is far from destitute of "thought" in the latter sense.   Mr. Muir's trouble is that he has never realised with Fr. Rolfe—and as Scottish poetry incomparably exemplifies—that "Life is Mind out for a lark", and strives instead to encase it in the strait-waistcoats of dull platitudes.)   I do not agree with him.   He only gives one example, and that a poor one (susceptible of a very different explanation than he supplies)—where, in *Tam o' Shanter*, Burns breaks into pure English for a few lines of reflective poetry. But in contemporary Scots verse I can show Mr. Muir scores of instances in which poets, writing in a thin medium of Scots, do not, like Burns, turn to English, but plunge into passages of denser Scots when they seek to express the core of the matter and come to grips with those profounder movements of their spirits for which, naturally, English or near-English Scots affords no possible medium. It is true that Scots is used in print for few purposes save poetry—though there has been a notable increase and great qualitative improvement in the use of Scots alike in novels and in plays in recent years, and I myself have written literary criticism in a full canon of Scots. Yet Scots is used for the full range of discourse by the great majority of Scots still (though, of course, they know English too and can screw themselves up to " speaking fine " when need be, albeit—in so far as thinking in any language is not a mere metaphor—they think in Scots and have to translate their thought into English utterance). The idea that Scots is an inadequate medium for any expressive purpose has been promulgated by the same agencies and for the same ends as the notion that the Anglo-Saxon age was a crude and uncouth period, a notion concerning which Vočadlo, in his essay on " Anglo-Saxon Terminology " (vide *Studies in English, by Members of the English Seminar of the Charles University*, Prague, 4th vol.), says, " in literary

culture the Normans were about as far behind the
people whom they conquered as the Romans were
when they made themselves masters of Greece ",[1]
and emphasises the significance of Aelfric's
Grammar as a test of the fitness of the West-
Saxon literary language for the higher functions
of science. These are, indeed, welcome re-
minders when we reflect that not only has English
pursued an Ascendancy Policy and refused practi-
cally all intercourse with Irish, Welsh, and
Scottish Gaelic, the Scots vernacular, and even
its own dialects, but that it attempted to disown
its own Anglo-Saxon sources in the same fashion,
and only the gallant fight put up by the " Saxon
Nymph ", Elizabeth Elstob (1683–1756), suc-
ceeded against the most obstinate opposition in
securing that place for Anglo-Saxon in English
Studies without which, today, the latter would
hardly be thinkable at all. Besides, Mr. Muir
gives his own case away—if he may be said to
have a case at all—since he contends that the

[1] As this introduction goes to the printer I note that
the same finding, expressed by Rudolf Bringmann in
his *Geschichte Irlands* (a book which incidentally is
throughout in complete keeping with the point of view
I am expressing here), makes a *Times Literary Supple-
ment* reviewer exclaim : " He makes the *remarkable state-
ment* [sic !] that the Normans were culturally inferior
to the Gaels ". Herr Bringmann predicts that " Irish
must and will become once more the living language
of Ireland ", which will thus regain the cultural im-
portance in the world (*Weltgeltung*) which she once
possessed—just as in my opinion Scottish literature
can only win to major forms by a like return to
Gaelic.

problem of Scots as a literary medium is insoluble,[1] involving this divorce between a language of the emotions and a different language to think in, yet he admits that at least one living poet has occasionally solved this difficulty ; and if that is so, then others can as well. Plenty are certainly trying to do so. The growing end of Scottish

[1] It is a profound mistake to disparage Scots because it has failed to evolve a prose literature and has remained almost entirely a vehicle for lyrical poetry. May not this be due to the influence of Gaelic just as the comparative lack of prose in old and mediaeval Bengali may be traced to the influence of Sanskrit where also prose works are disproportionately few ? As Professor Meiller said in his lecture on the composition of the Gāthās delivered in 1925 at the Upsala University : " The Buddhist style of composition, prose for explanations, verse for all that is suggestive and all that is to be pronounced with clearness, distinctness, and force, is not an isolated thing in the Indo-European world. It is an antique usage which is found again and again." Professor Meiller's " Essai de chronologie des langues indo-européennes ", in *Bull. de la Soc. de Linguistique*, 1931, xxxii, pp. 1 ff.. is one of the documents which, following the discoveries of Winckler and the decipherment of inscriptions by Hrozny, Forrer, and others, have helped to establish that clear conception of the antiquity, the kinship, and even the certain contacts of the Italo-Celtic and Indo-Iranian groups of languages, and their relations with the languages of Asia Minor and Hither Asia, commonly classed together as Hittite, which informs what I say here, apropos Colonel Waddell's and Roger O'Connor's books, of the need to realise that the impetus to civilisation was an Ur-Gaelic initiative and that in the Gaelic genius lies the reconciliation of East and West, in the light of which ineluctable mission of the Gaelic genius the English literary achievement is seen simply as the good which is the deadliest enemy of the best.

poetry is neither in English nor in Gaelic today but in Scots, and an ever-increasing number of our younger poets are reverting to that medium, and writing in a Scots which is a synthesis of all the dialects into which Scots has degenerated and of elements of Scots vocabulary drawn from all periods of our history. No recent Scottish poet writing in English has written poetry of the slightest consequence ; their contemporaries who write in Scots have shown a far higher creative calibre in the opinion of the highest critical authorities of many lands. These new Scots poets (A. D. Mackie, William Soutar, Marion Angus, Helen Cruickshank, and a dozen others) are inter-nationalists in their literary sympathies too, and have translated into Scots a great body of poetry from German, French, Russian, and other Euro-pean languages. Translations from the Russian of Boris Pasternak by William Soutar, from the Russian of Alexander Blok and the German of Rainer Maria Rilke by myself, from the German of Heine and others by Professor Alexander Gray, from the Dutch of P. C. Boutens and others by Emeritus-Professor Sir H. J. C. Grierson, and from a great array of French poets from Ronsard to Baudelaire by Miss Winefride Margaret Simpson, are included in this tale of recent renderings into Scots, and healthy intromissions with the whole range of European literature, which have been a notable feature of our recent literary history, like a veritable return to the Good Euro-peanism of our mediaeval ancestors. Scottish Gaelic has shown no similar movement yet, but

I have ample evidence that many brilliant young men in our Highlands and Islands are now addressing themselves to that great task. Scotland has idolised Burns but has failed to follow his great example in reverting from English to Scots ; this has been long overdue. Mr. Muir is only in the unfortunate position of resembling Sir John Squire, who thought it was a pity Burns wrote in Scots, not English. It is an important point that poetry in Scots has still an access, not only to a cultured section but to the working classes, in Scotland, that no English poetry has ever had or, to all appearances, can ever have.[1]   " Hugh

---

[1] Unlike Lenin himself, British Left-Wing critics (notoriously anti-intellectual and most incompetent theoreticians ; professed dialectical materialists destitute of dialectic) are prone to protest against learned poetry and literary allusiveness as being only for the few, and insusceptible of appealing to the big public. This was never the case in the Celtic countries—nor even in England in Elizabethan times, as the complex word-play and high allusiveness in the plays show. But as Henri Hubert says in *The Greatness and Decline of the Celts* (English translation, London, 1934) : " Celtic literature was essentially a poetic literature. . . . We must not think of Celtic poetry as lyrical outpourings, but as elaborately ingenious exercises on the part of rather pedantic literary men. Yet Celtic literature was popular as no other was." Professor Entwistle in *European Balladry*, pp. 227-228, points out that the same thing is true of the " rímur " in Iceland. " Relatively uninterested in the matter of the song, the Icelandic people were, and are, acute critics of the form. . . . If it is scarcely possible for a European taste to esteem these poems for their own merits, though we may coldly admire their intricacy, the ' rímur ' serve to remind us that there is no inevitability about the

Haliburton's " poems were cut out of the news-
papers as they appeared and hung up in cottar
houses and bothies all over Scotland. My own,
in by far the most difficult Scots written in modern
times, have won acceptance in every quarter of
the world. The use of Scots is no handicap to
international recognition. As to the usual objec-
tions or causes of disbelief in the practicability of
a return to Scots, these seem to me all disposed
of by a recent writer on my own work, who says :
" A poet can do what he pleases with language if
he can fit it to his purpose ". Mr. Muir himself,
in an article on " Literature from 1910 to 1935 "
which he contributed to the Jubilee supplement

' popular ' in poetry. . . . A ' people ' can be a people
of connoisseurs. . . . The case of Iceland goes further,
however, since it shows an undoubted ' people ' in-
terested in the niceties and subtleties of an advanced
art, to the exclusion of those ready appeals to the
understanding and senses which are normally supposed
to be popular." The significance of recent develop-
ments in Scottish poetry has been the abandonment of
the dreadful post-Burnsian practice of " lyrical out-
pourings " (the abyss of Grobianism and Eulenspiegel
into which we fell after the Reformation, and the
bottom of which we have not yet touched perhaps,
since that initial declension has been followed by the
long disastrous sway of the Common Sense Philosophy
which, in turn, has led to the terrible tyranny today
of that " omnitude "—to use Shestov's word—to
which apparently no term can be set and which indeed
may destroy civilisation altogether), the long-overdue
coming-together and intensified anglophobia of the
younger and more radical Irish, Welsh, Cornish,
and Scottish poets, and a return to " elaborately in-
genious exercises " on the part of these rather pedantic

of *The Scotsman* (1935), said : " It is in Scottish poetry, however, that the last twenty-five years have witnessed the greatest change . . . done something for Scottish poetry of quite unique value . . . made it a vehicle capable of expressing, like English or French, the feelings and thoughts of the contemporary world. . . . If an anthology of current Scots poetry were made, I think it would be found to be quite different in spirit from an anthology of Scots poetry written twenty years ago." I agree (albeit Mr. Muir himself in the volume which appeared only a few weeks after that *Scotsman* article wrote to very different effect, remarking of Scottish poetry that " an effort had recently been made to revive it by impregnating it

literary men, most of them intensely concerned with the social question and the desperate necessity of bridging the gulfs that have been allowed to develop between poetry and the people. The young Scottish poets of this new movement—none of whom have yet published in volume form (though they have collaborated in an annual group anthology, *Albannach*, the first issue of which appeared last year) and none of whom I have been able to represent in this volume—include James Findlay Hendry, Norman MacCaig, Neil Foggie, George Campbell Hay, and a dozen others, and their associates include Dylan Thomas and Keidrych Rhys in Wales, Dorian Cooke in Cornwall, Niall Montgomery, Philip O'Connor, and Donagh Mac-Donagh in Ireland, and Norman MacLeod and Kenneth Patchen in the U.S.A. This fact of the popularity of the elaborate technique of classical Gaelic poetry gives point to the contention that, as Herr Bringmann holds in his book to which I have referred, Gaelic civilisation, but for the English, might well have developed centuries ago into a model " People's State ".

with all the contemporary influences of Europe one after another, and thus galvanise it into life by a series of violent shocks . . . but . . . has left Scottish verse very much where it was " !)— though in an anthology covering the poetry of many centuries like this one, I have been unable, of course, to set side by side such representative selections of the best poems of these two relatively very brief periods to afford proof of the fact. I have not shirked the invidious task of including selections from a few of our living poets, however. The making of this Anthology was originally suggested to me by my friend the Irish poet A.E. (the late Mr. G. W. Russell), and, when he succeeded in interesting Messrs. Macmillan in the matter, he stipulated that I would at least include some of my own poems. I have, of course, had an entirely free hand and am entirely responsible for the particular choice that has been made in every case (though the selection I made initially has been greatly abridged to permit publication in the present series). I have not included work I do not personally esteem, no matter how highly it may have been praised, or esteemed (like so many most popular pieces) for other than purely literary reasons, by others.

Mr. Muir, in the book to which I have already referred, comments slightingly on " mere lyrics ", and one of the arguments on which he relies most is his contention that the lyric and the ballad are the two forms " which have been the almost unvarying staple of Scottish poetry since the sixteenth century, while England has produced a

variety of poetic forms, to indicate which one has
only to mention the names of some of its chief
poets. . . . In these the English tradition lives,
and lives in perpetual change. Can we say, then,
that Scottish poetry provides a satisfactory tradi-
tion for a native poet, when we consider that after
its first brilliant flowering it has remained station-
ary, and equally barren in variety and develop-
ment ? " The question seems to me perfectly
futile. Whatever the truth may be regarding
Scottish poetry *vis-à-vis* English poetry, certainly
recourse to the medium of the English language
has availed Scottish poets little, and many con-
temporary literary historians and literary critics
have found cause to observe with Professor B.
Ifor Evans, dealing with George MacDonald in
his *English Poetry in the Later Nineteenth Century*,
that " he writes a number of Scots songs and
ballads which have heartiness and rollicking move-
ment seldom discoverable in his English verse.
Like Stevenson, he seems, in his own tongue, to
penetrate to some parts of his nature, humorous,
satiric, which he can never release in English. . . .
One wishes that the Jacobite ancestor could have
dominated him more often and allowed him, in
writing Scottish ballads, to have grown into a
greater poet." That is the heart of the matter
indeed. And Mr. Muir would have done better
to remember that Mistral was speaking truths
neither local nor ephemeral, but as applicable to
Scots as to Provençal, when, in a speech made in
1877, he showed clearly why, to him and his
followers, the Félibrige was not a dabbling in

antiquarianism but the quickening of a true racial life : " A language is like the shaft of a mine, for at the bottom of it there have been deposited all the fears, all the feelings, all the thoughts of . . . generations. It is a pile, an ancient hoard, whither every passer-by has brought his gold or silver or leather coin . . . where a whole race has worked, body and soul, for hundreds and thousands of years. A language is the revelation of actual life, the manifestation of human thought, the all-holy instrument of civilisations, and the speaking testament of dead and living societies."

None of these things in relation to Scots presumably matters to Mr. Muir, who is not a Scot but an Orcadian, with a very different psychology and historical and linguistic background, and who has nowhere vouchsafed any evidence of any particular knowledge of the Scots language or any familiarity with its literature adequate to warrant his criticisms. So far as his deprecation of " mere lyrics " is concerned, however, Mr. Muir is on the worst possible ground. His argument about the various forms in English poetry as against the two forms which have formed the unvarying staple of Scottish poetry is perilously like contending that a centipede is necessarily more vital and more complete than a quadruped or a mere biped, and his whole thesis indeed is like condemning wild strawberries because they have not the attributes of peaches. With regard to lyrics, he ought at any rate to have remembered that he has laid himself open to such a rejoinder as that in this passage from Swinburne : " But it is useless to insist on such simple and palpable truths ; for ignorance will never understand that knowledge is attainable, and impotence will never admit that ability may be competent. ' Do you suppose it as easy to write a song as to write an epic ? ' said Béranger to Lucien Bonaparte. Nor would it be as easy for a most magnanimous mouse of a Calibanic poeticule to write a ballad, a roundel, or a virelai, after the noble fashion of Chaucer, as to gabble at any length like a thing most brutish in the blank and blatant jargon of epic or idyllic stultiloquence." Or, again, he might well have recalled those lines of Sir William Watson's quoted by Mr. Yeats in the preface to *The Oxford Book of Modern Verse, 1892–1935*—lines " to some journalist who had described some lyric elaborating or deepening its own tradition as of ' no importance to the age ' " :

> Great Heaven ! when these with clamour shrill
> Drift out to Lethe's harbour bar,
> A verse of Lovelace shall be still
> As vivid as a pulsing star.

The fact of the matter is that, as was pointed out long ago, " despite their proximity, there are no other two peoples in the world so different from each other as the Scots and the English ", and English poetry and Scottish are quite incomparable and have little or nothing to do with each other ; indeed their especial qualities are almost mutually exclusive. England may well be considered welcome to its greater range of forms when what England has made of the ballad, for example, is compared with what Scotland has made of it—a

comparison enough to give any necessary rein-
forcement to the counsel that Scotland will be
better advised to stick to her own last, and do no
whoring after alien literary forms. Mr. Muir's
whole argument indeed falls into precisely the
same category as Mr. R. L. Mackie's contention
in his preface to *A Book of Scottish Verse* in the
World's Classics series, that the reader of Scottish
poetry " would court only disappointment if he
looked for Alpine splendours in the ' honest gray
hills ' to which Scott gave his heart "—as if
England were a country with relatively magni-
ficent mountain scenery !—a remark only a trifle
less absurd, perhaps, than Dr. George S. Pryde's
statement, in the volume *Scotland* which he wrote
in collaboration with the late Sir Robert Rait, that
" distance meant isolation or at least very imperfect
contact (of Scotland) with the main stream of
European thought and progress "—whereas Eng-
land, of course, had the inestimable advantage of
being a few inches nearer.

I need not hesitate to say that I myself have
nothing in common with any of these writers and
that the Scots Muse replies to me as Alexander
Ross reports her replying to him when he invoked
her at the beginning of " Helenore, or the For-
tunate Shepherdess " :

> Speak my ain leid, 'tis gude auld Scots I mean,
> Your soudland gnaps I count not worth a preen.
> We've words a fouth we weel can ca' oor ain,
> Tho' frae them sair my bairns noo refrain,
> But are, to my gude auld proverb confeerin',
> Neither gude fish nor flesh nor yet salt herrin' !

—Gin this ye do, and line your rhyme wi' sense,
But ye'll mak' friends o' fremit folk wha kens ?
Wi' thir injunctions ye may set ye doun.
—Mistris, says I, I'm at your bidding boun'.

And the following verses from the lines addressed
to Ross by his editor, Dr. John Longmuir, put
the whole matter fairly and squarely, and, I think,
unanswerably :

> Ye shak your heid ; but, o' my fegs,
> Ye've set auld Scota [1] on her legs.
> Lang had she lain, wi' beffs and flegs
>   Bumbazed and dizzie ;
> Her fiddle wanted strings and pegs,
>   Wae's me, puir hizzie.
>
> Since Allan's death, naebody cared
> For aince to speir hoo Scota fared ;
> Nor plack nor thristled turner wared
>   To quench her drouth ;
> For, frae the cottar to the laird,
>   We a' run South.
>
> The Southland chiels indeed hae mettle,
> And brawly at a sang can ettle ;
> Yet we right couthily might settle
>   On this side Forth.
> The devil pay them wi' a pettle
>   That slight the North.
>
> Oor country leid [2] is far frae barren,
> 'Tis even right pithy and auldfarren
> Oorsels are neiper-like, I warran,
>   For sense and smergh,

[1] The name Ross gave to his Muse.
[2] leid = language.

In kittle times, when foes are yarrin',
     We're no' thought ergh.

.   .   .   .   .

Oor fine new-fangle sparks, I grant ye,
Gie puir auld Scotland mony a taunty;
They've grown sae ugertfu' and vaunty,
     And capernoited,
They guide her like a cankered aunty
     That's deaf and doited.

Sae comes of ignorance, I trow,
'Tis this that crooks their ill-fa'r'd mou'
Wi' jokes sae coarse they gar fouk spew
     For downright scunner;
For Scotland wantsna sons enew
     To do her honour.

I here might gie a skreed o' names,
Dawties o' Heliconian dames:
The foremost place Gavin Douglas claims,
     That pawky priest;
And what can match the First King James
     For sang or jest?

Montgomery grave, and Ramsay gay,
Dunbar, Scott, Hawthornden, and mae
Than I can tell; for o' my lay
     I maun brak aff;
'Twould tak' a live-lang simmer day
     To name the half.

The saucy chiels—I think they ca' them
Critics—the muckle sorrow claw them,
(For mense nor manners ne'er could awe them
     Frae their presumption),
They need not try thy jokes to fathom.
     They want rumgumption.

But ilka Mearns an' Angus bairn
Thy tales and sangs by hert shall learn,
And chiels shall come frae yont the Cairn—
———a-mounth, right vousty,
If Ross will be so kind as share in
        Their pint at Drousty.

It is an interesting fact that two poets who
exerted a tremendous influence throughout Europe
—Byron and " Ossian " Macpherson—were both
Scots, and that their treatment in English literary
rating has been strangely insignificant in com-
parison with their immense Continental vogue ;
another pointer to the incompatibility of Scottish
and English literary " direction " and achieve-
ment. Mr. T. S. Eliot recently had some wise
remarks to make on the essentially Scottish char-
acter of Byron as a poet. I entirely agree, and
have not included Byron in this anthology only
owing to considerations of space, and because his
work is relatively well known and easy of access,
and because he is of less consequence to Scottish
poetry in and for itself than as a unique mani-
festation of Scottish poetic genius " finding
itself " in a high degree through the medium of
the English language.

But for considerations of space too I would have
acted upon an idea, in which I entirely concur,
expressed by Dr. Agnes Mure Mackenzie in her
excellent *Historical Survey of Scottish Literature
to 1714* (1933) when, writing of " The Pearl "—" a
great poem, and a deep one—deeper, intellectually
and emotionally, than anything in Chaucer "—
she says : " I have described *The Pearl* at length

not only because of its intrinsic beauty and the
fact that it is one of the noblest examples of
a favourite and characteristic mediaeval literary
form, but because its author's work is technically,
so far as we know, the earliest example of the type
of verse and of poetic diction associated with Scots
literary poetry in the next century, though for
English descendants he had to wait until Swin-
burne ". Elsewhere she speculates as to the
authorship of " The Pearl " by Hucheone of the
Awle Ryale (identified, plausibly enough, with a
Sir Hugh of Eglinton, known to have died in
1381) and says : " If Hucheone wrote *Gawaine
and the Green Knight* and *The Pearl*—and the
weight of evidence is that he did—he was the
greatest Scots poet before Dunbar, and though
not such a master of technique was no mean
artist, and capable of a power of poetic emotion
of which Dunbar was not. . . . The extra-
ordinary intricacy of form in *The Pearl* has no
parallel in known English work until Swinburne,
but plenty in Dunbar, and finally, though the
argument is one that never convinces anyone but
the arguer, I recognise in it that indefinable but
perceptible quality, the mentality of a countryman,
as I do in *The Testament of Cresseid* and not in
Troylus and Creseyde."

I find Dr. Mure Mackenzie's argument
thoroughly convincing, and, as I say, but for
considerations of space, would have had no hesi-
tation whatever in planting " The Pearl " in the
forefront of this anthology. (I may add for the
benefit of those specially interested that R. Wellek's

essay " The Pearl: An Interpretation of the Middle-English Poem " in the volume of studies in English issued by the Caroline University, Prague, already referred to, is one of the best balanced papers that have been written on that thorny subject.)

With regard to bawdy verse, I have been unable for legal and other reasons to give a fair representation here to this most essential and exhilarating and important element of our poetic corpus. I have no sympathy whatever with any bowdlerisers or any of the slick gentry at fitting up ancient bawdry for " ears polite ". I would fain have included a good dose of it with all the old virility most scandalously intact. The Scots have never been squeamish in this direction, and to omit it is sadly to emasculate and misrepresent the splendid " gallus " body of Scottish poetry at a time when it is more than ever urgently necessary to resist all efforts to turn Scots into stots. Like all my predecessors of any consequence in the ranks of the Scottish poets, I regard the Merry Muses as quite indispensable—and by no means the least important—members of the Sacred Sisterhood.

HUGH MacDIARMID

SUDHEIM,
  ISLAND OF WHALSAY,
    THE SHETLAND ISLANDS

ACKNOWLEDGMENTS

ACKNOWLEDGMENTS for permission to use copyright poems are due to Mr. Douglas Ainslie for " The Stirrup-Cup ", from *Chosen Poems* (Hogarth Press) ; Miss Marion Angus and Messrs. Faber & Faber, Ltd., for " Alas ! Poor Queen " ; the Clarendon Press, Oxford, for " Hesiod ", from the Oxford Translation Series *Hesiod*, translated by A. W. Mair ; Miss Helen B. Cruickshank and Messrs. Methuen & Co., Ltd., for " Shy Geordie ", from *Up the Noran Water* ; Mrs. John Davidson and Mr. Grant Richards, for "A Runnable Stag ", by John Davidson, and for " The Last Journey ", from *The Testament of John Davidson* ; Professor Alexander Gray, for " Scotland ", from *Gossip*, and "Lassie, what mair wad you hae ? ", and " The Kings from the East ", from *Songs and Ballads, chiefly from Heine*; Mrs. Violet Jacob and Mr. John Murray, for " Tam i' the Kirk ", from *Songs of Angus* ; Messrs. John Lane, The Bodley Head, Ltd., for " In Romney Marsh ", by John Davidson ; Messrs. Longmans, Green & Co., Ltd., for " Clevedon Church ", from Andrew Lang's *Poetical Works* ; the late Dr. Ronald Campbell Macfie and the Cayme Press Ltd., for " In Memoriam, John Davidson ", from the author's *Collected Poems* ;

the late Dr. Pittendrigh Macgillivray, for " The
Return ", from *A Piper's Vaunting* ; Mr. Albert D.
Mackie and the Darien Press, Edinburgh, for
" Molecatcher ", from *Poems in Two Tongues* ;
Messrs. Alex. MacLaren & Sons, Glasgow, for
" The Path of the Old Spells ", by the late Donald
Sinclair ; Dr. Charles Murray and Messrs. Con-
stable & Co., Ltd., for " The Whistle ", from
Hamewith ; Mr. Will H. Ogilvie, for " The Blades
of Harden ", from *Whaup o' the Rede* ; Mr. Lloyd
Osbourne, for the poems by Robert Louis Steven-
son ; Mr. David Rorie and the Moray Press,
Edinburgh, for " The Pawky Duke ", from the
Scottish Students' Songbook ; Mr. William Soutar
and the Moray Press, Edinburgh ; Miss Muriel
Stuart, for " The Seed Shop", from *Poems*
(Heinemann) ; Miss Rachel Annand Taylor, for
" Ecstasy ", from *Rose and Vine* (Elkin Mathews),
and " The Princess of Scotland ", from *The End
of Fiammetta* (Richards Press) ; Messrs. William
Blackwood & Sons, Ltd., for poems by Hugh
MacDiarmid, Messrs. Victor Gollancz, Ltd., for
" The Skeleton of the Future ", from the same
author's *Stony Limits and Other Poems*, Messrs.
Aeneas Mackay, Stirling, for " Water Music ",
from his *Scots Unbound*, Mr. James H. Whyte, the
Modern Scot quarterly, and the Abbey Bookshop,
St. Andrews, for Mr. MacDiarmid's translations
of Alexander MacDonald's *Birlinn Chlann-Ragh-
naill* and Duncan Ban MacIntyre's " The Praise
of Ben Dorain ", and to the *Voice of Scotland*
quarterly, for his translations of poems by Iain
Lom, William Livingston, and Donald Sinclair.

CONTENTS

xlvii

AULD LANG SYNE

SHOULD auld acquaintance be forgot,
   And never brought to mind ?
Should auld acquaintance be forgot,
   And days o' lang syne ?

CHORUS

And for auld lang syne, my jo,
For auld lang syne,
We'll tak a cup o' kindness yet,
For auld lang syne.

And surely ye'll be your pint-stowp !
   And surely I'll be mine !
And we'll tak a cup o' kindness yet,
   For auld lang syne.

We twa hae run about the braes
   And pu'd the gowans fine ;
But we've wander'd mony a weary foot,
   Sin auld lang syne.

We twa hae paidl'd i' the burn
   Frae mornin' sun till dine ;

But seas between us braid hae roar'd,
    Sin auld lang syne.

And there's a hand, my trusty fiere !
    And gie's a hand o' thine,
And we'll tak a right gude-willy waught,
    For auld lang syne.

                                    Robert Burns.

II

WHEN ALEXANDER OUR KING
        WAS DEAD [1]

QWHEN Alexander our kynge was dede,
    That Scotland lede in lauche and le,
Away was sons of alle and brede,
    Of wyne and wax, of gamyn and gle.
Our golde was changit into lede.
    Crist, borne into virgynyte,
Succoure Scotlande and ramede,
    That is stade in perplexite.

                                    Anonymous.

---

[1] The earliest extant piece of Scottish verse.   Quoted
in *The Original Chronicle* of Andrew of Wyntoun, com-
pleted about 1420.

III

EPITHALAMIUM FOR MARY STUART AND THE DAUPHIN OF FRANCE [1]

(*Franscisci Valesii et Mariae Stuartae, regum Franciae et Scotiae, Epithalamium*)

(Translated from the Latin)

WHENCE the sudden stir that roars through my vitals ? Why is my breast, unused to the experience of Apollo's inspiration, by breathless excitement agitated, and amid Parnassus' long silent shade do the mob raise anew the Paean in their secret caves ? But lately, I remember, the laurels were untended, drooping, dumb the tortoise-shell, glum Apollo, and the lyre's inventor an Arcadian. . . . You, do you without backwardness, no belier of your royal progenitors, and like a true-born Frenchman, wholeheartedly take as your wedded wife this woman whom law has made spouse to you, nurture sister, sex servant of your command, courtesy mistress of your life, whom as life-partner to you have united her parents, and pedigree and goodness and beauty and eligible age and promise

[1] Out of this poem of 283 hexameters I submit over 100 lines—the introduction, the address to Francis, and the conclusion—including the noble passage in which, in Gibbon's words, Buchanan " celebrated the unviolated independence of his native land ". In the original, the metre is used with a remarkable vigour of rhetoric.

to obey and what, fastening these many chains
together, makes tighter and faster the fastenings on
all these individual chains—namely her love. If
unto you the Goddesses with unanimous consent
to suit you with a wife made offer—the three whom
Paris saw on shady Ida—and allowed you to join
the nuptial torches according to your free choice,
what, however ambitious are your desires, could
you ask for that would be better ? Is the charm
of exceptional beauty your delight ? See the great
nobility of her brow, what charm through her win-
some cheeks is suffused, how ripe a flame from
eyes how lovely flashes its lightnings, in what
friendly alliance harmonises with fresh youth
mature seriousness, and soft, easy gracefulness with
queenly dignity ! No whit behind her body is her
brain, being well trained in the employments of
Pallas, and, as it has received the culture of the
Muses' arts, so tranquillises her moods as to render
them gentle and obedient to wisdom's rule. If
unbroken family-tree and long pedigree are looked
for, this royal house from its one stock a hundred
descendants, who all successively bore the sceptre,
can reckon ; this is the only house that covers in
its historical records twice ten centuries, it alone,
often as it was hit by the storms its neighbours felt,
maintaining itself free from foreign domination ;
whatever antiquity is claimed for the other nations
by traditions, tales or the boldness of myth, or is
credited to them by our generation on the strength
of old records—compared with our antiquity—is
mere modernity. If splendour of dowry is what
stirs you, take as your dowry these war-brave

hearts, the Scots. Not here will I tell you about
the country's acres of fertile land, about its glens
fruitful in cattle, its waters fruitful in fish, its
copper- and lead-laden fields, its hills where is
found bright gold and hard iron, its rivers flow-
ing through metalliferous veins—enriching com-
modities which other nations besides ours possess.
These things let the numbskull mob admire, and
those who despise everything but wealth—those
whom constantly the keen thirst for possessions
is making thick and muddy-witted with deadly
poison. But the real boast of the quivered Scots
is this : to encircle the glens in the hunting, to
cross, by swimming, the rivers, to bear hunger, to
despise the variations of cold and hot weather ; not
by moat and walls, but by fighting to defend their
native land, and to hold life cheap when their good
name has to be maintained unimpaired ; once a
promise has been made, to keep faith ; to revere
the holy spirit of friendship ; and to love not
magnificence but character. It was due to these
qualities that, when wars roared throughout all
the world, and there was no land but changed its
ancestral laws, made subject to a foreign yoke—
one solitary nation in its old home still bade on,
and still enjoyed its traditional freedom. Here the
fury of the Angles halted, here stuck fast the deadly
onset of the Saxons, here the Danes stuck after
defeating the Saxons, and when the fierce Danes
were subjugated, the Normans too. If to turn the
pages of history books disgusts not, here too
Roman victoriousness halted its headlong march :
that onrush which the unhealthy sirocco repelled

c

not, and not Arabia's rough desert plains, not the Sudan with its heat, not the Rhine and Elbe with their cold delayed—to Italy's onrush Scotland put a stop, and is the only nation in the world along whose frontiers not with mountain summit, not with a rapid river's banks, not with the barrier of a forest, not with stretches of desert plain did the Roman power defend the marches of its empire, but with walls and a trench ; and though the other nations it drove by force of arms from their homes or else defeated and preserved for a disgraceful life of slavery, here content to protect its own territories, Rome built a long wall as defence against the battle-axes of the Scots. Here all hopes of advancing further were abandoned, and by the Solway water the boundary stone marks the limit of the Roman Empire. And think not that, so accustomed as they are to cruel Mars' pursuits, their hearts have attained not to the refinement of the cultural arts. Scotland too, when barbarian invasions shook the Roman world, almost alone among nations gave hospitality to the banished muses. From here the teachings of Greek culture and Latin culture, and teachers and shapers of unlearned youth, Charlemagne brought across to the Gauls ; Charlemagne too, who to the French the Latin fasces and Quirinus' robe gave to bear, to the French joined by treaty the Scots ; a treaty which neither the War-God with iron, nor unruly sedition can undo, nor mad lust for power, nor the succession of years, nor any other force, but a holier treaty, binding with closer bonds. Tell over the list of your nation's triumphs since that age and of the conspiracies of the world in all its airts for the destruction of the French name—without the help of Scottish soldiers never victory shone upon the French camp ; never really cruel disaster crushed the French without the shedding of Scottish blood ; it has shared the brunt of all the vicissitudes of French fortune, has this one nation ; and the swords that threatened the French it has often diverted against itself. The bellicose English know this, the wild Netherlanders know this, to this the Po's waters are witness, and Naples, attacked again and again by unsuccessful invasion. This is the dowry your wife offers you, a nation for so many centuries faithful to your subjects and conjoined with them by a treaty of alliance—happy omen of agreement between you in wedlock—a people unsubjugated by arms throughout so many dangerous crises—happy omen for wars and presage that to you will come victory's palm.

Rejoice ! now she is yours to kiss, and more than kiss. But check your haste. Give *us* a share of the happiness today ; *you* will monopolise all the joys tonight—and yet you won't monopolise all the joys today ! The people's disposition is determined by the ruler's disposition as much as the state of landscape and seascape is determined by the state of the sky. Let there be untroubled bright sunshine, and smiling is the countryside, placidly rippling the sea, bland, untempestuous the air. But if the heavens are cloudy and overcast with storms, the fields bear a mournful, sullen aspect, the waves are angry and the atmosphere dark with fog and oppressive. Thus to your people as a whole the contentment wedlock brings you assures corresponding contentment. Hence the present outburst of popular rejoicing. Nature, too, is throughout agog with eagerness to honour this wedding : see how the sun comes northward and daily lengthens his stay in the sky as if to behold the honeymoon couple ! how the earth puts forth buds and greenery as if to promise happiness and fruitfulness to the union ! Lucky couple ! I pray that no quarrels will shake your concord and that your wedlock will endure steadfastly and long, like the alliance that joins your respective nations. Bride, your beauty and ability will doubtless so impress your husband that he will offer to let you control his life and guide his kingdom. Be you true to the nature of your sex and refuse to exercise rule. Land, where it presents a rough craggy front, has to suffer Sea's buffets and fierce waves, but where it makes no stand but lies open, sand-strewn with a fine beach, then Sea puts away its violent moods and woos Land with gentle kisses. Ivy by clinging and obeying climbs as high as the tree to which it is wedded. So too in marriage, submission is the woman's role. Do not be too dismayed by your absence from your native land. In France you have many noble kinsmen (the Guises), there too you will everywhere find the allies of your own race, and memorials of historic exploits by members of your own nation, and there besides you have a husband who will soon mean more to you than either kinsmen or native land, and soon too you will have children to delight you with their baby ways.

[The poem then concludes :]

Grant me, Fates, this length of days—until Scotland and France, joined through so many centuries by mutual kindnesses, and by poets and by the fetters of laws, are now ruled by the sceptres of brothers and are growing one in spirit ; and those whom sea with waves, and sky and earth by huge distances sunder, unity of purpose unites into one people, unity of purpose destined to endure as long as the everlasting fires of the stars.

George Buchanan.

IV

IT WAS A' FOR OUR RIGHTFU' KING

It was a' for our rightfu' King
    We left fair Scotland's strand ;
It was a' for our rightfu' King
    We e'er saw Irish land, my dear,
    We e'er saw Irish land.

Now a' is done that men can do,
    And a' is done in vain ;
My Love and Native Land fareweel,
    For I maun cross the main, my dear
    For I maun cross the main.

He turn'd him right and round about,
    Upon the Irish shore ;

And gae his bridle reins a shake,
   With adieu for evermore, my dear
   And adieu for evermore.

The sodger frae the wars returns,
   The sailor frae the main ;
But I hae parted frae my love,
   Never to meet again, my dear,
   Never to meet again.

When day is gane, and night is come,
   And a' folk bound to sleep ;
I think on him that's far awa',
   The lee-lang night and weep, my dear,
   The lee-lang night and weep.
                Robert Burns.

v

A DESCRIPTION OF WALLACE

(Passage from " Schir William Wallace ",
written c. 1490)

WALLACE stature of greatness, and of hicht,
Was jugit thus, be discretioun of richt,
That saw him baith dissembill and in weid ;
Nine quarteris large he was in lenth indeed ;
Thrid part lenth in shouldris braid was he,
Richt seemly, strang, and lusty for to see ;
His limbis great, with stalwart pace and sound,
His browis hard, his armes great and round ;
His handis made richt like till a pawmer,
Of manlike mak, with nailes great and clear ;

Proportionit lang and fair was his visage ;
Richt sad of speech, and able in courage ;
Braid breist and heich, with sturdy crag and great ;
His lippis round, his nose was square and great ;
Bowand broun hairit, on browis and breeis licht,
Clear aspre een, like diamondis bricht.
Under the chin, on the left side, was seen,
Be hurt, a wain ; his colour was sanguine.
Woundis he had in mony divers place,
Bot fair and weil keepit was his face.
Of riches he keepit no proper thing ;
Gave as he wan, like Alexander the king.
In time of peace, meek as a maid was he ;
Whar weir approachit the right Ector was he.
To Scottis men a great credence he gave ;
Bot knawin enemies they couth him nocht dissave.

Henry the Minstrel.

VI

WALLACE'S LAMENT FOR THE GRAHAM

(Passage from " Schir William Wallace " :
written *c.* 1490)

WHEN they him fand, and gude Wallace him saw,
He lychtit doun, and hynt him fra them a'
In armis up ; beholdand his pale face
He kissit him, and cry'd full oft : 'Allace !
My best brother in warld that ever I had !
My ae fald friend when I was hardest stad !
My hope, my heal, thou wast in maist honour !
My faith, my help, strenthiest in stour !

In thee was wit, fredome, and hardiness ;
In thee was truth, manheid, and nobleness ;
In thee was rule, in thee was governance ;
In thee was virtue withouten variance ;
In thee lawtie, in thee was great largesse ;
In thee gentrice, in thee was steadfastnesse.
In thee was great cause of winning of Scotland,
Though I began and took the war on hand.
I vow to God, that has the warld in wauld
Thy deid sall be to Southeron full dear sauld.
Martyr thou art for Scotlandis richt and me ;
I sall thee venge, or ellis therefore to die.'

Henry the Minstrel.

VII

BRUCE CONSULTS HIS MEN

" I TROW that gude ending
Sall follow till our beginning.
The whether I say nocht this you till
For that ye suld follow my will
To fecht, for in you sall all be ;
For gif ye think speedful that we
Fecht, we sall fecht ; and, gif ye will,
We leave, your liking to fulfil
I sall consent on alkyn wise,
To do richt as ye will devise ;
Therefore say on your will plainly."
Then with ane voice all can they cry :
" Gude king, forouten mair delay,
To-morn, as soon as ye see day,

Ordain you haill for the battaile,
For doubt of deid we sall not fail,
Na nane pain sall refusit be
Till we have made our country free."

John Barbour.

VIII

BRUCE ADDRESSES HIS ARMY

" AND when it comis to the ficht
Ilk man set his heart and mycht
To stynt our fayis mekill pride.
On horse they sall arrayit ride
And come on you in weill great hy :
Meet them with speris hardily,
And wreak on them the mekill ill
That they and theiris has done us till,
And are in will yet for to do,
Gif they have mycht till come there-to.
And, certis, me think weill that we
For-out abasing oucht till be,
Worthy and of great vassalage,
For we have three great avantage :
The first is that we have the richt ;
And for the richt ilk man suld ficht.
The tothir is, they are comin here
For lypning in their great power,
To seek us in our awne land,
And has broucht here, rycht till our hand,
Riches into so great plenty,
That the poorest of you sall be

c 2

Baith rich and mychty therewithal
Gif that we win, as weill may fall.
The thrid is, that we for our lyvis
And for our children and our wivis,
And for the fredome of our land,
Are strenyeit in battail for to stand ;
And they for their mycht anerly,
And for they leit of us lichtly,
And for they wald destroy us all,
Mais them to ficht ; bot yet may fall
That they sall rue their barganing.

   .   .   .   .   .

And menis on your great manheid
Your worship and your doughty deed,
And of the joy that ye abyde,
Gif that us fallisk, as weill may tide,
Hap to vanquish the great battail.
Intil your handis forouten fail
Ye bear honour, pryss and richess,
Fredome, wealth and great blythness,
Gif ye conteyn you manfully ;
And the contrar all halely
Sall fall gif ye let cowardice
And wickedness your hertis surprise.
Ye micht have livit into thraldom
Bot, for ye yearnit till have fredome,
Ye are assemblit here with me ;
Therefore is needful that ye be
Worthy and wicht, but abaysing.
I warn you weill yet of a thing,
That mair mischief may fall us nane
Than in their handis to be tane.

   .   .   .   .   .

Bot when I meyn of your stoutness,
And on the mony great prowess
That ye have done so worthily,
I trust, and trowis siccarly,
Till have plain victor in this ficht ;
For though our fais have mekill mycht,
They have the wrang, and succudry
And covatise of senyory
Amovis them forouten mor.

.   .   .   .   .

I wot nocht what mair say sall I ?
Ye wot weill all what honour is :
Conteyn you therefore on sic wise
That your honour aye savit be."

John Barbour

IX

THE PRINCESS OF SCOTLAND

" WHO are you that so strangely woke,
    And raised a fine hand ? "
Poverty wears a scarlet cloke
        In my land.

" Duchies of dreamland, emerald, rose
    Lie at your command ? "
Poverty like a princess goes
        In my land.

" Wherefore the mask of silken lace
    Tied with a golden band ? "

Poverty walks with wanton grace
In my land.

" Why do you softly, richly speak
  Rhythm so sweetly-scanned ? "
Poverty hath the Gaelic and Greek
In my land.

" There's a far-off scent about you seems
  Born in Samarkand."
Poverty hath luxurious dreams
In my land.

" You have wounds that like passion-flowers
      you hide :
  I cannot understand."
Poverty hath one name with Pride
In my land.

" Oh ! Will you draw your last sad breath
  'Mid bitter bent and sand ? "
Poverty begs from none but Death
In my land.
                              Rachel Annand Taylor.

X

THE STIRRUP CUP

LADY, whose ancestor
Fought for Prince Charlie,

Met once and never more,
No time for parley !

Yet drink a glass with me
" Over the water " :
Memories pass to me,
Chieftain's granddaughter !

" Say, will he come again ? "
Nay, lady, never.
" Say, will he never reign ? "
Yea, lady, ever.

Yea, for the heart of us
Follows Prince Charlie ;
There's not a part of us
Bows not as barley.

Under the breeze that blew
Up the Atlantic,
Wafting the one, the true
Prince, the romantic,

Back to his native land
Over the water :
Here's to Prince Charlie and
Lochiel's granddaughter !

Douglas Ainslie.

XI

THE PATH OF THE OLD SPELLS

(Translated from the Gaelic)

RICH the peace of the elements tonight on the
Land-of-Joy, and the repose of the musics of the
calms winds round the Isles of Love, and active is
each wing in the stayless service of fate, while the
path of the old spells increases its westering re-
moteness yet.   Rich the body of the hills with the
memory of old days.   Happy the face of the seas
rapt in a dream of the days that are gone, the
peace upon it amassing a greater lustre with each
hour that goes past.   O days of my love, your
pride, your nobleness, your love so steadfast !   O
white days of love with your pure, kindly ways !
O times of joy with your laughter, your cheer,
your music !   Full of knowledge and guidance, O
world of grace, why have you gone and left only
the memory of the high noon of your glories ?
Is it a wonder that desire and expectation go over
after you, longing for the secrets that filled your
lap with esteem ?   Is it a wonder that the music
of the elements sings of the fame of your sway,
and that the curved lash of each eye is moist under
the darkening of jewels ?   O days that departed with
the time-store of the wisdom of my people, why
did your desire light on every ear of most worthy
virtue ?   Is it a wonder that the western firma-
ment is tonight in splendour, and that your abodes
in the far-distance are lit with an everlasting light ?

Is it a wonder that the bareness of every floor speaks of the fullness of your story ? Is it a wonder that hills have the words of the twilight in their mouths ? Is it a wonder that the harp of the songs is silent under the covering of the cloud, and that the song-voice of the bards is without spell, without excellence of art ? It is no wonder that the churchyard of my people by the sea is dumb. It is no wonder that the breast of the tombs is in swelling abundance with the worth of what is gone. O world, it is a woe that there will not return one hour that has withered, and that my desire, however lasting, will not light on one message from the sleep of the dead.

Donald Sinclair.

XII

ALAS ! POOR QUEEN

She was skilled in music and the dance
And the old arts of love
And the court of the poisoned rose
And the perfumed glove,
And gave her beautiful hand
To the pale Dauphin
A triple crown to win—
And she loved little dogs
        And parrots
    And red-legged partridges
And the golden fishes of the Duc de Guise
And a pigeon with a blue ruff
She had from Monsieur d'Elbœuf.

Master John Knox was no friend to her ;
She spoke him soft and kind,
Her honeyed words were Satan's lure
The unwary soul to bind.
" Good sir, doth a lissome shape
And a comely face
Offend your God His Grace
Whose wisdom maketh these
Golden fishes of the Duc de Guise ? "

She rode through Liddesdale with a song ;
" Ye streams sae wondrous strang,
Oh, mak' me a wrack as I come back
But spare me as I gang."
While a hill-bird cried and cried
Like a spirit lost
By the grey storm-wind tost.

Consider the way she had to go.
Think of the hungry snare,
The net she herself had woven,
Aware or unaware,
Of the dancing feet grown still,
The blinded eyes.
Queens should be cold and wise,
And she loved little things,
Parrots
    And red-legged partridges
And the golden fishes of the Duc de Guise
And the pigeon with the blue ruff
She had from Monsieur d'Elbœuf.

Marion Angus.

XIII

LAMENT FOR THE MAKARIS

" Quhen He Wes Sek "

I THAT in heill wes and gladnes,
Am trublit now with gret seiknes,
And feblit with infermite ;
   Timor mortis conturbat me.

Our plesance heir is all vane glory,
This fals warld is bot transitory,
The flesche is brukle, the Fend is sle ;
   Timor mortis conturbat me.

The stait of man dois change and vary,
Now sound, now seik, now blith, now sary
Now dansand mery, now like to dee ;
   Timor mortis conturbat me.

No stait in erd heir standis sickir ;
As with the wynd wavis the wickir,
Wavis this warldis vanite ;
   Timor mortis conturbat me.

On to the ded gois all Estatis,
Princis, Prelotis, and Potestatis,
Baith riche and pur of al degre ;
   Timor mortis conturbat me.

He takis the knychtis in to feild,
Anarmit under helme and scheild ;

Victour he is at all mellie ;
  Timor mortis conturbat me.

That strang unmercifull tyrand
Takis, on the moderis breist sowkand,
The bab full of benignite ;
  Timor mortis conturbat me.

He takis the campion in the stour,
The capitane closit in the tour,
The lady in bour full of bewte ;
  Timor mortis conturbat me.

He sparis no lord for his piscence,
Na clerk for his intelligence ;
His awfull strak may no man fle ;
  Timor mortis conturbat me.

Art, magicianis, and astrologgis,
Rethoris, logicianis, and theologgis,
Thamé helpis no conclusionis sle ;
  Timor mortis conturbat me.

In medicyne the most practicianis,
Lechis, surrigianis, and phisicianis,
Thame self fra ded may not supple ;
  Timor mortis conturbat me.

I se that makaris amang the laif
Playis heir ther pageant, syne gois to graif ;
Sparit is nocht ther faculte ;
  Timor mortis conturbat me.

He hes done petuously devour,
The noble Chaucer, of makaris flour,
The Monk of Bery, and Gower, all thre
    Timor mortis conturbat me.

The gude Syr Hew of Elgintoun,
And eik Heryot, and Wyntoun,
He hes tane out of this cuntre ;
    Timor mortis conturbat me.

That scorpion fell hes done infek
Maister Johne Clerk, and James Afflek,
Fra balat making and tragidie ;
    Timor mortis conturbat me.

Holland and Barbour he hes berevit ;
Allace ! that he nocht with us levit
Schir Mungo Lokert of the Le ;
    Timor mortis conturbat me.

Clerk of Tranent eik he hes tane,
That maid the Anteris of Gawane ;
Schir Gilbert Hay endit hes he ;
    Timor mortis conturbat me.

He hes Blind Hary and Sandy Traill
Slaine with his schour of mortall haill,
Quhilk Patrik Johnestoun mycht nocht fle
    Timor mortis conturbat me.

He hes reft Merseir his endite,
That did in luf so lifly write,

So schort, so quyk, of sentence hie ;
   Timor mortis conturbat me.

He hes tane Roull of Aberdene,
And gentill Roull of Corstorphin ;
Two bettir fallowis did no man se ;
   Timor mortis conturbat me.

In Dumfermelyne he hes done roune
With Maister Robert Henrisoun ;
Schir Johne the Ros enbrast hes he ;
   Timor mortis conturbat me.

And he hes now tane, last of aw,
Gud gentill Stobo and Quintyne Schaw,
Of quham all wichtis hes pete ;
   Timor mortis conturbat me.

Gud Maister Walter Kennedy
In poynt of dede lyis veraly,
Gret reuth it wer that so suld be ;
   Timor mortis conturbat me.

Sen he hes all my brether tane,
He will nocht lat me lif alane,
On forse I man his nyxt pray be ;
   Timor mortis conturbat me.

Sen for the deid remeid is none,
Best is that we for dede dispone,
Eftir our deid that lif may we ;
   Timor mortis conturbat me.

                    William Dunbar.

XIV

OF THE SAD LOT OF THE HUMANISTS IN PARIS

(*Quam misera sit conditio docentium literas
humaniores Lutetiae*)

(Translated from the Latin)

AWAY, useless trifles ! Farewell, barren Muses !
and the Castalian spring, favourite haunt of
Apollo's choir ! Away with you ! I've had
enough of you—I've passed youth in your com-
pany and the best years of my life have been wasted.
Seek someone who sees attractiveness in a life of
song in hungry solitude ; seek someone who can
write lyrics with nothing to drink but water.
With sweet blandishments you seduce raw youth
into following the alluring lyre's unmilitary
strains. Properly the age for soldiering, youth
becomes listless in an enervating retreat, and
drains away, robbed of its strength by lazy
rhythms. Prematurely, a disillusioned old age
drags along a twisted frame ; there is the threat of
death's approach accelerated, prematurely. Pale-
ness stains the cheeks, emaciation is throughout
the whole body, and in the gloomy face sits the
image of death. Seek to win leisure, and you
rush headlong among a thousand toils, and find
yourself tortured by new and ever new worries.
At night the ditcher is freed from the chain and
enjoys easy slumbers, and in mid-ocean the sailor
takes a rest. At night the worn-out ploughman

enjoys easy slumbers, at night peace sometimes
falls on the winds and the Ionian sea. But at
night you must inhale a grimy lamp's soot-reek
even if it is a mere camp-follower of Calliope that
you think to be, and as if you were guarding the
boughs bent by the gold's weight—the apples that
were the destined prey of Hercules' hand—
staying awake till dawn, you will read, re-read,
and reflect, and rummage through manuscripts
buried in crumbling decay. Often you will
scratch your head and bite your nails to the
quick, with angry hand you will often strike the
desk. It's this that causes sudden deaths and
destroys hopes of seeing old age, and neither Clio
nor Phoebus helps one here. If the head sinks
down with tired neck on the elbow and scant sleep
shuts the weary eyes, hark ! the watchman sud-
denly announces it's four o'clock, and with
terrifying peals disturbs the closed eyes : thunder-
struck as you are, the piercing bronze's sound
shakes sleepiness away and gives warning to lift
limbs from the soft couch. There's barely a
silence, when five o'clock sounds ; now the porter
clashes the cymbals, summoning the raw recruits
to their standards. Soon the master follows them
in, fearsome in his long gown, from his left
shoulder his satchel hangs against his back. In
his right hand is his weapon for attacking the lads
—the cruel tawse ; his left hand grasps great
Virgil's stirring work. Now he is in his chair and
shouting loud enough to burst his lungs ; he
proceeds with all his wits to examine the compli-
cated passages, he emends and deletes, alters, the

points he has worked on while others slept he clearly explains—points which have long been doubtful and hidden. Important facts, facts discovered not by the previous age's wits he digs out, and does not hide away for his own use the treasures he has found. In the meantime the lazy young men for the most part snore, or else many things take priority in their thoughts over the work before them. One is absent, there is a search for another who has bribed a neighbour to call his name, and by cleverness to make the teacher swallow the wily pretence. This fellow has no boots ; in one of that man's shoes a hole yawns wide where the leather has burst ; another has a pain and another is writing home. Hence rods and roarings sound, and cheeks are wet with tears and there's nothing but sobbing all day long. Next a religious service summons us, then lessons again—and blows again ; there is hardly any time allowed for taking a meal. No sooner is the table removed than a lesson begins, and this lesson is succeeded in its turn by another ; then a hasty supper—we rise and prolong our unconscionable work till late at night—as if the hours of day-light had been too short for really hard work. Why should I mention just now our toils' thousand scunners which a free spirit one would think oughtn't to have to suffer ? See the solid phalanxes of " galoches " from the city : the ground trembles under the tramp of their iron-shod heels ; in rushes the mob and lends to the lesson stolid ears—ears such as of yore Phrygian Marsyas directed to Phoebus' lyre—and complains that street corners have not been posted with placards, that their old friend Alexander is held in no honour, that the text-book is not big-bellied with full marginal notes, and that Guido's worthless manual is neglected and suppressed. Off they run with loud murmuring to Montaigne or some other college where things are near the A B C level. Why should I recount how often Orestes' passion is defended or the number of times that their verses are unmetrical? Because there's no throbbing in the left side of the youthful bumpkin's chest, both parents grow angry and clamorous; they complain of the years passing without producing any fruit and that all their expenditure has long been wasted; but they don't use a similar scale to weigh our labours, and repay loss of time with no emolument. Add that poverty marches in the company of the Muses, never quitting their side, and is a soldier in the Muses' camp, whether you sing of armies ready for fighting with the Turks, or write tender verses for the sweet-toned lyre to accompany, or woo the people's gaze with sportive Sock or bombastically sweep the ground with tragic robe—whatever line, in short, you pursue, unconscionable want stays by your side as a comrade—whether you are writing poetry or teaching poetry. Seven cities put in rival claims to be Homer's native land, but while he lived he had no home, far less native place. Ailing and penniless, Virgil weeps for the loss of his father's farm; Statius barely by recourse to his art escapes the onset of hunger. Ovid, cast forth in exile to Northern regions, blames his

banishment on the muses. The very god of bards
is believed to have been a cow-herd at Pherae, and
to have counted flocks in Haemonian plains. Why
has Calliope lived her length of days in spinster-
hood ? Because she has never had anything to
reckon on as making up her dowry. Meanwhile
life slips past with swift pace, and slow-moving
age complains how hard hunger is to bear and
laments the idle pursuits wherewith it amused
itself in youth and sorrows that its seeds were
cast on deceitful soil and that no money has been
gathered to aid ripe old age on its journey and that
its ship no longer finds harbours easy of access.
Away, therefore, barren Muses ! and seek someone
else to do your bidding : as for me, my lot as well
as my will summons me elsewhere.

George Buchanan.

XV

THE FLOWERS OF THE FOREST

I've heard the lilting at our yowe-milking,
  Lasses a-lilting before the dawn o' day ;
But now they are moaning in ilka green loaning :
  " The Flowers of the Forest are a' wede away."

At buchts in the morning, nae blythe lads are
      scorning ;
  The lasses are lonely, and dowie, and wae ;
Nae daffin', nae gabbin', but sighing and sabbing :
  Ilk ane lifts her leglen and hies her away.

In hairst, at the shearing, nae youths now are
      jeering,
  The bandsters are lyart, and runkled and grey ;
At fair or at preaching, nae wooing, nae fleeching :
  " The Flowers of the Forest are a' wede away."

At e'en, in the gloaming, nae swankies are
      roaming
  'Bout stacks wi' the lasses at bogle to play,
But ilk ane sits drearie, lamenting her dearie :
  " The Flowers of the Forest are a' wede away."

Dule and wae for the order sent our lads to the
      Border ;
  The English, for ance, by guile won the day ;
The Flowers of the Forest, that foucht aye the
      foremost,
  The prime o' our land, are cauld in the clay.

We'll hear nae mair lilting at the yowe-milking,
  Women and bairns are heartless and wae ;
Sighing and moaning on ilka green loaning ;
  " The Flowers of the Forest are a' wede away."
Jean Elliot.

XVI

THE BLADES OF HARDEN

(From *Whaup o' the Rede*)

Ho ! for the blades of Harden !
  Ho ! for the driven kye !
The broken gate and the lances' hate,
  And a banner red on the sky !

The rough road runs by the Carter ;
   The white foam creams on the rein ;
Ho ! for the blades of Harden !
   " There will be moonlight again."

The dark has heard them gather,
   The dawn has bowed them by,
To the guard on the roof comes the drum of a
       hoof
   And the drone of a hoof's reply.
There are more than birds on the hill tonight,
And more than winds on the plain !
The threat of the Scotts has filled the moss,
   " There will be moonlight again."

Ho ! for the blades of Harden !
   Ho ! for the ring of steel !
The stolen steers of a hundred years
   Come home for a Kirkhope meal !
The ride must risk its fortune,
   The raid must count its slain,
The March must feed her ravens,
   " There will be moonlight again ! "

Ho ! for the blades of Harden !
   Ho ! for the pikes that cross !
Ho ! for the king of lance and ling
   —A Scott on the Ettrick moss !
The rough road runs by the Carter,
   The white foam creams on the rein ;
And aye for the blades of Harden
   " There will be moonlight again ! "
                Will. H. Ogilvie.

XVII

THE DAY OF INVERLOCHY

(Translated from the Gaelic)

HAVE you heard of the manly turning taken by the camp that was in Cille Chuimein ? Far went the fame of their treatment of the foes they put to flight.

I ascended early on the Sunday morning to the top of the castle of Inverlochy. I saw the whole affair, and the battle's triumph was with Clan Donald.

Climbing up the slope of Cul-Eachaidh, I knew you were in the full inspiration of your valour. Although my country was in flames, a requital for that was the outcome of your action.

Even though the estate of the Brae were to remain for seven years as it is now, without sowing, harrowing, or cultivation, still good would be the interest with which we now are paid.

As for your side, Lord of Lawers, though great your boast in your sword, many is the young man of your father's clan now in Inverlochy lying.

Many's the man of gorget and pillion, as good as was ever of your clan, that was not suffered to take his boots over dry, but was taught to swim on Bun Nibheis.

A tale most joyful to receive of the Campbells of the wry mouths—every troop of them as they came having their heads broken under the blows of the swords.

On the day they had reckoned to triumph, they were being chased on the ice, and many a big dun sloucher of them was lying in Ach' an Todhair.

Whoso climbed Tom na-h-aire? Many were the new paws there badly salted, the death-cloud on their eyes, lifeless after being scourged with sword-blades.

You made a hot fray about Lochy, striking them on the noses. Many were the blue-fluted even swords striking in the hands of Clan Donald.

When gathered the great trouble of the blood-feud, in time of unsheathing the thin blades, the nails of the Campbells were to the earth after their sinews' cutting.

Many is the naked corpse without clothing that is lying on Cnoc an Fhraoiche from the field where the heroes hastened to the end of Litir Blar a' Chaorainn.

I'd tell another tale with truth, as well as clerk can write. Those heroes went to their utmost and they made the men they hated erupt like water in rout.

John of Moidart of the bright sails that would sail the ocean on a dark day, there was no tryst-breaking with you ! And joyful to me was the news of Barbreck in your power.

That was no unlucky journey that brought Alasdair to Alba, plundering, burning and slaying, and he laid down the Cock of Strathbogie.

> The bad bird that lost his comeliness
> In England and Scotland and Ireland,
> A feather is he of the wing's corner,
> I am not the worse of it that he yielded !

Alasdair of the sharp biting blades, you promised yesterday to destroy them. You put the rout past the Castle, guiding right well the pursuit.

Alasdair of the sharp galling blades, if you had had Mull's heroes with you, you had made those who escaped of them wait, while the rabble of the dulse retreated.

Alasdair, noble son of Colla, right hand for cleaving the castles, you put rout on the grey Saxons and if they drank kail-broth you emptied it out of them.

Did you know the Goirtein Odhar ? Well was

it manured, not with dung of sheep or goats, but
with blood of Campbells frozen !

Curse you if I pity your condition, listening to
the distress of your children, wailing for the band
that was in the battlefield, the howling of the
women of Argyle !

Iain Lom.

XVIII

LINES ON THE EXECUTION OF KING
CHARLES I

GREAT, good, and just, could I but rate
My grief, and thy too rigid fate,
I'd weep the world in such a strain
As it should deluge once again.
But since thy loud-tongued blood demands supplies
More from Briareus' hands than Argus' eyes,
I'll sing thine obsequies with trumpet sounds,
And write thine epitaph in blood and wounds.

James Graham, Marquis of Montrose.

XIX

IN THE HIGHLANDS

IN the highlands, in the country places,
Where the old plain men have rosy faces,
    And the young fair maidens
        Quiet eyes ;

Where essential silence chills and blesses,
And for ever in the hill-recesses
　　Her more lovely music
　　　Broods and dies—

O to mount again where erst I haunted ;
Where the old red hills are bird-enchanted,
　　And the low green meadows
　　　Bright with sward ;
And when even dies, the million-tinted,
And the night has come, and planets glinted,
　　Lo, the valley hollow
　　　Lamp-bestarr'd !

O to dream, O to awake and wander
There, and with delight to take and render,
　　Through the trance of silence,
　　　Quiet breath !
Lo ! for there, among the flowers and grasses,
Only the mightier movement sounds and passes ;
　　Only winds and rivers,
　　　Life and death.
　　　　　　　Robert Louis Stevenson.

XX

SCOTLAND

Here in the uplands
The soil is ungrateful ;
The fields, red with sorrel,
Are stony and bare.

A few trees, wind-twisted—
Or are they but bushes ?—
Stand stubbornly guarding
A home here and there.

Scooped out like a saucer,
The land lies before me ;
The waters, once scattered,
Flow orderedly now
Through fields where the ghosts
Of the marsh and the moorland
Still ride the old marches,
Despising the plough.

The marsh and the moorland
Are not to be banished ;
The bracken and heather,
The glory of broom,
Usurp all the balks
And the fields' broken fringes,
And claim from the sower
Their portion of room.

This is my country,
The land that begat me.
These windy spaces
Are surely my own.
And those who here toil
In the sweat of their faces
Are flesh of my flesh,
And bone of my bone.

D

Hard is the day's task
Scotland, stern Mother—
Wherewith at all times
Thy sons have been faced :
Labour by day,
And scant rest in the gloaming
With Want an attendant,
Not lightly outpaced.

Yet do thy children
Honour and love thee.
Harsh is thy schooling,
Yet great is the gain :
True hearts and strong limbs,
The beauty of faces,
Kissed by the wind
And caressed by the rain.
                              Alexander Gray.

XXI

COMPLAINT OF THE COMMON WEILL OF SCOTLAND

AND thus as we were talking to and fro
We saw a busteous berne come owre the bent,
But horse, on fute, as fast as he micht go,
Whose raiment was all raggit, riven and rent,
With visage lean, as he had fastit Lent :
And forwart fast his wayis he did advance,
With ane richt malancolious countenance.

With scrip on hip, and pykestaff in his hand,
As he had purposit to pass fra hame.
Quod I : " Gude man, I wald fain understand,
Gif that ye plesit, to wit what were your name ? "
Quod he : " My son, of that I think great shame ;
Bot sen thou wald of my name have ane feill,
Forsooth, they call me John the Common weill ".

" Schir Common weill, who has you so disguisit ? "
Quod I : " or what makis you so miserabill ?
I have marvel to see you so supprysit,
The whilk that I have seen so honorabill.
To all the warld ye have been profitable,
And weill honorit in everilk natioun :
How happenis, now, your tribulatioun ? "

" Allace ! " quod he, " thou sees how it does stand
With me, and how I am disherisit
Of all my grace, and mon pass of Scotland,
And go, afore whare I was cherisit.
Remain I here, I am bot perisit ;
For there is few to me that takis tent,
That garris me go so raggit, riven and rent.

" My tender friendis are all put to flycht ;
For Policy is fled again to France.
My sister, Justice, almost hath tint her sicht,
That she can nocht hold evenly the balance.
Plain wrang is plain capitane of Ordinance,
The whilk debarris Lawtie and Reason,
And small remeid is found for open treason.

" Into the South, allace, I was near slain :
Owre all the land I culd find no relief ;
Almost betwixt the Merse and Lochmabane
I culd nocht knaw ane leill man be ane thief.
To schaw their reif, thift, murder, and mischief,
And vicious werkis, it wald infect the air :
And als langsum to me for to declare.

" Into the Highland I culd find no remeid,
Bot suddenly I was put to exile.
Tha sweir swyngeoris they took of me none heed,
Nor amangs them let me remain ane while.
Als, in the out Ilis and in Argyle,
Unthrift, sweirness, falset, poverty and strife
Put Policy in danger of her life.

" In the Lawland I come to seek refuge,
And purposit there to mak my residence ;
Bot singular profit gart me soon disluge,
And did me great injuries and offence,
And said to me : ' Swith, harlot, hie thee hence :
And in this country see thou tak no curis,
Sa lang as my auctoritie enduris.

" ' Therefore, adieu, I may no langer tarry.' "
" Fare weill ", quod I, and with Sanct John to
    borrow.
Bot wit ye weill my heart was wonder sarye,
When Common weill so sopit was in sorrow.
Yit after the nicht comis the glad morrow ;
" Wharefore, I pray you, shaw me in certain,
When that ye purpose for to come again."

" That questioun, it sall be soon decidit ",
Quod he : " thare sall na Scot have comforting
Of me, till that I see the country guidit
By wisdom of ane gude, auld prudent king,
Whilk sall delight him maist abune all thing,
To put justice till executioun,
And on strang traitouris mak punitioun.

" Als yet to thee I say ane other thing :
I see richt weill that proverb is full true.
Woe to the realm that has owre young a king."
With that he turnit his back and said " adieu ".
Over firth and fell richt fast fra me he flew,
Whose departing to me was displesand.
With that, Remembrance took me by the hand.

And soon, me thocht, she brocht me to the roche,
And to the cove where I began to sleep.
With that ane ship did speedily approach,
Full plesandlie sailing upon the deep ;
And syne did slack her sailis, and gan to creep
Towart the land, anent where that I lay :
Bot, wit you weill, I gat ane felloun fray.

All her cannounis she let crack off at onis :
Down shook the streameris from the top-castell ;
They sparit nocht the poulder nor the stonis ;
They shot their boltis and doun their anchoris
    fell ;
The marineris they did so youte and yell,
That hastily I stert out of my dream,
Half in ane fray, and speedily past hame.

And lichtly dinit, with lyste and appetite,
Syne efter, past intil ane oritore,
And took my pen, and than began to write
All the visioun that I have shawin before.
Sir, of my dream as now thou gettis no more,
Bot I beseik God for to send thee grace
To rule thy realm in unity and peace.

Sir David Lyndsay.

XXII

FREEDOM

A ! FREDOME is a noble thing !
Fredome maiss man to have liking :
Fredome all solace to man givis :
He livis at ease that freely livis !
A noble heart may have nane ease,
Na ellis nocht that may him please,
Gif fredome failye ; for free liking
Is yearnit owre all other thing.
Na he, that ay has livit free,
May nocht knaw weill the propertie,
The anger, na the wrechit doom,
That is couplit to foul thralldom.
Bot gif he had assayit it,
Than all perquer he suld it wit ;
And suld think fredome mair to prize
Than all the gold in warld that is.

John Barbour.

· XXIII

THE PRAISE OF BEN DORAIN [1]

URLAR

OVER mountains, pride
Of place to Ben Dorain !
I've nowhere espied
A finer to reign.
In her moorbacks wide
Hosts of shy deer bide ;
While light comes pouring
Diamond-wise from her side.

Grassy glades are there
With boughs light-springing,
Where the wild herds fare
(Of these my singing !),
Like lightning flinging
Their heels on the air
Should the wind be bringing
Any hint to beware.

Swift is each spirited one
Clad in a fine fitting
Skin that shines like the sun
Of its glory unwitting.
Like a banner when they run
Of flame-red is their flitting.
A clever deed would be done
A shot in these small bellies getting.

[1] Translated from the Gaelic by Hugh MacDiarmid

It calls for a prime gun
In a young man's gripping
—A flint with a breach-run
And trigger hard-clipping
On the hammer with none
Of hesitation or slipping ;
A sound-stocked eight-sided one
To catch a stag skipping.

Yet one born for the game,
The man to outwit them,
Who whene'er he took aim
Was certain to hit them,
Lived here, Patrick by name,
Swiftly though when he came
With his boys and dogs they might flit them.

SIUBHAL

Keenest of careering
Of smelling and hearing
Is the little hind rearing
Among the peaks, peering
Along the wind, fearing
Whatever is nearing,
Lightly the ground clearing
'Mid summits sky-shearing,
But never descending
Where a ball might be rending
Past mending, or ending,
The grace she is tending
Here where it's blending
With the light to which, wending,

She seems to be lending
More than the sun's sending.

She makes no complaining
Of any speed straining
The mettle obtaining
In one that's not waning
From the standard pertaining
To a breed that has lain in
These high tops each aeon in
Since Time began feigning
Eternity's reign in
A separate rule to be gaining.

I love when she stretches
Her breath and the wind fetches
A ghost of her bellowing,
But it's not for us wretches
Of men that the mellowing
Call sounds o'er the vetches
As she seeks her listening
Lover in rutting-time, glistening
With loving-kindness.
His no deafness nor blindness,
The stag of the proud head tapering,
White-flash-buttocked one, capering,
High-stepper showing his paces
With reverberant roaring.
He's always on Ben Dorain
And knows all her choice places.

It would be a masterpiece
To tell all the stags one sees

Here on Ben Dorain, and with these
Every hind going at ease,
Slim, neat, a sight to please,
With her fawns by her knees,
Or all with white tails on the breeze
Filing up through the passes.

Start yon one on the edge
Of Harper's Corrie ; I'll pledge
Hardly a man in the kingdom
But would need to sing dumb
Telling truth of his trying
To follow her fast flying
That of her hoofs on the grass
Puts scarce a flick as they pass.

On a lush level straying
A fair band of them playing,
Quick-footed, cunning,
Restless, age on their running
No weight will be laying,
No sorrow essaying
To shadow their sunning ;
No mental troubles are theirs,
Aching hearts or sad cares.

They owe their glossy
Coats to the cosy
Forest quiet and mossy
So broad and bossy.
—At peace there toss you
Where scarce man knows you
Nor dangers engross you,

Free heads and clean bodies
Wholesome as the sod is
To whose bounty all owed is
Your sleek flesh that no load is !

It's lush àsainn that's keeping
The breast to the fawns—leaping
Speckled ones !—heaping
Them invisibly deep in
Warmth that, though sleeping
In the rude waste, can creep in
No least twinge of cramp
From the cold wind or damp.

To milk of the club-rush they're owing
What keeps their lives going
Pure as the hill-streams' flowing.
It holds their hearts glowing ;
Even in nights of wild snowing
In no house they'd be stowing
But in Corrie Altrum, showing
There's still snug beds for knowing
Among the bare jutting rocks
For creatures the right food stocks ;
Finding by the Fall of the Fairies
What subtle shelter there is
No one less groundwise and windwise
Than they ever descries.

URLAR

The hind as she should be
  Is in the forest

Where there's plenty free
    Of the food that's fittest.
Hill-grass bladed cleanly
    She will eat with zest ;
Club-rush, heath-rush, juicy,
    Of rare virtues possessed,
Cunning with right fat to see
    Her kidneys drest ;
Watercress more highly
    Than wine assessed.
She fares contentedly
    On all that is best ;
Cultivated grass would be
    A plague and pest
To her so amply and meetly
    Nourished and blest
On crisp herbs of purity
    No manure has messed ;
With many a tit-bit too
    Of St John's wort, primrose,
Daisy-tops the greenswards strew,
    And orchid that grows
—Towers with flowers that as fawns do
    Have speckles in rows—
In boglands she goes to
    That no man knows.
These are the tonics true
    To which instinct goes
In trying times ; they endue
    Lean frames with fat that glows
Prettily on them, without rue
    From any weight it throws.

There's no more pleasing fellowship
    Than theirs at gloaming-tide
And when through deepening shades they slip
    In safety they'll abide
Long though the night, sharp the wind's nip,
    Well sheltered by a hillside
In the place that's deemed their agile trip
    For centuries its greatest pride
—Not preferring hardship or want,
But Ben Dorain, their beloved haunt !

Siubhal

The mountain high-towered,
Well-turfed and flowered,
Stream-lit and bowered,
None other is dowered
Like her in Christendom.
I'm overpowered as I roam
Bemused by her beauty
That the maps don't acclaim
Her transcending fame
As is their bare duty
With a special sign
As the queen of her line.
All the storms that have lowered
Have found her no coward
And whatever is toward
Will find her the same.

She's exuberant in fruits
Far beyond the measure
Usually found

On like areas of ground,
And rich in rare roots
And the tenderest of shoots
And has many a treasure
Of light-woven woodlands.
Oh, hers are the good lands
For all kinds of pleasure.
The cock is high-breasted
That on her has nested
With splendid torrent invested
Of music that springs unarrested
Between him and the sun,
And other birds, many a one,
A full repertoire run.
And hers is the brisk little buck
Who could have no better luck
With such greenswards for prancing on
Without slipping or mishap,
Without failing or falling, yon
Cloven-hoofed clever chap !
Then deep corries for ranging
To the heights, or, changing,
Dallying in copsewood and bracken
Of variety there's no lack in
Ben Dorain for all his wants.
Every winding gully he haunts
On every crag-top balances
With audacious curtsies,
And has ample distances
To put behind him should
Aught to startle him intrude.
Every second tussock he takes
As over the moss-quakes he makes

On hoofs nonpareil thin
In his eagerness to win
To where his love will be found
Come up from the low ground
—Every second tussock, or third ;
Light and easy as a bird !

As for the little growling doe
And her young fawns who bide
In a hidden glen ill to know
High up the mountain side,
The ear she has !   And the eye !
And the quick deft feet to ply
Over the boggling peat-hags !
Lightning behind her lags.
Though Caoilte and Cuchullin
Sought her they'd be fooling.
The sight would not daunt her
Of them and every hunter,
With all the men and horses
Hire-bound by King George ; their forces
Would include nothing to catch her
If she wished to escape ; watch her,
Gallant, long-legged, swift-turning,
Incalculable, her white-flared hips burning
Like stars in the distance !   No matter
How precipitous the uplands may be
Lured by no level land she'll be
Where they might win at her.
She is the incarnate spirit
Of the heights her kind inherit,
Analysing every breath of air
With instant unerring nose.

Volatile, vigilant, there
One with the horizon she goes
Where horizons horizons disclose.
Or lies like a star hidden away
By the broad light of day.
Earth has nothing to match her.

URLAR

The hind loves to wander
Among the saplings yonder.
The passes of the braes
Are her dwelling-place.
The leaflets of the trees
And fresh heather-stems—these
Are the fare she prefers,
To cattle-fodder averse.
Blithe and gentle her nature,
A glad gloomless creature,
Mercurial and thoughtless,
Going like a knotless
Thread through the landscape,
Yet bearing herself always
Circumspect and comely in shape,
With the hues of health ablaze ;
Knowing precisely how far to press
Her vital force to fill out,
Without straining, her formal niceness,
At rest or in revel or rout.
In the glen of the sappiest
Green copsewood she's happiest,
Yet often goes by the Great Rock
Where bush-clumps break the shock

Of the North Wind and let
No icy jet of it get
On her slumbering there
In some favourite lair ;
Or she trips up the dell
Of the hazels to the well
She loves to drink at ; cold and clear,
Far better than beer.
No one could think of
Better for her to drink of.
It inspires her lithe wiles,
Her sheer grace that beguiles,
Her constant strength and speed
In every hazard of need.
The honour of the best ears
In all Europe is hers !

SIUBHAL

Graceful to see to me was a group
Lined up in the order of march to troop
Down by the Sron rock south through the loop
'Twixt Craobh-na-h-ainnis moor and the scoop
Of Corrie-dhaingean ; no goog on that herd,
And none with a staring hide covered,
That for bite and sup never begged or chaffered
Nor yet lacked though to that they'd not stoop.
That was the fine line to be watching oop
The seen parts of a path between noop and noop.
Then along Corrie Rannoch's either side
About the wing of the pass and the wide
Corrie of Ben Achalader and over
By Conn Lonn on the Laoidhre's spur,

What a host to delight a deer-lover,
Everyone in a radiant red jupe !
On to the hollow of the Feinne there
And in the Creag-sheilich beyond that
Where gather the winsome hinds that care
Nothing for grass that dunghills begat,
But whose joy it is to be strutting
On a grassy level, butting
And playing with each other or in
The rutting-bogs make a right din
Of spirited lewdness, keen, wanton,
Lusty, with no care or cant on.

No tongue could keep on thirsting
On the lower side of Meall Eanail where spring
The wine-streams of Annet, honey-tasted to drink ;
A flow efficacious, white, narrow,
Filtering over sand, brim to the brink,
Sweeter than cinnamon, a draught to make marrow.
This is the water to cure all thirst
That from the bottom of the earth has burst.
There's plenty of it here on the mountain top,
Free—not for sale in a shop !
This is the loveliest thing to see
In all this quarter of Europe to me,
The fresh water, mild with limpidity,
Welling so pure and harmless
From the dark roots of the watercress,
With various mosses waving about the lips
Of every ripple as it slips
From the wards of the rock and swells the pool
Uninflaming, delicious, and cool,
Coming in an eddy from the gravel,

On the shoulder of Ben Dorain,
The great demesne where you have all
The good life can set store in.

The hither side of the hill slope
Has goodliness without stint or stop ;
The tumultuous tumbled moor-corrie
Opens by it—a corrie of glory.
Grouty through-other rocks, all points and pits
Shaggy and counter and ravelled—oh, it's
Easy enough for me to praise
Steep defiles such variety arrays,
For there's felicity enough on them,
All manner of fine stuff on them.
One could spend endless love on them.
Full of bells, full of buds, they are,
With everywhere the dainty clear star
Of the daisy so ruddy and fair
Twinkling in the tapestry there,
And the moorland busked in a great
Rough-figured mantle that suits her estate
What tongue can ever hope
For words with the like to cope ?—
The grandest scene in all Europe !

URLAR

The lonely moorland ringed round
With glen-mouths and hill-ends,
Corrie Fraoich, will be found
Best of all.   Fawns' presence lends
It that smiling look that ground

They favour aye commends.
Its southerly setting defends
It from cold ; hence they abound.
Glad is the little hind here.
Pure her body, healthy, clear,
True womanly in virtue she.
Taintless her breath would appear
To anyone who might kiss her.
It is here that, once they see
It, young men always wish to be.
Like pipes' sticks are its fanwise
Ravines through which the wind sighs.
Stags' chief meeting-ground and place
That's source of every great chase.
Rich in all that comes out with rain,
Wild berries and flowers perfume this plain.
There's heaps of fish in near-by streams
To get with a torch's gleams
And the narrow pine-shafted spear
Plied by men used to such gear.
Fine to see the trout leaping
Light flies in clusters catching
On waters so smoothly sweeping !
I've said as I stood watching,
The best things in land or sea found
All in you, Ben Dorain, abound !

CRUNN-LUTH

Who would stalk the hind in this glen
    Needs good knowledge and cunning
To steal softly within her ken
    Without starting her running,

Carefully and cleverly inveigling
   Himself forward, her notice shunning,
Using each least thing in turn then
   To hide himself and his gun in.
Bush, rock, and hollow all in taken,
   Vastly ingenious, there's great fun in.

Details of the land all well gauged,
   Clouds' direction duly noted,
His wits are thenceforth all engaged
   In covering the space allotted,
And getting the finale staged
   Before the hind can have thought it
Enplotted—aye, all the campaign waged
   Ere hint of danger is brought it.

The hind's own instincts outplaying,
   In spite of herself she's taken
By the stalker, not without paying
   Full due to her wits wide-waken,
With tribute of stilly delaying
   And coolness never forsaken
And frame to wriggle a worm's way in
   Without affront or aching.

At last he puts the eye steadily
   To the hind on the stag still intent,
And the peg is drawn out readily
   The butt-iron's kick to relent.
A new flint's just tightened, and deadly
   The down-blow of the hammer's sent.
The spark to the packed powder flies redly
   And the hail from the barrel is sprent.

It was well loved by the quality
   To be up Ben Dorain's passes
In the hey-day of their vitality
   Where the deer troop by in masses,
While hunters of such judicality
   In the sport where nothing crass is
Stalk them with the right mentality
   That alone their wariness outclasses.

And the brisk keen dogs behind them,
   Creatures so surly and slaughtering,
Frantic at jaws' grip to find them
   With the herd like wild-fire scattering,
Till speed it seems has combined them
   —Their hair-on-end howling, shattering
The golden silence of deer-flight, entwined them
   With the foes their rabid foam's spattering.

Furious in high career that conjunction
   Of leaping dogs and fugitive deer,
And the peaks and passes echoed with unction
   The baying of the hounds exciting to hear
As they drove down their quarries without com-
      punction
   In to the icy pools that bottomless appear
And rocked on their necks in relentless function
   While they floundered and bloodied the waters
      there !
. . . Though I've told a little of Ben Dorain here,
Before I could tell all it deserves I would be
In a delirium with the strange prolixity
Of the talking called for, I fear.
                Duncan Ban MacIntyre.

XXIV

A RUNNABLE STAG

WHEN the pods went pop on the broom, green
　　broom,
　　And apples began to be golden-skinned,
We harboured a stag in the Priory coomb,
　　And we feathered his trail up-wind, up-wind,
　　We feathered his trail up-wind—
　　　　A stag of warrant, a stag, a stag,
　　　　A runnable stag, a kingly crop,
　　　　Brow, bay and tray and three on top,
　　　　A stag, a runnable stag.

Then the huntsman's horn rang yap, yap, yap,
　　And " Forwards " we heard the harbourer
　　　　shout ;
But 'twas only a brocket that broke a gap
　　In the beechen underwood, driven out,
　　From the underwood antlered out
　　　　By warrant and might of the stag, the stag,
　　　　The runnable stag, whose lordly mind
　　　　Was bent on sleep, though beamed and tined
　　　　He stood, a runnable stag.

So we tufted the covert till afternoon
　　With Tinkerman's Pup and Bell-of-the-North ;
And hunters were sulky and hounds out of tune
　　Before we tufted the right stag forth,
　　Before we tufted him forth,
　　　　The stag of warrant, the wily stag,

The runnable stag with his kingly crop,
Brow, bay and tray and three on top,
The royal and runnable stag.

It was Bell-of-the-North and Tinkerman's Pup
   That stuck to the scent till the copse was drawn.
" Tally ho ! tally ho ! " and the hunt was up,
   The tufters whipped and the pack laid on,
   The resolute pack laid on,
      And the stag of warrant away at last,
      The runnable stag, the same, the same,
      His hoofs on fire, his horns like flame,
      A stag, a runnable stag.

" Let your gelding be : if you check or chide
   He stumbles at once and you're out of the hunt ;
For three hundred gentlemen, able to ride,
   On hunters accustomed to bear the brunt,
   Accustomed to bear the brunt,
      Are after the runnable stag, the stag,
      The runnable stag with his kingly crop,
      Brow, bay and tray and three on top,
      The right, the runnable stag."

By perilous paths in coomb and dell,
   The heather, the rocks, and the river-bed,
The pace grew hot, for the scent lay well,
   And a runnable stag goes right ahead,
   The quarry went right ahead—
      Ahead, ahead, and fast and far ;
      His antlered crest, his cloven hoof,
      Brow, bay and tray and three aloof,
      The stag, the runnable stag.

For a matter of twenty miles and more,
  By the densest hedge and the highest wall,
Through herds of bullocks he baffled the lore
  Of harbourer, huntsman, hounds and all,
  Of harbourer, hounds and all—
    The stag of warrant, the wily stag,
    For twenty miles, and five and five,
    He ran, and he never was caught alive,
    This stag, this runnable stag.

When he turned at bay in the leafy gloom,
  In the emerald gloom where the brook ran deep,
He heard in the distance the rollers boom,
  And he saw in a vision of peaceful sleep,
  In a wonderful vision of sleep,
    A stag of warrant, a stag, a stag,
    A runnable stag in a jewelled bed,
    Under the sheltering ocean dead,
    A stag, a runnable stag.

So a fateful hope lit up his eye,
  And he opened his nostrils wide again,
And he tossed his branching antlers high
  As he headed the hunt down the Charlock glen,
  As he raced down the echoing glen
    For five miles more, the stag, the stag,
    For twenty miles, and five and five,
    Not to be caught now, dead or alive,
    The stag, the runnable stag.

Three hundred gentlemen, able to ride,
  Three hundred horses as gallant and free
Beheld him escape on the evening tide,

Far out till he sank in the Severn Sea,
    Till he sank in the depths of the sea—
        The stag, the buoyant stag, the stag
        That slept at last in a jewelled bed
        Under the sheltering ocean spread,
        The stag, the runnable stag.

                                    John Davidson.

XXV

CLEVEDON CHURCH

Westward I watch the low green hills of Wales,
    The low sky silver grey,
The turbid Channel with the wandering sails
    Moans through the winter day.
There is no colour but one ashen light
    On tower and lonely tree,
The little church upon the windy height
    Is grey as sky or sea.

But there hath he that woke the sleepless Love
    Slept through these fifty years,
There is the grave that has been wept above
    With more than mortal tears.
And far below I hear the Channel sweep
    And all his waves complain,
As Hallam's dirge through all the years must keep
    Its monotone of pain.

        .   .   .   .   .

Grey sky, brown waters, as a bird that flies,
    My heart flits forth from these

Back to the winter rose of northern skies,
  Back to the northern seas.
And lo, the long waves of the ocean beat
  Below the minster grey,
Caverns and chapels worn of saintly feet,
  And knees of them that pray.

And I remember me how twain were one
  Beside that ocean dim,
I count the years passed over since the sun
  That lights me looked on him,
And dreaming of the voice that, safe in sleep,
  Shall greet me not again,
Far, far below I hear the Channel sweep
  And all his waves complain.

Andrew Lang.

XXVI

IRELAND WEEPING

(Eirinn a' Gul)

(Translated from the Gaelic)

UTMOST island of Europe, loveliest land under the
canopy of the skies, often did I see your coast over
the great roaring sound of the sea.

When a mild wind blew from the south-east and
the firmament was without mist or cloud, the
Gaels in the Rhinns of Islay told one another of
your loveliness,

Of your grassy goodly plains, level Lag an Rotha and Magh Aoidh, and your branchy dells that gave shelter to the winged minstrels of the trees.

Of your pure fountains gurling spring-water, your numerous herds among your glens, your woods and hills and meads and greenery from end to end.

In the guiltless morning of youth I got the tales of the ages gone by at the hearth of Islay of Clan Donald, ere the Gaels were exiled from their heritage,

The welcoming company who loved to tell the tale of Innis Fail ; the fables of the worthy hospitable ones told in the harmonious modes of the bards.

We little ones believed the stories we thus heard from the mouths of the old, and believed, therefore, that you were still as in these heroic tales— joyful, exultant, happy.

To-day I see unchanged your sky-line over the sea from the wave-beaten shore of south Islay, but gloomy to tell is your condition now.

A tale of the woe of yoke and exile, of famine, grief, and injustice, with no way to relieve your pain, since you yourself broke your strength.

Where is the heroism of the three Hughs, heroic

O'Donell and O'Neill, and MacGuidhir hurling himself without hestation upon the foe and standing to death before he yielded ?

Where is the race of the brave that did not evade battle at Dun a' Bheire, when they poured down like a mountain flood under the rims of their speckled shields ?

The rocks answering with an echo, to the triumphant shout on the field ; the foxes stretched without breath, and their blood humming on the ground !

William Livingston.

XXVII

BIRLINN CHLANN-RAGHNAILL [1]

(The Birlinn of Clanranald)

Being a ship-blessing, together with a sea-incitement made for the crew of the Birlinn of the Lord of Clanranald

> GOD bless the craft of Clanranald
> When brangled first with the brine,
> Himself and his heroes hurling ;
> The pick of the human line !
>
> The blessing of holy Triune
> On the fury of the air ;
> The sea's ruggedness smoothed away
> Ease us to our haven there !

[1] Translated from the Gaelic by Hugh MacDiarmid.

Father who fashioned the ocean
And winds that from all points roll,
Bless our lean ship and her heroes,
Keep her and her whole crew whole !

Your grace, O Son, on our anchor,
Our rudder, sails, and all graith
And tackle to her masts attached,
And guard us as we have faith !

Bless our mast-hoops and our sail-yards
And our masts and all our ropes,
Preserve our stays and our halyards,
And confirm us in our hopes !

Holy Ghost, be you our helmsman
To steer the course that is right.
You know every port under Heaven.
We cast ourselves on your sleight !

THE BLESSING OF THE ARMS

God's blessing be on our claymores
And flexible grey toledos
And heavy coats of mail-harness
Through which no dull blade can bleed us.

Bless our shoulder-belts and gorgets
And our well-made bossy targes,
Bless each and all of our weapons,
And the man who with it charges.

Bless our gleaming bows of yew-wood
Good to bend in battle-mêlée,

And birchen arrows, not to splinter
In the surly badger's belly.

Bless every dirk, every pistol,
Every kilt of noble pleating,
Every martial apparatus
With us under this ship's sheeting.

Lack no knowledge then or mettle
To do brave deeds with hardihood
While still four planks of her remain
Or pair of overlaps holds good.

With her drowned boards yet for footstools
Or a thole-pin above water
Let ocean not numb your resource,
Your hearts inchoate horror shatter.

Keep up a herculean struggle.
If the sea detects no weakness,
Her pride at last will be overcome
And reward your prowess with meekness.

As your foe in a land battle
Seeing your strength is left untouched
Is more apt to weaken in onslaught
Than be in fiercer furies clutched,

So with the sea ; if you maintain
Set resolve and dauntless spirits
She will at length, as God's ordained,
Humble herself to your merits.

INCITEMENT FOR ROWING TO SAILING-PLACE

To put the black well-fashioned yewship
  To the sailing-place
Thrust you out flexible oarbanks
  Dressed to sheer grace ;
Oars smooth-shafted and shapely,
  Grateful for gripping,
Made for lusty resolute rowing,
  Palm-fast, foam-whipping ;
Knocking sparks out of the water
  Towards Heaven
Like the fire-flush from a smithy
  Updriven,
Under the great measured onstrokes
  Of the oar-lunges
That confound the indrawn billows
  With their plunges,
While the shrewd blades of the white woods
  Go cleaving
The tops of the valleyed blue-hills
  Shaggily heaving.
O stretch you, pull you, and bend you
  Between the thole-pins,
Your knuckles snow with hard plying
  The pinewood fins ;
All the big muscular fellows
  Along her lying
With their hairy and sinewy
  Arms keep her flying,
Raising and lowering together
  With a single motion

Their evenly dressed poles of pinewood
  Mastering the ocean.

A Herculean planked on the fore-oar
  Roaring : " Up, on with her ! "
Makes all the thick shoulder muscles
  Glide better together,
Thrusting the birlinn with snorting
  Through each chill sea-glen ;
The hard curved prow through the tide-lumps
  Drives inveighing,
On all hands sending up mountains
  Round her insistence.
Hugan, the sea says, like Stentor ;
  Heig, say the thole-pins.
Rasping now, on the timbers,
  Of the shirred surges !
The oars jib ; blood-blistering
  Slowly emerges
On each hard hand of the rowers
  In berserk fettle
Hurling on the trembling oakplanks,
  Caulking, and metal,
Though nailheads spring with the thunder
  Thumping her thigh.
A crew to make a right rocking
  The deeps to defy,
Working the lean ship like an auger
  Through walls of water,
The bristling wrath of blue-black billows
  No daunting matter.
They are the choice set of fellows
  To hold an oarage

E

Outmanœuvring the dark swirlings
   With skill and courage,
Without a point lost or tiring,
   Timely throughout,
Despite all the dire devilment
   Of the waterspout !

[Then after the sixteen men had sat at the oars to row her against the wind to a sailing-place, Calum Garbh, son of Ranald of the Seas, who was on the fore-oar, recited an iorram (or rowing song) for her, as follows :]

And now since you're selected
—No doubt true choice effected !—
Let rowing be directed
         Bold and set.

Give a rocking pointedly,
Without lapse or lack of netteté,
So all sea-problems set yet be
         More than met.

A well-gripped stubborn rocking
From bones and sinews yoking,
The steps from her oarbank knocking
         Foam to fire.

Incite each other along
And a good so-go-all song
From the fore man's mouth fall strong
         To inspire.

Oar's sawdust on the rowlocks,
Hands run with sores like golochs,

Waves' armpits like any mollusc
        Screw the oars.

Cheeks be lit all blazing red,
Palms of skin all casing shed,
While sweat off every face and head
        Thumping pours.

Stretch you, pull you, and bend you
The blades the pine-trees lend you,
Ascend, descend, and wend you
        Through the sea.

Banks of oars on either side
Set your labour to her tide
And spray on ocean's thorter-pride
        Throw freely.

Row as one, cleanly, clearly ;
Through flesh-thick waves cut sheerly ;
A job that's not done wearily
        Nor snail-wise.

Strike her evenly without fluther.
Often glance at one another
So in your thews still further
        Vim may rise.

Let her oak go skelping through
Big-bellied troughs of swingeing blue ;
In their two thighs pounding too
        Each spasm down.

Though the hoary heaving ocean
Swell with even more commotion,
Toppling waves with drowning notion
          Roar and frown,

And incessant wash pour in
O'er her shoulders and the din
Groan all round and sob to win
          Through her keel,

Stretch you, pull you, and bend you.
The red-backed sleek shafts tend you.
With the pith strong arms lend you
          Victory feel.

Put that headland past your prow
Where you strain with sweat-drenched brow
And lift the sails upon her now
          From Uist of the sheldrakes !

[Then they rowed to a sailing-place. They took
in the sixteen oars which were swiftly pruned down
against her thigh to avoid sheet-ropes. Clanranald
ordered his gentlemen to see to the disposition in
the places for which they were qualified of men
who would not be daunted by any spectre from the
deep nor any chaos in which the ocean might in-
volve them. After the selection every man was
ordered to take up his appointed place, and accord-
ingly the steersman was summoned to sit at the
rudder in these words :]

        Set at the rudder a brawny
          Grand fellow,
      Top nor trough of sea can unhorse,
          Coarse skelp nor bellow ;

Broad-beamed, well-set, full of vigour
    Wary withal ;
Who hearing the shaggy surges
    Come roaring
Her prow expertly to the rollers
    Keeps shoring ;
Who will even keep her going
    As if unshaken,
Adjusting sheet and tack—glances
    Windward taken ;
Yielding no thumb-long deviation
    Of her true course
Despite the bounding wave-summits'
    Opposing force ;
Who will go windward so stoutly
    With her when needed,
Though nailhead nor rib in her oak
    But shrieks—unheeded ;
Whom no spectre sprung from the abyss
    Could shift or dismay,
Or grey sea to his ears upswoln
    E'er tear away
From his set place while yet alive
    Helm under armpit !
Under his charge whatever's been placed
    Nothing has harmed it.
A match for old ocean rough-glenned
    With inclemency !
Who no rope strains tackwindwarding
    But easily
Lets run and tacks under full canvas
    None so meetly

And her tacking on each wavetop
    Binds so featly,
Straight harbourwards under spray-showers
    Running so sweetly !

[There was appointed a shrouds-man.]

Set another stalwart fellow
    For shrouds-grasping ;
With finger-vices, great hand-span,
    For such clasping ;
Sage, quick ; to help with the yard's end
    When that's needed,
With masts and gear, leave no neighbour
    Task unheeded ;
Wind-wise, and aptly adjusting
    With shrouds-manning
The sheet's-man's slackings—and t'assist
    In all ways scanning.

[A sheet's-man was set apart.]

Set too on the thwart a sheet's-man
    With great arms ending
In horny compulsive fingers
    For the sheet-tending ;
Pull in, let out, as is wanted,
    With strength of grabbing ;
Draw in when beating to windward,
    The blast crabbing ;
And release when the gust again
    Ceases rending.

[There was ordered out a tacksman.]

Dispose another sturdy sailor,
    Masterfully

To keep the tack to her windward,
　And deal duly ;
The tack to each cleat his changing
　Up and down bringing,
As a fair breeze may favour
　Or ill come swinging ;
And if he sees tempest threaten
　Against the shock
Let him shear the tack without mercy
　Down to the stock.

[There was ordered to the prow a pilot.]

A pilot in the prow be standing.
　Let him afford
Us ever reliable knowledge
　Of what's toward
And keep confirming the steersman
　In our right going,
For he is the veritable Pole Star
　We must have showing ;
Suresightedly taking a landmark
　With the trained vision
That is the God of all weathers
　On such a mission.

[There was set apart a halyard-man.]

Take place at the main halyard
　A clear-headed
Athletic fellow, with vigour
　And care wedded,
An able fellow without flurry,
　Grim and alert,

To take from her and give to her
    Just and expert,
To lie with hand of due power
    There on the halyard,
The weight of his grasp decisive
    Rive oakwoodward ;
Not tie the halyard about the cleat
    Tight beyond use
But fix it firmly, cunningly,
    With running noose ;
Thus over the pin squirting, humming,
    Now as it's roped,
Yet should perchance the prop be sundered
    It may be stopped !

[There was set apart a teller-of-the-waters, since the
sea was becoming too rough, and the steersman said
to him :]

I'll have at my ear a teller
    Of the waters ;
Let him keep close watch windward
    On these matters ;
A man somewhat timid, cautious,
    Not altogether
A coward however !—Keeping
    Stock of the weather,
Whether in his fore or stern quarter
    The fair breeze is,
Blurting out without hesitation
    Aught he sees is
Peril-spelling to his notion ;
    Or, should he spy

The likeness of a drowning sea
   Roaring down, cry
To put our stem swiftly to it.
   Insistently
Clamorous at the least threat of danger
   This man must be,
And not fear to give the steersman
   Any hint of hazard.
—But let him be the one teller
   Of the waters heard,
And not the whole of you bawling
   Advices mixed,
A distraught steersman not knowing
   Who to heed next !

[There was ordered out a baler, since the sea was
rushing over them fore and aft :]

Let attend on the baling space
   A hardy hero
Not to be cramped or benumbed
   By cold at zero,
Raw brine or stinging hail dashing
   In thrashing showers
Round his chest and neck,—but armoured
   In dogged powers,
A thick round wooden baling-can
   In his swarthy hands,
Throwing out the sea forever
   As soon as it lands ;
Never straightening his lithe backbone
   Till his task's o'er,
Not one drop left in her bottom
   —Or keelson-floor !

Were her planks holed till for a riddle
  She well might pass
He'd keep her all dry as a bottle's
  Outside glass !

[Two men were appointed for hauling the peak-downhauls, since it appeared that the sails would be torn from them by the exceeding boisterousness of the weather :]

Put a pair of hefty fellows
  Thick-boned, strong-thewed,
To take charge of her peak-downhauls
  With force and aptitude ;
With the power of great fore-arms
  In till of need
To haul them in or let them run,
  But always lead
When wayward back to the middle ;
  For this two men
Of the Canna men, Donnchadh Mac Chomaig
  And Iain Mac Iain,
Were chosen—deft and definite fellows
  In brawn and brain.

[Six men were chosen to man the ship's floor as a precaution against the failing of any of those mentioned, or lest the raging of the sea might pluck one overboard, one of these six might take his place :]

Let's have six men, quick and clever
  To give a hand,
Going through the ship in all directions,
  A nimble band,

Each like a hare on a mountain top
    And dogs copping him,
Dodging this way and that, and having
    Nothing stopping him ;
Handy men, quick in the uptake,
    Spry and observant,
To fill any breach as needed
    Are who we want ;
Men who can climb the hard smooth ropes
    Of the slender hemp
As in May trees of a thick-wood
    Only squirrels can attempt ;
Gleg fellows, shrewd to take from her
    As desired
Or give respite meet and restful ;
    Keen, untired.
Such the six the ship of MacDonald
    Has now acquired.

[Now that every convenience pertaining to sailing
had been put in good order and every brave depend-
able fellow had taken up the duty assigned to him,
they hoisted the sails about sunrise on St. Bride's
Day, beginning their course from the mouth of
Loch Ainort in South Uist.]

THE VOYAGE

The sun bursting golden-yellow
    Out of his husk,
The sky grew wild and hot-breathing,
    Unsheathing a fell tusk,
Then turned wave-blue, thick, dun-bellied,
    Fierce and forbidding,

Every hue that would be in a plaid
   In it kneading ;
A " dog's tooth " in the Western quarter
   Snorters prophesied ;
The swift clouds under a shower-breeze
   Multiplied.
Now they hoisted the speckled sails
   Peaked and close-wrought,
And stretched out the stubborn shrouds
   Tough and taut
To the long resin-red shafts
   Of the mast.
With adroit and firm-drawn knotting
   These were made fast
Through the eyes of the hooks and rings ;
   Swiftly and expertly
Each rope put right of the rigging ;
   And orderly
The men took up their set stations
   And were ready.
Then opened the windows of the sky
   Pied, grey-blue,
To the lowering wind's blowing,
   A morose brew,
The sea pulled on his grim rugging
   Slashed with sore rents,
That rough-napped mantle, a weaving
   Of loathsome torrents.
The shape-ever-changing surges
   Swelled up in hills
And roared down into valleys
   In appalling spills.

The water yawned in great craters,
  Slavering mouths agape
Snatching and snarling at each other
  In rabid shape.
It were a man's deed to confront
  The demented scene,
Each mountain of them breaking
  Into flamy lumps.
Each fore-wave towering grey-fanged
  Mordantly grumps
While a routing comes from the back-waves
  With their raving rumps.
When we would rise on these rollers
  Soundly, compactly,
It was imperative to shorten sail
  Swiftly, exactly.
When we would fall with one swallowing
  Down into the glens
Every topsail she had would be off.
  —No light task the men's !
The great hooked big-buttocked ones
  Long before
They came at all near us were heard
  Loudly aroar
Scourging all the lesser waves level
  As on they tore.
It was no joke to steer in that sea
  When the high tops to miss
Seemed almost to hear her keel scrape
  The shelly abyss !
The sea churning and lashing itself
  In maniacal states,

Seals and other great beasts were even
    In direr straits,
The wild swelth and the pounding waves
    And the ship's nose
Scattering their white brains callous
    Through the billows.
They shouted to us loudly, dreadfully,
    The piteous word :—
" Save us or we perish.   We are subjects.
    Take us aboard."
Small fish that were in the waters,
    Murderously churned,
Floated on the top without number
    White bellies upturned.
The stones and shells of the floor even
    Came up to the top
Torn up by the all-grabbing motion
    That would not stop.
The whole sea was a foul porridge
    Full of red scum
With the blood and ordure of the beasts,
    Ruddy, glum,
While screaming with their gill-less mouths,
    Their jaws agape,
Even the air's abyss was full of fiends
    That had no shape.
With the paws and tails of great monsters
    Gruesome to hear
Were the screeching towerers. They would
    strike
Fifty warriors with fear.
The crew's ears lost all appetite
    For hearing in that din,

Rabble of mad sky-demons,
   And their watery kin
Making a baying so unearthly,
   Deeper than the sea-floor,
Great notes lower than human hearing
   Ever heard before.
What then with the ocean's turmoil
   Pounding the ship,
The clamour of the prow flenching whales
   With slime-foiled grip,
And the wind from the Western quarter
   Restarting her windward blast,
Through every possible ordeal
   It seemed we passed.
We were blinded by the sea-spray
   Ever going over us ;
With, beyond that, like another ocean,
   Thunders and lightnings to cover us,
The thunderbolts sometimes singeing
   Our rigging till the smoke
And stench of the reefs smouldering
   Made us utterly choke.
Between the upper and lower torments
   Thus were we braised,
Water, fire, and wind simultaneously
   Against us raised.
—But when it was beyond the sea's power
   To make us yield
She took pity with a faint smile
   And truce was sealed,
Though by that time no mast was unbent,
   No sail untorn,

Yard unsevered, mast-ring unflawed,
　　Oar not shag-shorn,
No stay unstarted, halyard or shroud unbroken.
　　Fise.　Faise.
Thwart and gunwale made confession
　　In similar wise.
Every mast-rigging and tackle
　　The worse of wear ;
Not a beam-knee or rib of her
　　Unloosened there ;
Her gunwale and bottom-boards
　　Were confounded ;
Not a helm left unsplit,
　　A rudder unwounded.
Every timber creaked, moaned, and warped.
　　Not a tree-nail
Was unpulled, no plank had failed
　　To give in the gale.
Not a part that pertained to her
　　But had suffered
And from its first state and purpose
　　Sadly differed.
The sea proclaimed peace with us
　　At the fork of Islay Sound
And the hostile barking wind
　　Was ordered off the ground.
It went to the upper places of the air
　　And became a quiet
Glossy-white surface to us there
　　After all its riot,
And to God we made thanksgiving
　　That good Clanranald

Was spared the brutal death for which
    The elements had wrangled.
Then we pulled down the speckled canvas
    And lowered
The sleek red masts and along her bottom
    Safely stored,
And put out the slender well-wrought oars
    Coloured, and smooth to the hand,
Made of the pine cut by Mac Bharais
    In Finnan's Island,
And set up the right-royal, rocking, rowing,
    Deft and timeous,
And made good harbour there at the top
    Of Carrick-Fergus.
We threw out anchors peacefully
    In that roadstead.
We took food and drink unstinting
    And there we stayed.

Alexander MacDonald
(Alasdair MacMhaighstir Alasdair).

XXVIII

A WET SHEET AND A FLOWING SEA

A WET sheet and a flowing sea,
    A wind that follows fast,
And fills the white and rustling sail,
    And bends the gallant mast ;
And bends the gallant mast, my boys,
    While, like the eagle free,

Away the good ship flies, and leaves
  Old England on the lee.

O for a soft and gentle wind !
  I heard a fair one cry ;
But give to me the snoring breeze,
  And white waves heaving high ;
And white waves heaving high, my boys,
  The good ship tight and free—
The world of waters is our home,
  And merry men are we.

There's tempest in yon hornèd moon,
  And lightning in yon cloud ;
And hark the music, mariners,
  The wind is piping loud ;
The wind is piping loud, my boys,
  The lightning flashing free—
While the hollow oak our palace is,
  Our heritage the sea.
                              Allan Cunningham.

XXIX

SHIP-BROKEN MEN WHOM STORMY
SEAS SORE TOSS

SHIP-BROKEN men whom stormy seas sore toss
Protests with oaths not to adventure more ;
Bot all their perils, promises, and loss
They quite forget when they come to the shore :

Even so, fair dame, whiles sadly I deplore
The shipwreck of my wits procured by you,
Your looks rekindleth love as of before,
And dois revive which I did disavow ;
So all my former vows I disallow,
And buries in oblivion's grave, but groans ;
Yea, I forgive, hereafter, even as now
My fears, my tears, my cares, my sobs, and moans,
In hope if anes I be to shipwreck driven,
Ye will me thole to anchor in your heaven.
William Fowler.

xxx

IN ORKNAY

Upon the utmost corners of the warld,
And on the borders of this massive round,
Where fate and fortune hither has me harled
I do deplore my griefs upon this ground ;
And seeing roaring seas from rocks rebound
By ebbs and streams of contrar routing tydes,
And Phoebus' chariot in their waves lie drown'd
Wha equally now night and day divides,
I call to mind the storms my thoghts abydes,
Which ever wax and never dois decrease,
For nights of dole day's joys ay ever hides,
And in their vayle doith all my weill suppress :
So this I see, wherever I remove,
I change bot seas, bot cannot change my love.
William Fowler.

XXXI

IN ROMNEY MARSH

(From *Ballads and Songs*)

As I went down to Dymchurch Wall,
    I heard the South sing o'er the land ;
I saw the yellow sunlight fall
    On knolls where Norman churches stand.

And ringing shrilly, taut and lithe,
    Within the wind a core of sound,
The wire from Romney town to Hythe
    Alone its airy journey wound.

A veil of purple vapour flowed
    And trailed its fringe along the Straits ;
The upper air like sapphire glowed ;
    And roses filled Heaven's central gates.

Masts in the offing wagged their tops ;
    The swinging waves pealed on the shore ;
The saffron beach, all diamond drops
    And beads of surge, prolonged the roar.

As I came up from Dymchurch Wall,
    I saw above the Downs' low crest
The crimson brands of sunset fall,
    Flicker and fade from out the west.

Night sank : like flakes of silver fire
    The stars in one great shower came down ;

Shrill blew the wind ; and shrill the wire
   Rang out from Hythe to Romney town.

The darkly shining salt sea drops
   Streamed as the waves clashed on the shore ;
The beach, with all its organ stops
   Pealing again, prolonged the roar.
                        John Davidson.

XXXII

CANADIAN BOAT SONG

FAIR these broad meads—these hoary woods are
   grand ;
But we are exiles from our fathers' land.

Listen to me, as when you heard our father
     Sing long ago the song of other shores—
Listen to me, and then in chorus gather
     All your deep voices, as ye pull your oars.

From the lone sheiling of the misty island
     Mountains divide us, and the waste of
       seas—
Yet still the blood is strong, the heart is Highland,
     And we in dreams behold the Hebrides.

We ne'er shall tread the fancy-haunted valley,
     Where 'tween the dark hills creeps the
       small clear stream,

In arms around the patriarch banner rally,
    Nor see the moon on royal tombstones
      gleam.

When the bold kindred, in the time long vanish'd,
    Conquered the soil and fortified the
      keep,—
No seer foretold the children would be banish'd
    That a degenerate lord might boast his
      sheep.

Come foreign rage—let Discord burst in slaughter !
    O then for clansmen true, and stern clay-
      more—
The hearts that would have given their blood like
    water,
    Beat heavily beyond the Atlantic roar.
                Anonymous.

XXXIII

THE REEDS IN THE LOCH SAYIS

Though raging stormes movis us to shake,
    And wind makis waters overflow ;
We yield thereto bot dois not break
    And in the calm bent up we grow.

So baneist men, though princes rage,
    And prisoners, be not despairit.
Abide the calm, whill that it 'suage,
    For time sic causis has repairit.
                Anonymous.

XXXIV

HESIOD, 1908

DEATH at the headlands, Hesiod, long ago
  Gave thee to drink of his unhonied wine :
Now Boreas cannot reach thee lying low,
  Nor Sirius' heat vex any hour of thine :
  The Pleiads rising are no more a sign
For thee to reap, nor when they set to sow :
  Whether at morn or eve Arcturus shine,
To pluck the vine or prune thou canst not know.

Vain now for thee the crane's autumnal flight,
  The loud cuckoo, the twittering swallow—vain
    The flowering scolumus, the budding trees,
Seed-time and Harvest, Blossoming and Blight,
  The mid, the early, and the later rain,
    And strong Orion and the Hyades.
                            Alexander Mair.

XXXV

WATER MUSIC

ARCHIN' here and arrachin' there,
  Allevolie or allemand,
Whiles appliable, whiles areird,
  The polysemous poem's planned.

Lively, louch, atweesh, atween,
  Auchimuty or aspate,

Threidin' through the averins
Or bightsom in the aftergait.

Or barmybrained or barritchfu'
Or rinnin' like an attercap,
Or shinin' like an Atchison,
Wi' a blare or wi' a blawp.

They ken a' that opens and steeks,
Frae Fiddleton Bar to Callister Ha',
And roon aboot for twenty miles
They bead and bell and swaw.

Brent on or boutgate or beschacht,
Bellwaverin' or borne-heid,
They mimp and primp, or bick and birr,
Dilly-dally or show speed.

Brade up or sclafferin', rouchled, sleek,
Abstraklous or austerne,
In belths below the brae-hags
And bebbles in the fern.

Bracken, blackberries, and heather
Ken their amplefeysts and toves.
Here gangs ane wi' aiglets jinglin'
Through a gowl anither goves.

Lint in the bell whiles hardly vies
Wi' ane the wind amows,
While blithely doon abradit linns
Wi' gowd begane anither jows.

Cougher, blocher, boich, and croichle,
Fraise in ane anither's witters,
Wi' backthraws, births, by-rinnin's,
Beggar's broon or blae—the critters!

Or burnet, holine, watchet, chauve,
Or wi' a' the colours dyed
O' the lift abune and plants and trees
That grow on either side.

Or coinyelled wi' the midges,
Or swallows a' aboot,
The shadow o' an eagle,
The aiker o' a troot.

Toukin' ootrageous face
The turn-gree o' your mood
I've climmed until I'm lost
Like the sun ahint a clood.

But a tow-gun frae the boon-tree
A whistle frae the elm,
A spout-gun frae the hemlock
And, back in this auld realm,
Dry leafs o' dishielogie
To smoke in a " partan's tae ".

And you've me in your creel again,
Brim or shallow, bauch or bricht,
Singin' in the mornin',
Corrieneuchin' a' the nicht.
                              Hugh MacDiarmid.

XXXVI

TULLOCHGORUM

Come, gie's a sang, Montgomery cry'd,
And lay your disputes a' aside ;
What signifies't for folks to chide
   For what was done before them ?
Let Whig and Tory a' agree,
   Whig and Tory, Whig and Tory,
   Whig and Tory a' agree
     To drop their whigmigmorum ;
Let Whig and Tory a' agree
To spend this night wi' mirth and glee,
And cheerfu' sing, alang wi' me,
     The Reel o' Tullochgorum.

O Tullochgorum's my delight,
It gars us a' in ane unite,
And ony sumph that keeps up spite,
   In conscience I abhor him.
Blithe and merry we'll be a',
   Blithe and merry, blithe and merry,
   Blithe and merry we'll be a'
     And mak a cheerfu' quorum.
For blithe and merry we'll be a'
As lang as we hae breath to draw,
And dance, till we be like to fa',
     The Reel o' Tullochgorum.

What needs there be sae great a fraise
Wi' dringing dull Italian lays,

I wadna gie our ain strathspeys
   For half a hunder score o' them :
They're dowf and dowie at the best,
   Dowf and dowie, dowf and dowie,
   Dowf and dowie at the best,
     Wi' a' their variorum ;
They're dowf and dowie at the best,
Their allegros and a' the rest ;
They canna please a Scottish taste
     Compared wi' Tullochgorum.

Let warldly worms their minds oppress
Wi' fears o' want and double cess,
And sullen sots themselves distress
   Wi' keeping up decorum.
Shall we sae sour and sulky sit,
   Sour and sulky, sour and sulky,
   Sour and sulky shall we sit
     Like auld philosophorum ?
Shall we sae sour and sulky sit,
Wi' neither sense, nor mirth, nor wit,
Nor ever rise to shake a fit
     To the Reel o' Tullochgorum ?

May choicest blessings aye attend
Each honest, open-hearted friend,
And calm and quiet be his end,
   And a' that's good watch o'er him ;
May peace and plenty be his lot,
   Peace and plenty, peace and plenty,
   Peace and plenty be his lot,
     And dainties a great store o' them ;
May peace and plenty be his lot,

Unstained by any vicious spot,
And may he never want a groat,
  That's fond o' Tullochgorum!

But for the sullen, frumpish fool,
Who wants to be oppression's tool,
May envy gnaw his rotten soul,
  And discontent devour him ;
May dule and sorrow be his chance,
 Dule and sorrow, dule and sorrow,
 Dule and sorrow be his chance,
  And nane say, Wae's me for him !
May dule and sorrow be his chance,
And a' the ills that come frae France,
Whae'er he be that winna dance
  The Reel o' Tullochgorum.
      John Skinner.

XXXVII

THE BONNY EARL O' MORAY

I

YE Highlands and ye Lawlands,
 O where hae ye been ?
They hae slain the Earl o' Moray,
 And hae laid him on the green.

II

Now wae be to thee, Huntley !
 And whairfore did ye sae !
I bade you bring him wi' you,
 But forbade you him to slay.

III

He was a braw gallant,
 And he rid at the ring ;
And the bonny Earl o' Moray,
 O he might hae been a king !

IV

He was a braw gallant,
 And he play'd at the ba' ;
And the bonny Earl o' Moray
 Was the flower amang them a'

V

He was a braw gallant,
 And he play'd at the gluve ;
And the bonny Earl o' Moray,
 O he was the Queen's luve !

VI

O lang will his Lady
 Look owre the Castle Downe,
Ere she see the Earl o' Moray
 Come sounding through the town !
 Anonymous.

XXXVIII

TO MACKINNON OF STRATH

(Translated from the Gaelic)

DISTANT and long have I waited without going to
visit you, O Lachlan from the northern airt.

The snow of the cairns came down with every stream, and every mountain lost her gloom.

If the moorland grew dark and the sun would bend down it were time for me to go on a round of visiting.

It is not the plains of the Saxons that I would make for, but the braes of the glens up yonder,

And the hall of the generous one, the destination of hundreds of travellers, Kilmaree under the wing of the bay.

Bear this greeting over the Kyle, since they cannot hear my cry, to the company that is without surliness or gloom,

To the noble son of Alpin, of the stainless royal blood, feather of the eagle that is not feeble to tell of.

You did not follow the custom of others in being strict for the rent on tenantry.

They knew your worth ; in the time of the sun's going under, the sound of the harpstrings was heard about your ear.

Your young men would be drinking, full stoups on the table, and horns of silver going round in their fists.

But if strife arose for you, they were up at once in your behalf, Clan Gregor of the pipes and the routs.

Likewise the Grants of Strath Spey, and they stubborn and brave, three score and three hundred in time of need.

That's the band not scanty, that would put pine to the flagpole, and bend the bossed yew to the ear.

You got a gift from Clan Leod of the banners of satin, of the cups of the horns, of the goblets.

You took the white pebble for wife, she of the level regard. Lovely is your wife by your side, and courteous,

Sweet mouth to raise the song, side like the swan of the waves, thin brow that will not bend with gloom !

Iain Lom.

XXXIX

THE RETURN

(A Piper's Vaunting)

Och hey ! for the splendour of tartans !
And hey for the dirk and the targe !
The race that was hard as the Spartans
Shall return again to the charge :

Shall come back again to the heather,
　　Like eagles, with beak and with claws
To take and to scatter for ever
　　The Sasunnach thieves and their laws.

Och, then, for the bonnet and feather !—
　　The Pipe and its vaunting clear :
Och, then, for the glens and the heather !
　　And all that the Gael holds dear.
　　　　　　　　　Pittendrigh Macgillivray.

XL

SIR PATRICK SPENS

THE King sits in Dunfermline town,
　　Drinking the blude-red wine ;
" O whare will I get a skeely skipper,
　　To sail this new ship of mine ? "—

O up and spake an eldern knight,
　　Sat at the King's right knee,—
" Sir Patrick Spens is the best sailor
　　That ever sailed the sea."—

Our King has written a braid letter,
　　And seal'd it with his hand,
And sent it to Sir Patrick Spens,
　　Was walking on the strand.

' To Noroway, to Noroway,
　　To Noroway o'er the faem ;

The King's daughter of Noroway,
  'Tis thou maun bring her hame."

The first word that Sir Patrick read,
  Sae loud loud laughed he ;
The neist word that Sir Patrick read,
  The tear blinded his ee.

" O wha is this has done this deed,
  And tauld the King o' me,
To send us out, at this time of the year,
  To sail upon the sea ?

" Be it wind, be it weet, be it hail, be it sleet,
  Our ship must sail the faem ;
The King's daughter of Noroway,
  'Tis we must fetch her hame."—

They hoysed their sails on Monenday morn,
  Wi' a' the speed they may ;
They hae landed in Noroway,
  Upon a Wodensday.

They hadna been a week, a week,
  In Noroway, but twae,
When that the lords o' Noroway
  Began aloud to say,—

" Ye Scottishmen spend a' our King's gowd,
  And a' our Queenis fee."—
" Ye lie, ye lie, ye liars loud !
  Fu' loud I hear ye lie ;

F

" For I brought as much white monie
  As gane my men and me,
And I brought a half-fou of gude red gowd,
  Out o'er the sea wi' me.

" Make ready, make ready, my merrymen a'.
  Our gude ship sails the morn."—
" Now, ever alake, my master dear,
  I fear a deadly storm !

" I saw the new moon, late yestreen,
  Wi' the auld moon in her arm ;
And, if we gang to sea, master,
  I fear we'll come to harm."

They hadna sail'd a league, a league,
  A league but barely three,
When the lift grew dark, and the wind blew
    loud,
  And gurly grew the sea.

The ankers brak, and the topmasts lap,
  It was sic a deadly storm ;
And the waves cam o'er the broken ship,
  Till a' her sides were torn.

" O where will I get a gude sailor,
  To take my helm in hand,
Till I get up to the tall top-mast,
  To see if I can spy land ? "—

" O here am I, a sailor gude,
  To take the helm in hand,

Till you go up to the tall top-mast ;
    But I fear you'll ne'er spy land."—

He hadna gane a step, a step,
    A step but barely ane,
When a bout flew out of our goodly ship,
    And the salt sea it came in.

" Gae, fetch a web o' the silken claith,
    Another o' the twine,
And wap them into our ship's side,
    And let nae the sea come in."—

They fetch'd a web o' the silken claith,
    Another o' the twine,
And they wapp'd them round that gude ship's
    side,
    But still the sea cam in.

O laith, laith, were our gude Scots lords
    To weet their cork-heel'd shoon !
But lang or a' the play was play'd,
    They wat their hats aboon.

And mony was the feather bed,
    That flatter'd on the faem ;
And mony was the gude lord's son,
    That never mair cam hame.

The ladyes wrang their fingers white,
    The maidens tore their hair,
A' for the sake of their true loves ;
    For them they'll see nae mair.

O lang, lang, may the ladyes sit,
  Wi' their fans into their hand,
Before they see Sir Patrick Spens
  Come sailing to the strand !

And lang, lang, may the maidens sit,
  With their gowd kaims in their hair,
A' waiting for their ain dear loves !
  For them they'll see nae mair.

Half-owre, half-owre to Aberdour,
  'Tis fifty fathoms deep,
And there lies gude Sir Patrick Spens,
  Wi' the Scots lords at his feet.

Anonymous.

XLI

THE BATTLE OF OTTERBOURNE

It fell about the Lammas tide,
  When the muir-men win their hay,
The doughty Douglas bound him to ride
  Into England, to drive a prey.

He chose the Gordons and the Græmes,
  With them the Lindesays, light and gay,
But the Jardines wald not with him ride,
  And they rue it to this day.

And he has burn'd the dales of Tyne,
  And part of Bambrough shire ;

And three good towers on Reidswire fells,
   He left them all on fire.

And he march'd up to Newcastle,
   And rode it round about ;
" O wha's the lord of this castle,
   Or wha's the lady o't ? "—

But up spake proud Lord Percy, then,
   And O but he spake hie !
" I am the lord of this castle,
   My wife's the lady gay."

" If thou'rt the lord of this castle,
   Sae weel it pleases me !
For, ere I cross the Border fells,
   The tane of us shall die."—

He took a lang spear in his hand,
   Shod with the metal free,
And for to meet the Douglas there,
   He rode right furiouslie.

But O how pale his lady look'd,
   Frae aff the castle wa',
When down before the Scottish spear
   She saw proud Percy fa'.

" Had we twa been upon the green,
   And never an eye to see,
I wad hae had you, flesh and fell ;
   But your sword sall gae wi' me."—

" But gae ye up to Otterbourne,
    And wait there dayis three ;
And, if I come not ere three dayis end,
    A fause knight ca' ye me."—

" The Otterbourne's a bonnie burn ;
    'Tis pleasant there to be ;
But there is nought at Otterbourne,
    To feed my men and me.

" The deer rins wild on hill and dale,
    The birds fly wild from tree to tree :
But there is neither bread nor kale,
    To fend my men and me.

" Yet I will stay at Otterbourne,
    Where you shall welcome be ;
And, if ye come not at three dayis end,
    A fause lord I'll ca' thee."—

" Thither will I come," proud Percy said,
    " By the might of Our Ladye ! "—
" There will I bide thee," said the Douglas,
    " My troth I plight to thee."

They lighted high on Otterbourne,
    Upon the bent sae brown ;
They lighted high on Otterbourne,
    And threw their pallions down.

And he that had a bonnie boy,
    Sent out his horse to grass ;

And he that had not a bonnie boy,
   His ain servant he was.

But up then spake a little page,
   Before the peep of dawn—
" O waken ye, waken ye, my good lord
   For Percy's hard at hand."—

" Ye lie, ye lie, ye liar loud !
   Sae loud I hear ye lie :
For Percy had not men yestreen
   To dight my men and me.

" But I have dream'd a dreary dream,
   Beyond the Isle of Skye ;
I saw a dead man win a fight,
   And I think that man was I."

He belted on his guid braid sword,
   And to the field he ran ;
But he forgot the helmet good,
   That should have kept his brain.

When Percy wi' the Douglas met,
   I wat he was fu' fain !
They swakked their swords, till sair they swat,
   And the blood ran down like rain.

But Percy with his good broad sword,
   That could so sharply wound,
Has wounded Douglas on the brow,
   Till he fell to the ground.

Then he call'd on his little foot-page,
  And said—" Run speedilie,
And fetch my ain dear sister's son,
  Sir Hugh Montgomery.

" My nephew good," the Douglas said,
  " What recks the death of ane !
Last night I dream'd a dreary dream,
  And I ken the day's thy ain.

" My wound is deep ; I fain would sleep ;
  Take thou the vanguard of the three,
And hide me by the braken bush,
  That grows on yonder lilye lee.

" O bury me by the braken bush,
  Beneath the blooming brier,
Let never living mortal ken
  That ere a kindly Scot lies here."

He lifted up that noble lord,
  Wi' the saut tear in his e'e ;
He hid him in the braken bush,
  That his merrie-men might not see.

The moon was clear, the day drew near
  The spears in flinders flew,
But mony a gallant Englishman
  Ere day the Scotsmen slew.

The Gordons good, in English blood,
  They steep'd their hose and shoon ;

The Lindsays flew like fire about,
  Till all the fray was done.

The Percy and Montgomery met,
  That either of other were fain ;
They swapped swords, and they twa swat,
  And aye the blood ran down between.

" Now yield thee, yield thee, Percy," he said,
  " Or else I vow I'll lay thee low ! "—
" To whom must I yield," quoth Earl Percy,
  " Now that I see it must be so ? "—

" Thou shalt not yield to lord nor loun,
  Nor yet shalt thou yield to me ;
But yield thee to the braken bush,
  That grows upon yon lilye lee ! "—

" I will not yield to a braken bush,
  Nor yet will I yield to a brier ;
But I would yield to Earl Douglas,
  Or Sir Hugh the Montgomery, if he were here."

As soon as he knew it was Montgomery,
  He struck his sword's point in the gronde ;
The Montgomery was a courteous knight,
  And quickly took him by the honde.

This deed was done at the Otterbourne
  About the breaking of the day ;
Earl Douglas was buried at the braken bush,
  And the Percy led captive away.

Anonymous.

F 2

XLII

EDWARD

I

" Why does your brand sae drop wi' blude,
      Edward, Edward ?
Why does your brand sae drop wi' blude,
    And why sae sad gang ye, O ? "—
" O I hae kill'd my hawk sae gude,
      Mither, mither ;
O I hae kill'd my hawk sae gude,
    And I had nae mair but he, O."

II

" Your hawk's blude was never sae red,
      Edward, Edward ;
Your hawk's blude was never sae red,
    My dear son, I tell thee, O."—
" O I hae kill'd my red-roan steed,
      Mither, mither ;
O I hae kill'd my red-roan steed,
    That erst was sae fair and free, O."

III

" Your steed was auld, and ye hae got mair,
      Edward, Edward ;
Your steed was auld, and ye hae got mair ;
    Some other dule ye dree, O."
" O I hae kill'd my father dear,
      Mither, mither ;

O I hae kill'd my father dear,
    Alas, and wae is me, O ! "

IV

" And whatten penance will ye dree for that,
    Edward, Edward ?
Whatten penance will ye dree for that ?
    My dear son, now tell me, O."—
" I'll set my feet in yonder boat,
    Mither, mither ;
I'il set my feet in yonder boat,
    And I'll fare over the sea, O."

V

" And what will ye do wi' your tow'rs and your ha',
    Edward, Edward ?
And what will ye do wi' your tow'rs and your ha',
    That were sae fair to see, O ? "—
" I'll let them stand till they doun fa',
    Mither, mither ;
I'll let them stand till they doun fa',
    For here never mair maun I be, O."

VI

" And what will ye leave to your bairns and your
    wife,
    Edward, Edward ?
And what will ye leave to your bairns and your
    wife,
    When ye gang owre the sea, O ? "—
" The warld's room : let them beg through life,
    Mither, mither ;

The warld's room : let them beg through life ;
    For them never mair will I see, O."

VII

" And what will ye leave to your ain mither dear,
    Edward, Edward ?
And what will ye leave to your ain mither dear,
    My dear son, now tell me, O ? "—
" The curse of hell frae me sall ye bear,
    Mither, mither ;
The curse of hell frae me sall ye bear :
    Sic counsels ye gave to me, O ! "

                    Anonymous.

XLIII

BONNY GEORGE CAMPBELL

I

Hie upon Hielands,
    And laigh upon Tay,
Bonny George Campbell
    Rade out on a day :
Saddled and bridled,
    Sae gallant to see,
Hame cam' his gude horse,
    But never cam' he.

II

Down ran his auld mither,
    Greetin' fu' sair ;

Out ran his bonny bride,
   Reaving her hair ;
" My meadow lies green,
   And my corn is unshorn,
My barn is to bigg,
   And my babe is unborn."

III

Saddled and bridled
   And booted rade he ;
A plume in his helmet,
   A sword at his knee ;
But toom cam' his saddle
   A' bluidy to see,
O hame cam' his gude horse,
   But never cam' he !

Anonymous.

XLIV

OMNIA VANITAS

(Translated from the Gaelic)

Is not man's greatest heart's desire
A bitter guerdon when 'tis won ?
A crown bequeathed by royal sire
Is nought compared with dreams you've spun.

Even as the rose in garden fair
When plucked soon sheds its lovely bloom,
And marred by hand beyond repair,
Will swiftly lose its sweet perfume.

No man of high or low estate
Can hope from sorrow to be free :
Kings have their heart-breaks just as great
As commoners of low degree.

Each sod of peat in smoke must burn.
Each human blessing pain will bring.
Each rose-bud has its prickly thorn.
Who gathers honey dares the sting.

What though yon man be rich in gold ?
Sadness is writ upon his face.
The clearest well your eyes behold
Has sand to foul it at the base.

Dugald Buchanan.

XLV

THE BONNIE BROUKIT BAIRN

Mars is braw in crammasy,
Venus in a green silk goun,
The auld mune shak's her gowden feathers,
Their starry talk's a wheen o' blethers,
Nane for thee a thochtie sparin',
Earth, thou bonnie broukit bairn !
—*But greet, an' in your tears ye'll droun
The haill clanjamfrie !*

Hugh MacDiarmid.

XLVI

FROM " ANE SATIRE OF THE THREE ESTAITIS "

(Oppression betrays Theft)

Oppressioun

Have I nocht made ane honest shift
That has betrasit Commoun Thift,
For thar is nocht under the lift
    And curster corse.
I am richt sure that he and I
Within this half-year craftily
Has stolen ane thousand sheep and kye
    By maris and hors.
Wald God that I were sound and haill,
Now liftit into Liddesdale,
The Merse suld find me beef and kale
    Whatrack of bread.
Where I there liftit with my life,
The Devil suld stick me with a knife
And ever I come again in Fife
    Whill I were deid :
Adew, I leave the Devil amang you
That in his fingaris he may fang you
With all leill men that dois belang you,
    For I may rue
That evir I come into this land ;
For why ye may weill understand
I gat na gear to turn mine hand
    Yet anis adew.

THEFT

(Speaks from the gallows)

Allace, this is ane fellon rippat.
The widdefow wardens tuk my gear
And left me nowdir hors nor meir,
   Nor erdly gude that me belangit,
     Now wallaway I mon be hangit.
Repent your livis all plain oppressiouris
All murdressaris and strang transgressouris
Or ellis ga choose you gude confessouris,
   And mak you ford :
For and ye tarry in this land
And come under correctiounis hand
   Your grace sall be I understand
     Ane gude sharp cord.
Adew, my brether commoun thievis
That helpit me in my mischievis
Adew Grossaris, Niksonis and Bellis,
Oft have we fairne out through the fellis ;
Adew Robsonis, Hawis and Pylis
That in our craft has mony wylis ;
Littillis, Trumbillis and Armestrangis
Adew, all thievis that me belangis,
Tailyouris, Erewynis and Elwandis,
Speedy of feet and slicht of handis,
The Scottis of Eskdale and the Grames
I have na time to tell your names,
With King Correctioun be ye fangit
Believe richt sure ye will be hangit.

FALSET

(*After Theft is hanged*)

Wae's me for good Commoun Thift
Was never man made more honest shift
    His living for to win.
There was nocht in all Liddesdale
That kye more craftily could steal
    Where thou hangs on that pin.
                Sir David Lyndsay.

XLVII

TAM I' THE KIRK

O Jean, my Jean, when the bell ca's the con-
    gregation,
Owre valley an' hill wi' the ding frae its iron mou',
When a'body's thochts is set on his ain salvation,
    Mine's set on you.

There's a reid rose lies on the Buik o' the Word
    afore ye
That was growin' braw on its bush at the keek o'
    day,
But the lad that pu'd yon flower i' the mornin's
    glory
        He canna pray.

He canna pray; but there's nane i' the kirk will
    heed him
Whaur he sits his lane at the side o' the wa'.

For nane but the reid rose kens what my lassie
    gie'd him :
        It an' us twa !

He canna sing for the sang that his ain he'rt
    raises,
He canna see for the mist that's afore his een,
And a voice drouns the hale o' the psalms an' the
    paraphrases,
        Cryin' " Jean, Jean, Jean ! "
                          Violet Jacob.

XLVIII

TO LUVE UNLUVIT

To luve unluvit is ane pain ;
For she that is my soverane,
    Some wanton man so hie has set her
That I can get no luve again,
    Bot breaks my hairt, and nocht the better.

When that I went with that sweet may,
To dance, to sing, to sport and play,
    And oft-times in my armis plet her ;
I do now murne both nicht and day,
    And breaks my hairt, and nocht the better.

Where I was wont to see her go
Richt trimly passand to and fro,
    With comely smilis when that I met her ;
And now I live in pain and woe,
    And breaks my hairt, and nocht the better.

Whatten ane glaikit fule am I
To slay myself with melancholy,
　　Sen weill I ken I may nocht get her !
Or what suld be the cause, and why,
　　To brek my hairt, and nocht the better ?

My hairt sen thou may nocht her please,
Adieu, as gude luve comis as gais,
　　Go choose ane other and forget her ;
God gif him dolour and disease
　　That breaks their hairt, and nocht the better.
Alexander Scott.

XLIX

WHA IS PERFYTE

WHA is perfyte to put in writ
The inwart murning and mischance,
Or to endite the great delight
Of lusty luvis observance,
Bot he that may, certain, patiently suffer pain
To win his soverane in recompanse.

Albeit I know of luvis law
The pleasure and the painis smart,
Yet I stand awe for to furthshaw
The quiet secretis of my heart.
For it may Fortune raith to do her body skaith
Whilk wat that of them baith I am expert.

She wat my woe that is ago,
She wat my welfare and remead,

She wat also, I luve no mo
    Bot her, the well of womanheid.
She wat withouten fail, I am her luvar laill,
She has my hairt all haill till I be deid.

    That bird of bliss in beauty is
        In erd the only a per se,
    Whase mouth to kiss is worth, I wis,
        The warld full of gold to me.
Is nocht in erd I cure, bot please my lady pure,
Syne be her servitour unto I dee.

    She has my luve at her behufe,
        My hairt is subject bound and thrall,
    For she dois move my hairt abuve
        To see her proper persoun small.
Sen she is wrocht at will, that Nature may fulfil
Gladly I give her till, body and all.

    There is nocht wie can estimie
        My sorrow and my sighingis sair,
    For I am so done faithfully
        In favouris with my lady fair
That baith our hairtis are ane, locknyt in luvis
        chain,
And everilk grief is gane for evermair.
                                    Alexander Scott.

L

ALL MY LUVE, LEAVE ME NOT

    ALL my luve, leave me not,
        Leave me not, leave me not,

All my luve, leave me not
   Thus mine alone.
With ane burden on my back,
I may not bear it I am sa waik,
Luve, this burden fra me take
   Or ellis I am gone.

With sinnis I am laden sore,
Leave me not, leave me not,
With sinnis I am laden sore
   Leave me not alone.
I pray Thee, Lord, therefore,
Keep not my sinnis in store,
Loose me or I be forlore,
   And hear my moan.

With Thy handis Thou has me wrocht,
Leave me not, leave me not,
With Thy handis Thou has me wrocht,
   Leave me not alone.
I was sold and Thou me bocht,
With Thy blude Thou has me coft,
Now am I hither socht
   To Thee, Lord, alone.

I cry and I call to Thee,
To leave me not, to leave me not,
I cry and I call to Thee
To leave me not alone.
   All they that laden be
Thou biddis come to Thee
Then sall they savit be
   Through Thy mercy alone.

Anonymous.

LI

O MISTRESS MINE

O MISTRESS mine, till you I me commend
All haill, my hairt sen that ye have in cure,
For, but your grace, my life is near the end ;
Now let me nocht in danger me endure.
Of lifelik luve suppois I be sure
Wha wat na God may me some succour send,
Then for your luve why wald ye I forfure ?
O mistress mine ! till you I me commend.

The winter nicht ane hour I may nocht sleep
For thocht of you, bot tumbland to and fro,
Me-think ye are into my armis, sweet,
And when I wauken, ye are so far me fro ;
Alas ! alas ! then waukenis my woe,
Then wary I the time that I you kend ;
War nocht gude hope, my heart wad burst in two,
O mistress mine ! till you I me commend.

Sen ye are ane that has my hairt alhaill,
Without feigning I may it nocht ganestand,
Ye are the bounty bliss of all my bale,
Baith life and death standis into your hand.
Sen that I am sair bunden in your hand,
That nicht or day, I wat nocht where to wend,
Let me anis say that I your friendship fand.
O mistress mine ! till you I me commend.

Anonymous.

LII

MY HEART IS HEICH ABOVE

My heart is heich above,
  My body is full of bliss,
For I am set in luve,
  As well as I wald wiss ;
I luve my lady pure,
  And she luvis me again ;
I am her serviture,
  She is my soverane.

She is my very heart,
  I am her hope and heal ;
She is my joy inwart,
  I am her luvar leal ;
I am her bound and thrall,
  She is at my command ;
I am perpetual
  Her man, both fute and hand.

The thing that may her please
  My body sall fulfil ;
Whatever her disease,
  It dois my body ill.
My bird, my bonnie ane,
  My tender babe venust,
My luve, my life alane,
  My liking and my lust.

We interchange our hairtis
  In otheris armis soft ;

Spreitless we twa depairtis
   Uand our luvis oft ;
We murne when licht day dawis,
   We plain the nicht is short,
We curse the cock that crawis,
   That hinderis our disport.

I glowffin up agast,
   When I her miss on nicht,
And in my oxter fast
   I find the bowster richt ;
Then languor on me lies,
   Like Morpheus the mair,
Whilk causis me uprise
   And to my sweet repair :

And then is all the sorrow
   Furth of remembrance,
That ever I had aforrow
   In luvis observance.
Thus never do I rest,
   So lusty a life I lead,
When that I list to test
   The well of womanheid.

Luvaris in pain, I pray
   God send you sic remead
As I have nicht and day,
   You to defend from deid ;
Therefore be ever true
   Unto your ladies free,
And they will on you rue,
   As mine has done on me.
             Anonymous.

LIII

OF A' THE AIRTS THE WIND CAN BLAW

OF a' the airts the wind can blaw,
  I dearly like the west,
For there the bonnie lassie lives,
  The lassie I lo'e best ;
There wild-woods grow, and rivers row,
  And mony a hill between :
But day and night my fancy's flight
  Is ever wi' my Jean.

I see her in the dewy flowers,
  I see her sweet and fair :
I hear her in the tunefu' birds,
  I hear her charm the air :
There's not a bonnie flower that springs,
  By fountain, shaw, or green ;
There's not a bonnie bird that sings,
  But minds me o' my Jean.

Robert Burns.

LIV

O MY LUVE'S LIKE A RED, RED ROSE

O MY luve's like a red, red rose,
  That's newly sprung in June :
O my luve's like the melodie
  That's sweetly play'd in tune.

As fair art thou, my bonnie lass,
　　So deep in luve am I ;
And I will luve thee still, my dear,
　　Till a' the seas gang dry.

Till a' the seas gang dry, my dear,
　　And the rocks melt wi' the sun ;
And I will luve thee still, my dear,
　　While the sands o' life shall run.

And fare thee weel, my only luve !
　　And fare thee weel a while !
And I will come again, my luve,
　　Tho' it were ten thousand mile.

Robert Burns

LV

MY AIN KIND DEARIE, O

(AIR—" The Lea Rig ")
[Based upon an old song]

WHEN o'er the hill the eastern star
　　Tells bughtin' time is near, my jo ;
An' owsen frae the furrow'd field
　　Return sae dowf an' weary, O ;
Down by the burn, where scented birks
　　Wi' dew are hanging clear, my jo,
I'll meet thee on the lea rig,
　　My ain kind dearie, O.

In mirkest glen, at midnight hour,
　　I'd rove, an' ne'er be earie, O,

If thro' that glen I gaed to thee,
  My ain kind dearie, O.
Altho' the night was ne'er sae wild,
  An' I were ne'er sae wearie, O,
I'd meet thee on the lea rig,
  My ain kind dearie, O.

The hunter lo'es the morning sun,
  To rouse the mountain deer, my jo :
At noon the fisher seeks the glen,
  Along the burn to steer, my jo ;
Gi'e me the hour o' gloamin' gray,
  It mak's my heart sae cheery, O,
To meet thee on the lea rig,
  My ain kind dearie, O.

Robert Burns.

LVI

IF DOUGHTY DEEDS

If doughty deeds my lady please
  Right soon I'll mount my steed ;
And strong his arm, and fast his seat,
  That bears frae me the meed.
I'll wear thy colours in my cap,
  Thy picture in my heart ;
And he that bends not to thine eye
  Shall rue it to his smart.
    Then tell me how to woo thee, love ;
      O tell me how to woo thee !
    For thy dear sake, nae care I'll take,
      Thro' ne'er another trow me.

If gay attire delight thine eye
   I'll dight me in array ;
I'll tend thy chamber door all night,
   And squire thee all the day.
If sweetest sounds can win thine ear,
   These sounds I'll strive to catch ;
Thy voice I'll steal to woo thysell,
   That voice that nane can match.

But if fond love thy heart can gain,
   I never broke a vow ;
Nae maiden lays her skaith to me,
   I never loved but you.
For you alone I ride the ring,
   For you I wear the blue ;
For you alone I strive to sing,
   O tell me how to woo !
     Then tell me how to woo thee, love ;
      O tell me how to woo thee !
     For thy dear sake, nae care I'll take,
      Tho' ne'er another trow me.
         R. Graham of Gartmore

LVII

THE COMING OF LOVE

(From *The Kingis Quhair*)

BEWAILLING in my chamber thus allone,
   Despeired of all my joye and remedye,
For-tiret of my thought and wo-begone,
   And to the wyndow gan I walk in hye,

To see the warld and folk that went forbye,
  As for the tyme though I of mirthis fude
Mycht have no more, to luke it did me gude.

Now was there maid fast by the Touris wall
  A gardyn faire, and in the corner's set
Ane herbere greene, with wandis long and small,
  Railit about, and so with treis set
Was all the place, and hawthorn hegis knet,
  That lyf was non walkyng there forbye,
  That mycht within scarce any wight aspy.

So thick the bewis and the levis grene
  Beschadit all the allyes that there were,
And myddis every herbere mycht be sene
  The scharpe grene suete jenepere,
Growing so fair with branchis here and there,
  That, as it semyt to a lyf without,
  The bewis spred the herbere all about.

And on the smale grene twistis sat
  The lytil suete nyghtingale, and song
So loud and clere, the ympnis consecrat
  Of luvis use, now soft now lowd among,
That all the gardynis and the wallis rong
  Ryght of thair song, and on the copill next
  Of thaire suete armony, and lo the text :

" Worschippe, ye that loveris bene, this May,
  For of your bliss the kalendis are begonne,
And sing with us, away winter, away,
  Come somer, come, the suete seson and sonne,
Awake, for schame ! that have your hevynis wonne,

And amourously lift up your hedis all,
    Thank Lufe that list you to his merci call.

When thai this song had song a littil thrawe,
    Thai stent a quhile, and therewith unafraid,
As I beheld, and kest myn eyen a-lawe,
    From beugh to beugh thay hippit and thai plaid,
And freschly in thair birdis kynd araid
    Thair fatheris new, and fret thame in the sonne,
    And thankit Lufe, that had their makis wonne.

And therewith kest I doun myn eye ageyne,
    Whare as I saw walkyng under the Toure,
Full secretely, new cumyn hir to playne,
    The fairest or the freschest younge floure
That ever I sawe, methought, before that houre,
    For which sodayne abate, anon astert
    The blude of all my body to my hert.

And though I stood abaisit tho a lyte,
    No wonder was ; for why ? my wittis all
Were so ouercome with plesance and delyte,
    Only through latting of myn eyen fall,
That sudaynly my hert become hir thrall,
    For ever of free wyll, for of manace
    There was no takyn in her suete face.

And in my hede I drew rycht hastily,
    And eft sones I lent it out ageyne,
And saw hir walk that verray womanly,
    With no wight mo, bot only women tueyne,
Than gan I studye in myself and seyne :
    " Ah ! suete, are ye a warldly creature,
    Or hevinly thing in likeness of nature ?

" Or ye god Cupidis owin princess ?
　And cumyn are to louse me out of band,
Or are ye veray Nature the goddesse,
　That have depayntit with your hevinly hand
This gardyn full of flouris, as they stand ?
　What sall I think, allace ! what reverence
　Sall I minister to your excellence ?

" Giff ye a goddess be, and that ye like
　To do me payne, I may it not astert ;
Giff ye be warldly wight, that dooth me sike,
　Why lest God mak you so, my derest hert,
To do a sely prisoner thus smert,
　That lufis you all, and wote of nought but wo ?
　And, therefore, merci, suete ! sen it is so."

When I a lytill thrawe had maid my mone,
　Bewailing myn infortune and my chance,
Unknawin' how or what was best to done,
　So ferre I fallyng into lufis dance,
That sodaynly my wit, my contenance,
　My hert, my will, my nature, and my mynd,
　Was changit clene rycht in ane other kind.
　　　　　　　　　　James I. of Scotland.

LVIII

CUPID AND VENUS

FRA bank to bank, fra wood to wood I rin,
　Ourhailit with my feeble fantasie ;
　Like til a leaf that fallis from a tree,

Or til a reed ourblawin with the win'.
Twa gods guides me; the ane of them is blin',
   Yea and a bairn brocht up in vanitie ;
   The next a wife ingenrit of the sea,
And lichter nor a dauphin with her fin.

Unhappy is the man for evermair
   That tills the sand and sawis in the air ;
   But twice unhappier is he, I lairn,
That feedis in his hairt a mad desire,
And follows on a woman throw the fire,
   Led by a blind and teachit by a bairn.
               Mark Alexander Boyd.

LIX

THE WATERGAW

Ae weet forenicht i' the yow-trummle
I saw yon antrin thing,
A watergaw wi' its chitterin' licht
Ayont the on-ding ;
An' I thocht o' the last wild look ye gied
Afore ye deed !

There was nae reek i' the laverock's hoose
That nicht — an' nane i' mine :
But I ha'e thocht o' that foolish licht
Ever sin' syne ;
An' I think that mebbe at last I ken
What your look meant then.
               Hugh MacDiarmid.

LX

GO, HEART, UNTO THE LAMP OF LICHT [1]

Go, heart, unto the lamp of licht,
  Go, heart, do service and honour,
Go, heart, and serve him day and nicht,
  Go, heart, unto thy Saviour.

Go, heart, to thy only remeid
  Descending from the heavenly tour :
Thee to deliver from pyne and deide,
  Go, heart, unto thy Saviour.

Go, heart, but dissimulatioun,
  To Christ, that took our vile nature,
For thee to suffer passioun,
  Go, heart, unto thy Saviour.

Go, heart, richt humill and meek,
  Go, heart, as leal and true servitour,
To him that heill is for all seek,
  Go, heart, unto thy Saviour.

Go, heart, with true and haill intent,
  To Christ thy help and haill succour,

[1] From *The Gude and Godlie Ballatis*, 1567—a translation of Luther's hymn for Christmas Eve " Vom himel hoch da kom ich her ". The first six stanzas are omitted.

G

Thee to redeem he was all rent,
　Go, heart, unto thy Saviour.

To Christ, that raise from death to live,
　Go, heart, unto thy latter hour,
Whais great mercy can nane discrive,
　Go, heart, unto thy Saviour.

Anonymous.

LXI

BLEST, BLEST AND HAPPY HE

Blest, blest and happy he
Whose eyes behold her face,
But blessed more whose ears hath heard
The speeches framed with grace.

And he is half a god
That these thy lips may kiss,
Yet god all whole that may enjoy
　Thy body as it is.

Anonymous.

LXII

BAITH GUDE AND FAIR AND WOMANLY

Baith gude and fair and womanly,
Debonair, steadfast, wise and true,
Courteous, humill and lawlie,
And groundit weill in all virtue,

To whose service I sall pursue
Worship without villany,
And ever anon I sall be true,
Baith gude and fair and womanly.

Honour for ever unto that free
That nature formit has so fair ;
In worship of her fresh beautie
To Luvis court I will repair,
To serve and luve without despair,
Forthy I wat her most worthy
For to be callit our allwhere
Baith gude and fair and womanly.

Sen that I give my hairt her to,
Why wyte I her of my murning ?
Though I be woe what wyte has scho ?
What wald I more of my sweet thing
That wat not of my womenting.
When I her see comfort am I,
Her fair effeir and fresh having
Is gude and fair and womanly.

Thing in this warld that I best luve,
My very heart and comforting,
To whose service I sall pursue
Whill deid mak our depairting.
Faithful, constant, and bening
I sall be while the life is in me,
And luve her best attour all thing,
Baith gude and fair and womanly.

Anonymous.

LXIII

THE TRYST

O LUELY, luely, cam she in
And luely she lay doun :
I kent her be her caller lips
And her breists sae sma' and roun'.

A' thru the nicht we spak nae word
Nor sinder'd bane frae bane :
A' thru the nicht I heard her hert
Gang soundin' wi' my ain.

It was about the waukrife hour
Whan cocks begin to craw
That she smool'd saftly thru the mirk
Afore the day wud daw.

Sae luely, luely, cam she in
Sae luely was she gaen ;
And wi' her a' my simmer days
Like they had never been.

William Soutar.

LXIV

BARBARA

ON the Sabbath-day,
  Through the churchyard old and gray,
Over the crisp and yellow leaves I held my rustling
    way ;

And amid the words of mercy, falling on my soul
 like balms,
'Mid the gorgeous storms of music—in the
 mellow organ-calms,
'Mid the upward-streaming prayers, and the
 rich and solemn psalms,
   I stood careless, Barbara.

   My heart was otherwhere,
   While the organ shook the air,
And the priest, with outspread hands, bless'd
 the people with a prayer ;
But when rising to go homeward, with a mild
 and saint-like shine
Gleam'd a face of airy beauty with its heavenly
 eyes on mine—
Gleam'd and vanish'd in a moment—O that
 face was surely thine
   Out of heaven, Barbara !

   O pallid, pallid face !
   O earnest eyes of grace !
When last I saw thee, dearest, it was in another
 place.
You came running forth to meet me with my love-
 gift on your wrist :
The flutter of a long white dress, then all was lost
 in mist—
A purple stain of agony was on the mouth I kiss'd,
   That wild morning, Barbara.

   I search'd, in my despair,
   Sunny noon and midnight air ;

I could not drive away the thought that you were
lingering there.
O many and many a winter night I sat when you
were gone,
My worn face buried in my hands, beside the fire
alone—
Within the dripping churchyard, the rain plashing
on your stone,
    You were sleeping, Barbara.

    'Mong angels, do you think
    Of the precious golden link
I clasp'd around your happy arm while sitting by
yon brink ?
Or when that night of gliding dance, of laughter
and guitars,
Was emptied of its music, and we watch'd, through
lattice-bars,
The silent midnight heaven creeping o'er us with
its stars,
    Till the day broke, Barbara ?

    In the years I've changed ;
    Wild and far my heart has ranged,
And many sins and errors now have been on me
avenged ;
But to you I have been faithful whatsoever good I
lack'd :
I loved you, and above my life still hangs that love
intact—
Your love the trembling rainbow, I the reckless
cataract.
    Still I love you, Barbara.

Yet, Love, I am unblest ;
　　With many doubts opprest,
I wander like the desert wind without a place of
　　rest.
Could I but win you for an hour from off that
　　starry shore,
The hunger of my soul were still'd ; for Death
　　hath told you more
Than the melancholy world doth know—things
　　deeper than all lore
　　You could teach me, Barbara.

　　In vain, in vain, in vain !
　　You will never come again.
There droops upon the dreary hills a mournful
　　fringe of rain ;
The gloaming closes slowly round, loud winds
　　are in the tree,
Round selfish shores for ever moans the hurt and
　　wounded sea ;
There is no rest upon the earth, peace is with
　　Death and thee—
　　　　Barbara !

　　　　　　　　　　Alexander Smith.

LXV

ECSTASY

O ye that look on Ecstasy
　　The Dancer lone and white,
Cover your charmed eyes, for she
　　Is Death's own acolyte.

She dances on the moonstone floors
Against the jewelled peacock doors :
The roses flame in her gold hair,
The tired sad lids are overfair.
All ye that look on Ecstasy
    The Dancer lone and white,
Cover your dreaming eyes, lest she—
(*Oh ! softly, strangely !*)—float you through
These doors all bronze and green and blue
    Into the Bourg of Night.
                Rachel Annand Taylor.

LXVI

ROMANCE

I WILL make you brooches and toys for your
    delight
Of bird-song at morning and star-shine at night.
I will make a palace fit for you and me,
Of green days in forests and blue days at sea.

I will make my kitchen, and you shall keep your
    room,
Where white flows the river and bright blows the
    broom,
And you shall wash your linen and keep your body
    white
In rainfall at morning and dewfall at night.

And this shall be for music when no one else is
    near,

The fine song for singing, the rare song to hear !
That only I remember, that only you admire,
Of the broad road that stretches and the roadside
    fire.

                Robert Louis Stevenson.

LXVII

THE NIGHT IS NEAR GONE

HAY ! now the day dawis,
The jolly cock crawis,
Now shroudis the shawis
    Throw Nature anon.
The throstle-cock cryis
On lovers wha lyis ;
Now skaillis the skyis :
    The night is near gone.

The fieldis ourflowis
With gowans that growis
Where lilies like lowe is,
    As red as the ro'an.
The turtle that true is,
With notes that renewis,
Her pairtie pursueis :
    The night is near gone.

Now hartis with hindis,
Conform to their kindis,
Hie tursis their tyndis,
    On grund where they groan.

G 2

Now hurchonis, with haris,
Ay passes in pairis ;
Whilk duly declaris
   The night is near gone.

The season excellis
Through sweetness that smellis ;
Now Cupid compellis
   Our hairtis each one
On Venus wha wakis,
To muse on our makis,
Syne sing, for their sakis :
   " The night is near gone ".

All courageous knichtis
Aganis the day dichtis
The briest-plate that bricht is,
   To fecht with their fone.
The stoned steed stampis
Through courage, and crampis,
Syne on the land lampis :
   The night is near gone.

The freikis on fieldis
That wight wapins wieldis
With shining bright shieldis
   As Titan in trone ;
Stiff spearis in restis,
Owre courseris crestis,
Are broke on their breistis :
   The night is near gone,

So hard are their hittis,
Some swayis, some sittis,
And some perforce flittis
    On grund whill they groan.
Syne groomis that gay is,
On bonkis and brayis
With swordis assayis :
'The night is near gone.

Alexander Montgomerie.

LXVIII

THE ROYAL PALACE OF THE HIGHEST HEAVEN

(Probably by Montgomery)

THE royal palace of the highest heaven,
    The stately furneis of the starry round,
The lofty vault of wandering planetis seven,
    The air, the fire, the water and the ground ;
    Suppose of these the science be profound,
Surpassing far our gross and silly sense,
    The pregnant spreits yet of the learnit hes found
By age, by time, by long experience
Their pitch, their power, and their influence,
    The course of nature and her movingis all,
So that we need not now be in suspense
    Of earthly thingis, nor yet celestial :
Bot only of this monster love we doubt,
Whose crafty course no cunning can find out.

Alexander Montgomerie.

LXIX

FROM "THE CHERRY AND THE SLAE"

About ane bank, where birdis on bewis
Ten thousand timis their notis renewis
  Ilk hour into the day,
The merle and mavis micht be seen,
The progne and the philomene,
  Whilk causit me to stay.
I lay and leanit me to ane buss
  To hear the birdis beir ;
Their mirth was sa melodious
  Throw nature of the year :
    Some singing, some springing
      So heich into the sky ;
    So nim'ly and trimly
      Thir birdis flew me by.

I saw the hurcheon and the hare,
Wha fed amang the flouris fair,
  Were happing to and fro.
I saw the cunning and the cat,
Whase downis with the dew was wat,
  With mony beistis mo.
The hart, the hind, the doe, the roe,
  The fowmart, and the fox
Were skipping all fra brae to brae,
  Amang the water brocks ;
    Some feeding, some dreiding
      In case of sudden snares ;

With skipping and tripping
   They hantit all in pairs.

The air was sa attemperate,
But ony mist immaculate,
   Baith purifyit and clear ;
The fieldis fair were flourishit,
As Nature had them nourishit
   Baith delicate and deir ;
And every bloom on branch and beuch
   So prettily they spread,
And hang their heidis out-owre the heuch
   In Mayis colour cled ;
      Some knopping, some dropping
         Of balmy liquor sweet,
      Distelling and smelling
         Throw Phoebus' halesome heat.

The cuckoo and the cushat cried,
The turtle, on the other side,
   Na pleasure had to play ;
So schill in sorrow was her sang
That, through her voice, the roches rang ;
   For Echo answerit ay,
Lamenting still Narcissus' case,
   Wha starvit at the well ;
Wha through the shadow of his face
   For luve did slay himsel.
      Whiles weeping and creeping
         About the well he bade ;
      Whiles lying, whiles crying,
         Bot it na answer made.

The dew as diamonds did hing
Upon the tender twistis ying,
    Our-twinkling all the trees ;
And ay where flouris did flourish fair,
There suddenly I saw repair
    Ane swarm of sounding bees.
Some sweetly has the honey socht,
    Whill they were cloggit sore ;
Some willingly the wax has wrocht,
    To keep it up in store.
        So heaping with keeping,
            Into their lives they hide it,
        Precisely and wisely
            For winter they provide it.

To pen the pleasures of that park,
How every blossom, branch, and bark
    Against the sun did shine,
I leif to poetis to compile
In stately verse and ornate style :
    It passes my ingine.
Bot as I movit me alane,
    I saw ane river rin
Out-owre ane crag and rock of stane,
    Syne lichtit in ane linn,
        With tumbling and rumbling
            Amang the roches round,
        Devalling and falling
            Into that pit profound.

To hear the startling streamis clear
Me-thocht it music to the ear,
    Where descant did abound

With treble sweet, and tenor just,
And ay the echo repercust
  Her diapason sound,
Set with the Ci-sol-fa-uth cleif,
   Thereby to knaw the note ;
There soundit a michty semibreif
   Out of the elfis throat.
    Discreetly, mair sweetly
     Nor crafty Amphion,
    Or Muses that uses
     At fountain Helicon.
              Alexander Montgomerie.

LXX

ROBENE AND MAKYNE

Robene sat on gude green hill
Keepand a flock of fe :
Merry Makyne said him till,
" Robene, thou rue on me ;
I have thee luvit loud and still,
Thir yearis two or three ;
My dule in dern bot gif thou dill,
Doubtless but dreid I die."

Robene answerit, " Be the rude,
Naething of luve I knaw,
Bot keepis my sheep under yon wood,
Lo where they raik on raw :
What has marrit thee in they mood,
Makyne, to me thou shaw ;

Or what is luve, or to be lo'ed ?
Fain wald I leir that law."

" At luvis lair gif thou will leir,
Tak there ane *a b c* :
Be keynd, courteous, and fair of feir
Wise, hardy, and free ;
So that no danger do thee deir,
What dule in dern thou dree ;
Press thee with pain at all power
Be patient and privie."

Robene answerit her again,
" I wait nocht what is luve ;
Bot I have marvel in certain
What makis thee thus wanrufe :
The weddir is fair, and I am fain,
My sheep gois hale abufe ;
And we wald play us in this plain,
They wald us baith reprufe."

" Robene, tak tent unto my tale,
And work all as I rede,
And thou sall have my hairt all haill,
Eke and my maidenheid.
Sen God sendis bute for bale,
And for murning remeid,
In dern with thee bot gif I deal,
Doubtless I am bot deid."

" Makyne, to-morne this ilka tide,
An ye will meet me here,

Peradventure my sheep may gang beside,
Whill we have liggit full near ;
Bot maugre haif I, an I bide
Fra they begin to steir ;
What lyis on hairt I will nocht hide ;
Makyne, than mak gude cheer."

" Robene, thou reivis my roif and rest ;
I luve bot thee alane."
" Makyne, adieu, the sun gois west,
The day is near hand gané."
" Robene, in dule I am so drest,
That luve will be my bane,"
" Ga luve, Makyne, wherever thou list,
For leman I lo'e nane."

" Robene, I stand in sic a styll ;
I sich, and that full sair."
" Makyne, I have been here this while ;
At hame God gif I were."
" My honey, Robene, talk ane while ;
Gif thou will do na mair."
" Makyne, some other man beguile,
For hameward I will fare."

Robene on his wayis went,
As licht as leaf of tree ;
Makyne murnit in her intent,
And trow'd him never to see.
Robene braid attour the bent ;
Then Makyne cryit on hie,
" Now may thou sing, for I am shent !
What ailis luve at me ? "

Makyne went hame withouttin fail
Full weary eftir couth weep :
Then Robene in a full fair dale
Assemblit all his sheep.
Be that some pairt of Makyne's ail
Outthrow his hairt coud creep ;
He fallowit her fast there till assail,
And till her tuk gude keep.

" Abide, abide, thou fair Makyne,
A word for ony thing ;
For all my luve it sall be thine,
Withouttin depairting.
All haill thy heart for till have mine
Is all my coveting ;
My sheep to-morne whill houris nine
Will need of no keeping."

" Robene, thou has heard sung and say,
In gestis and storeis auld,
The man that will nocht when he may
Sall have nocht when he wald.
I pray to Jesu every day
Mot eke their cares cauld,
That first presses with thee to play,
Be firth, forest, or fauld."

" Makyne, the nicht is soft and dry,
The weddir is warm and fair,
And the green wood richt near us by
To walk attour all where ;

There may na janglour us espy,
That is to luve contrair ;
Therein, Makyne, baith ye and I
Unseen we may repair."

" Robene, that warld is all away
And quite brocht till ane end,
And never again thereto, perfay,
Sall it be as thou wend ;
For of my pain thou made it play,
And all in vain I spend ;
As thou has done, sa sall I say,
Murne on, I think to mend."

" Makyne, the hope of all my heal,
My hairt on thee is set,
And evermair to thee be leal,
While I may live but let ;
Never to fail, as otheris feill,
What grace that ever I get."
" Robene, with thee I will nocht deal ;
Adieu, for thus we met."

Makyne went hame blyth aneuch,
Attour the holtis hair ;
Robene murnit, and Makyne leuch ;
She sang, he sichit sair ;
And so left him, baith wo and wreuch,
In dolour and in care,
Keepand his herd under a heuch,
Amangis the holtis hair.

Robert Henryson.

LXXI

THE GARMONT OF GUDE LADIES

WALD my gude lady luve me best
And work eftir my will,
I suld ane garmont gudliest
Gar mak her body till.

Of hie honour suld be her hood,
Upon her heid to wear,
Garneist with governance so gude,
Na deeming suld her deir.

Her serk suld be her body nixt,
Of chastitie so white,
With shame and dreid togidder mixt,
The same suld be perfite.

Her kirtle suld be of clean constance,
Laced with leesome luve,
The mailyeis of continuance
For never to remove.

Her gown suld be of gudliness.
Weill ribbon'd with renoun,
Purfillit with pleasure in ilk place
Furrit with fine fassoun.

Her belt suld be of benignitie
About her middle meet ;
Her mantle of humilitie,
To thole baith wind and weet.

Her hat suld be of fair-having,
And her tepat of truth ;
Her patelet of gude-pansing ;
Her hals-ribbon of ruth.

Her sleevis suld be of esperance,
To keep her fra despair ;
Her glovis of gude governance,
To guide her fingeris fair.

Her shoon suld be of siccarness,
In sign that she nocht slide ;
Her hose of honestie, I guess,
I suld for her provide.

Wald she put on this garmont gay,
I durst swear by my seill,
That she wore never green nor grey
That set her half so weill.

Robert Henryson.

LXXII

O WHISTLE AN' I'LL COME TO YE, MY LAD

Chorus

O whistle an' I'll come to ye, my lad,
O whistle an' I'll come to ye, my lad,
Tho' father an' mother an' a' should gae mad
O whistle an' I'll come to ye, my lad.

But warily tent when ye come to court me,
And come nae unless the back-yett be a-jee ;
Syne up the back-stile, and let naebody see,
And come as ye were na comin to me,
And come as ye were na comin to me.

At kirk, or at market, whene'er ye meet me,
Gang by me as tho' that ye car'd na a flie ;
But steal me a blink o' your bonnie black e'e,
Yet look as ye were na lookin to me,
Yet look as ye were na lookin to me.

Aye vow and protest that ye care na for me,
And whiles ye may lightly my beauty a wee ;
But court na anither, tho' jokin ye be,
For fear that she wile your fancy frae me,
For fear that she wile your fancy frae me.

Robert Burns.

LXXIII

THE LOVELY LASS O' INVERNESS

THE lovely lass o' Inverness,
　　Nae joy nor pleasure can she see ;
For e'en to morn she cries " alas ! "
　　And aye the saut tear blin's her e'e.

" Drumossie moor, Drumossie day—
　　A waefu' day it was to me ;
For there I lost my father dear,
　　My father dear, and brethren three.

" Their winding-sheet the bluidy clay,
    Their graves are growin green to see ;
And by them lies the dearest lad
    That ever blest a woman's e'e !

" Now wae to thee, thou cruel lord,
    A bluidy man I trow thou be ;
For mony a heart thou has made sair,
    That ne'er did wrang to thine or thee ! "

Robert Burns.

LXXIV

ANOTHER SONG

(Oran Eile)

(Translated from the Gaelic)

It is I that am under sorrow at this time. Dram
will not be drunk by me with cheer. A worm is
brooding in my vitals that has told the world my
secret desire. I may not see passing the maiden of
softest eye. That is what has cast down my spirit
to the ground like foliage from the tops of trees.

O maiden, most ringleted of hair, I am missing
you most desperately, yet if you have chosen a
good place for yourself my blessing every morn be
with you ! I am sighing after you like a warrior
who has been wounded, lying useless on the field,
and who will fight no more.

And I am left like a fugitive from the herd,
like a man who gives no esteem to woman, through

your journey oversea under a kerchief. *That* took an incontinent shedding of tears from my eyes. Better were it that I did not observe your beauty, your sense, and your renown, nor the sweet courtesy of your mouth that is more melodious than all music put together.

Each evil man who hears of my state—the state that puts fear on my nature—says that I am not a bard and that no poem of worth will be engendered by me, that my grandfather was a payer of rent and my father always a pedlar ; they would put geldings in the plough, but I would cut a verse before a hundred.

Long is my spirit in gloom. My apprehension will not awaken to music, bewildered in dream like the distressed wanderer of the ocean on the tops of the waves in mist. It is remembering that your gaiety is far away that has changed the hue of my complexion, left without love-talk, without mirth, without pride, without music, without grace, without strength.

I shall not awaken the lay at will, I shall not put a poem in order, I shall not raise music on the harp, I shall not hear the laughter of the young, I shall not ascend the pass of the high hills as was my wont, but I shall depart to sleep forever in the hall of the dead bards.

William Ross.
(Uilleam Ros.)

LXXV

DUNCAN GRAY

DUNCAN GRAY cam' here to woo,
 Ha, ha, the wooing o't,
On blythe Yule-night when we were fou,
 Ha, ha, the wooing o't :
Maggie coost her head fu' heigh,
Look'd asklent and unco skeigh,
Gart poor Duncan stand abeigh ;
 Ha, ha, the wooing o't.

Duncan fleech'd and Duncan pray'd ;
 Ha, ha, the wooing o't,
Meg was deaf as Ailsa Craig,
 Ha, ha, the wooing o't :
Duncan sigh'd baith out and in,
Grat his e'en baith blear't an' blin',
Spak o' lowpin o'er a linn ;
 Ha, ha, the wooing o't.

Time and Chance are but a tide,
 Ha, ha, the wooing o't,
Slighted love is sair to bide,
 Ha, ha, the wooing o't :
" Shall I, like a fool," quoth he,
" For a haughty hizzie die ?
She may gae to—France for me ! "
 Ha, ha, the wooing o't.

How it comes let doctors tell,
   Ha, ha, the wooing o't ;
Meg grew sick, as he grew hale,
   Ha, ha, the wooing o't.
Something in her bosom wrings,
For relief a sigh she brings :
And O ! her een they spak sic things !
   Ha, ha, the wooing o't.

Duncan was a lad o' grace,
   Ha, ha, the wooing o't :
Maggie's was a piteous case,
   Ha, ha, the wooing o't :
Duncan could na be her death,
Swelling pity smoor'd his wrath ;
Now they're crouse and canty baith,
   Ha, ha, the wooing o't.
          Robert Burns.

LXXVI

SIC A WIFE AS WILLIE HAD
(AIR : " The Eight Men of Moidart ")

[The heroine of this song was the wife of a farmer
near Ellisland]

WILLIE WASTLE dwalt on Tweed,
   The spot they called it Linkum-doddie ;
Willie was a wabster gude,
   Could stown a clew wi' ony body.
He had a wife was dour an' din,
   Oh, Tinkler Madgie was her mither ;

Sic a wife as Willie had,
   I wad na gi'e a button for her.

She has an e'e—she has but ane,
   The cat has twa the very colour ;
Five rusty teeth, forbye a stump,
   A clapper tongue wad deave a miller :
A whiskin' beard about her mou',
   Her nose an' chin they threaten ither—
Sic a wife as Willie had,
   I wad na gi'e a button for her.

She's bough-hough'd, she's hem-shinn'd,
   Ae limpin' leg, a hand-breed shorter ;
She's twisted right, she's twisted left,
   To balance fair in ilka quarter ;
She has a hump upon her breast,
   The twin o' that upon her shouther ;
Sic a wife as Willie had,
   I wad na gi'e a button for her.

Auld baudrons by the ingle sits,
   An' wi' her loof her face a-washin' ;
But Willie's wife is na sae trig,
   She dights her grunzie wi' a hushion ;
Her walie nieves like midden-creels,
   Her face wad fyle the Logan Water ;
Sic a wife as Willie had,
   I wad na gi'e a button for her.
                      Robert Burns.

LXXVII

THE WIFE OF AUCHTERMUCHTY

In Auchtermuchty there dwelt ane man,
Ane husband, as I heard it tauld,
Wha weil could tipple out a can,
And neither luvit hunger nor cauld.
Whill anis it fell upon a day,
He yokit his pleuch upon the plain ;
Gif it be true as I heard say,
The day was foul for wind and rain.

He lousit the pleuch at the landis en',
And draif his oxen hame at even ;
When he come in he lookit ben,
And saw the wife baith dry and clean,
And sittand at ane fire beikand bauld,
With ane fat soup as I heard say :
The man being very weet and cauld,
Between thae twa it was na play.

Quoth he, " Where is my horses' corn ?
My ox has neither hay nor strae ;
Dame, ye maun to the pleuch to-morne,
I sall be hussy, gif I may."
" Husband," quod she, " content am I
To tak the pleuch my day about,
Sa ye will rule baith calvis and kye,
And all the house baith in and out.

" Bot sen that ye will hussif-skep ken,
First ye sall sift, and syne sall knead ;

And ay as ye gang but and ben,
Luik that the bairnis be snodly cled.
Ye'se lay ane soft wisp to the kiln,
We haif ane dear farm on our heid ;
And ay as ye gang furth and in,
Keep weil the gaislingis fra the gled."

The wife was up richt late at even,
I pray God gife her evil to fare,
She kirn'd the kirn, and scum'd it clean,
And left the gudeman bot the bledoch bare.
Than in the morning up she gat,
And on her hairt laid her disjeune,
She put as meikle in her lap,
As micht haif ser'd them baith at noon.

Sayis, " Jock, will thou be maister of wark,
And thou sall haud and I sall call ;
I'se promise thee ane gude new sark,
Either of round claith or of small ".
She lousit the oxen aucht or nine,
And hynt ane gadstaff in her hand ;
And the gudeman raise eftir syne,
And saw the wife had done command.

And ca'd the gaislingis furth to feed,
There was bot seven-some of them all,
And by there comis the greedy gled,
And lickit up five, left him bot twa.
Than out he ran in all his main,
How sune he heard the gaislingis cry ;
Bot than or he come in again,
The calvis brak louse and soukit the kye.

The calvis and kye being met in the loan
The man ran with ane rung to red ;
Than by their comis ane ill-willy cow,
And brodit his buttock whill that it bled.
Than hame he ran to ane rock of tow,
And he sat doun to 'say the spinning ;
I trow he loutit owre near the lowe,
Quod he, " This wark has ill beginning ".

Than to the kirn that he did stoure,
And jumlit at it whill he swat,
When he had jumlit a full lang hour,
The sorrow crap of butter he gat.
Albeit na butter he could get,
Yit he was cummerit with the kirn,
And syne he het the milk owre het,
And sorrow spark of it wald yirn.

Than ben there come ane greedy sow,
I trow he cun'd her little thank,
And in she shot her meikle mou',
And ay she winkit and she drank.
He cleikit up ane crukit club,
And thocht to hit the sow ane rout ;
The twa gaislingis the gled had left,
That straik dang baith their harnis out.

Than he bure kindling to the kiln,
Bot she start all up in ane lowe,
Whatever he heard, whatever he saw,
That day he had na will to mow.

Than he yeid to take up the bairnis,
Thocht to haif fund them fair and clean ;
The first that he gat in his armis
It was all dirt up to the een.

Than up he gat on ane knowe-heid,
On her to cry, on her to shout,
She heard him, and she heard him not,
Bot stoutly steer'd the stottis about.
She draif the day unto the nicht,
She lousit the pleuch and syne come hame ;
She fand all wrang that sould been richt,
I trow the man thocht richt great shame.

Quod he, " My office I forsake
For all the dayis of my life,
For I wald put ane house to wraik,
Had I been twenty dayis gudewife ",
Quod she, " Weil mot ye bruik the place,
For truly I will never accep' it ".
Quod he, " Fiend fall the liaris face,
Bot yit ye may be blyth to get it ".

Than up she gat an maikle rung,
And the gudeman made to the door ;
Quod he, " Dame, I sall hald my tongue,
For an we fecht I'll get the waur ".
Quod he, " When I forsook my pleuch,
I trow I bot forsook my seill,
And I will to my pleuch again,
For I and this house will never do weil ".

Anonymous.

LXXVIII

SHY GEORDIE

Up the Noran Water
In by Inglismaddy,
Annie's got a bairnie
That hasna got a daddy.
Some say it's Tammas's,
An' some say it's Chay's ;
An' naebody expec'it it,
Wi' Annie's quiet ways.

Up the Noran Water
The bonny little mannie
Is dandled an' cuddled close
By Inglismaddy's Annie.
Wha the bairnie's daddy is
The lassie never says ;
But some think it's Tammas's,
An' some think it's Chay's.

Up the Noran Water
The country folk are kind ;
An' wha the bairnie's daddy is
They dinna muckle mind.
But oh ! the bairn at Annie's breist,
The love in Annie's e'e—
They mak' me wish wi' a' my micht
The lucky lad was me !

Helen B. Cruickshank.

LXXIX

LOCHINVAR

O, YOUNG Lochinvar is come out of the west,
Through all the wide Border his steed was the
     best ;
And save his good broadsword he weapons had
     none,
He rode all unarm'd, and he rode all alone.
So faithful in love, and so dauntless in war,
There never was knight like the young Lochinvar.

He staid not for brake, and he stopp'd not for
     stone,
He swam the Eske river where ford there was
     none ;
But ere he alighted at Netherby gate,
The bride had consented, the gallant came late :
For a laggard in love, and a dastard in war,
Was to wed the fair Ellen of brave Lochinvar.

So boldly he enter'd the Netherby Hall,
Among bride's-men, and kinsmen, and brothers,
     and all :
Then spoke the bride's father, his hand on his
     sword,
(For the poor craven bridegroom said never a
     word,)
" O come ye in peace here, or come ye in war,
Or to dance at our bridal, young Lord Lochinvar ? "

H

" I long woo'd your daughter, my suit you
    denied ;—
Love swells like the Solway, but ebbs like its tide—
And now am I come, with this lost love of mine,
To lead but one measure, drink one cup of wine.
There are maidens in Scotland more lovely by far,
That would gladly be bride to the young Lochin-
    var."

The bride kiss'd the goblet : the knight took it up,
He quaff'd off the wine, and he threw down the
    cup.
She look'd down to blush, and she look'd up to
    sigh,
With a smile on her lips, and a tear in her eye.
He took her soft hand, ere her mother could bar,—
" Now tread we a measure ! " said young Lochin-
    var.

So stately his form, and so lovely her face,
That never a hall such a galliard did grace ;
While her mother did fret, and her father did
    fume,
And the bridegroom stood dangling his bonnet
    and plume ;
And the bride-maidens whisper'd, " 'Twere better
    by far,
To have match'd our fair cousin with young
    Lochinvar ".

One touch to her hand, and one word in her ear,
When they reach'd the hall-door, and the charger
    stood near ;

So light to the croupe the fair lady he swung,
So light to the saddle before her he sprung !
" She is won ! we are gone, over bank, bush, and
    scaur ;
They'll have fleet steeds that follow ", quoth young
    Lochinvar.

There was mounting 'mong Graemes of the
    Netherby clan ;
Forsters, Fenwicks, and Musgraves, they rode
    and they ran :
There was racing and chasing on Cannobie Lee,
But the lost bride of Netherby ne'er did they see.
So daring in love, and so dauntless in war,
Have ye e'er heard of gallant like young Lochin-
    var ?

Sir Walter Scott.

LXXX

THE TRETIS OF THE TUA MARIIT WEMEN AND THE WEDO

Apon the Midsummer evin, mirriest of nichtis,
I muvit furth allane, neir as midnicht wes past,
Besyd ane gudlie grein garth, full of gay flouris,
Hegeit, of ane huge hicht, with hawthorne treis ;
Quhairon ane bird, on ane bransche, so birst out
    hir notis
That never ane blythfullar bird was on the beuche
    harde :
Quhat throw the sugarat sound of hir sang glaid,

And throw the savour sanative of the sueit flouris,
I drew in derne to the dyk to dirkin efter mirthis ;
The dew donkit the daill and dynnit the feulis.
  I hard, under ane holyn hevinlie grein hewit,
Ane hie speiche, at my hand, with hautand
      wourdis ;
With that in haist to the hege so hard I inthrang
That I was heildit with hawthorne and with heynd
      leveis :
Throw pykis of the plet thorne I presandlie luikit,
Gif ony persoun wald approche within that plesand
      garding.
  I saw thre gay ladeis sit in ane grene arbeir,
All grathit in to garlandis of fresche gudlie flouris ;
So glitterit as the gold wer thair glorius gilt tressis,
Quhill all the gressis did gleme of the glaid hewis ;
Kemmit was thair cleir hair, and curiouslie sched
Attour thair schulderis doun schyre, schyning full
      bricht ;
With curches, cassin thair abone, of kirsp cleir and
      thin :
Thair mantillis grein war as the gress that grew in
      May sessoun,
Fetrit with thair quhyt fingaris about thair fair
      sydis :
Off ferliful fyne favour war thair faceis meik,
All full of flurist fairheid, as flouris in June ;
Quhyt, seimlie, and soft, as the sweit lillies
New upspred upon spray, as new spynist rose ;
Arrayit ryallie about with mony rich vardour,
That nature full nobillie annamalit with flouris
Off alkin hewis under hevin, that ony heynd knew,
Fragrant, all full of fresche odour fynest of smell.

Ane cumlie tabil coverit wes befoir tha cleir ladeis,
With ryalle cowpis apon rawis full of ryche wynis.
And of thir fair wlonkes, tua weddit war with
    lordis,
Ane wes ane wedow, I wis, wantoun of laitis.
And, as thai talk at the tabill of many taill sindry,
Thay wauchtit at the wicht wyne and waris out
    wourdis ;
And syne thai spak more spedelie, and sparit no
    matiris.

Bewrie, said the Wedo, ye woddit wemen ying,
Quhat mirth ye fand in maryage, sen ye war menis
    wyffis ;
Reveill gif ye rewit that rakles conditioun ?
Or gif that ever ye luffit leyd upone lyf mair
Nor thame that ye your fayth hes festinit for ever ?
Or gif ye think, had ye chois, that ye wald cheis
    better ?
Think ye it nocht ane blist band that bindis so
    fast,
That none undo it a deill may bot the deith ane ?

Than spak ane lusty belyf with lustie effeiris ;
It, that ye call the blist band that bindis so fast,
Is bair of blis, and bailfull, and greit barrat wirkis.
Ye speir, had I fre chois, gif I wald cheis better ?
Chenyeis ay ar to eschew ; and changeis ar sueit :
Sic cursit chance till eschew, had I my chois anis,
Out of the chenyeis of ane churle I chaip suld for
    evir.
God gif matrimony were made to mell for ane
    yeir !

It war bot merrens to be mair, bot gif our myndis
    pleisit :
It is agane the law of luf, of kynd, and of nature,
Togiddir hairtis to strene, that stryveis with uther :
Birdis hes ane better law na bernis be meikill,
That ilk yeir, with new joy, joyis ane maik,
And fangis thame ane fresche feyr, unfulyeit, and
    constant,
And lattis thair fulyeit feiris flie quhair thai pleis.
Cryst gif sic ane consuetude war in this kith
    haldin !
Than weill war us wemen that evir we war fre ;
We suld have feiris as fresche to fang quhen us
    likit,
And gif all larbaris thair leveis, quhen thai lak
    curage.
My self suld be full semlie in silkis arrayit,
Gymp, jolie, and gent, richt joyus, and gent(ryce).
I suld at fairis be found new faceis to se ;
At playis, and at preichingis, and pilgrimages greit,
To schaw my renone, royaly, quhair preis was of
    folk,
To manifest my makdome to multitude of pepill,
And blaw my bewtie on breid, quhair bernis war
    mony ;
That I micht cheis, and be chosin, and change
    quhen me lykit.
Than suld I waill ane full weill, our all the wyd
    realme,
That suld my womanheid weild the lang winter
    nicht ;
And when I gottin had ane grome, ganest of uther,
Yaip, and ying, in the yok ane yeir for to draw ;

Fra I had preveit his pitht the first plesand moneth,
Than suld I cast me to keik in kirk, and in markat,
And all the cuntre about, kyngis court, and uther,
Quhair I ane galland micht get aganis the nixt yeir,
For to perfurneis furth the werk quhen failyeit the
    tother ;
A forky fure, ay furthwart, and forsy in draucht,
Nother febill, nor fant, nor fulyeit in labour,
But als fresche of his forme as flouris in May ;
For all the fruit suld I fang, thocht he the flour
    burgeoun.

I have ane wallidrag, ane worme, ane auld wobat
    carle,
A waistit wolroun, na worth bot wourdis to clatter ;
Ane bumbart, ane dron bee, ane bag full of flewme,
Ane skabbit skarth, ane scorpioun, ane scutarde
    behind ;
To see him scart his awin skyn grit scunner I
    think.
Quhen kissis me that carybald, than kyndillis all
    my sorow ;
As birs of ane brym bair, his berd is als stif,
Bot soft and soupill as the silk is his sary lume ;
He may weill to the syn assent, bot sakles is his
    deidis.
With goreis his tua grym ene ar gladderrit all
    about,
And gorgeit lyk twa gutaris that war with glar
    stoppit ;
Bot quhen that glowrand gaist grippis me about,
Than think I hiddowus Mahowne hes me in
    armes ;

Thair ma na sanyne me save fra that auld Sathane ;
For thocht I croce me all cleine, fra the croun doun,
He wil my corse all beclip, and clap me to his
　breist.
Quhen schaiffyne is that ald schalk with a scharp
　rasour,
He schowis one me his schevill mouth and schedis
　my lippis ;
And with his hard hurcheone skyn sa heklis he my
　chekis,
That as a glemand gleyd glowis my chaftis ;
I schrenk for the scharp stound, bot schout dar I
　nought,
For schore of that auld schrew, schame him betide !
The luf blenkis of that bogill, fra his blerde ene,
As Belzebub had on me blent, abasit my spreit ;
And quhen the smy one me smyrkis with his smake
　smolet,
He fepillis like a farcy aver that flyrit one a gillot.
　Quhen that the sound of his saw sinkis in my eris,
Than ay renewis my noy, or he be neir cumand :
Quhen I heir nemmyt his name, than mak I nyne
　crocis,
To keip me fra the cummerans of that carll mangit,
That full of eldnyng is and anger and all evill
　thewis.
I dar nought luke to my luf for that lene gib,
He is sa full of jelusy and engyne fals ;
Ever ymagynyng in mynd materis of evill,
Compasand and castand casis a thousand
How he sall tak me, with a trawe, at trist of ane
　othir ;
I dar nought keik to the knaip that the cop fillis,

For eldnyng of that ald schrew that ever one evill
    thynkis ;
For he is waistit and worne fra Venus werkis,
And may nought beit worth a bene in bed of my
    mystirs.
He trowis that young folk I yerne yeild, for he
    gane is,
Bot I may yuke all this yer, or his yerd help.
  Ay quhen that caribald carll wald clyme one my
    wambe,
Than am I dangerus and daine and dour of my
    will ;
Yit leit I never that larbar my leggis ba betueene,
To fyle my flesche, na fumyll me, without a fee
    gret ;
And thoght his pene purly me payis in bed,
His purse pays richely in recompense efter :
For, or he clym on my corse, that carybald forlane,
I have conditioun of a curche of kersp allther
    fynest,
A goun of engranyt claith, right gaily furrit,
A ring with a ryall stane, or other riche jowell,
Or rest of his rousty raid, thoght he wer rede wod :
For all the buddis of Johne Blunt, quhen he abone
    clymis,
Me think the baid deir aboucht, sa bawch ar his
    werkis ;
And thus I sell him solace, thoght I it sour think :
Fra sic a syre, God yow saif, my sueit sisteris
    deir !

  Quhen that the semely had said her sentence to
    end,

Than all thai leuch apon loft with latis full mery,
And raucht the cop round about full of riche
    wynis,
And ralyeit lang, or thai wald rest, with ryatus
    speche.

  The wedo to the tothir wlonk warpit ther
      wordis ;
Now, fair sister, fallis yow but fenyeing to tell,
Sen man ferst with matrimony yow menskit in
    kirk,
How haif ye farne be your faith ? confese us the
    treuth :
That band to blise, or to ban, quhilk yow best
    thinkis ?
Or how ye like lif to leid in to leill spousage ?
And syne my self ye exeme one the samyn wise,
And I sall say furth the south, dissymyland no
    word.

  The plesand said, I protest, the treuth gif I
      schaw,
That of your toungis ye be traist. The tothir twa
    grantit ;
With that sprang up hir spreit be a span hechar.
To speik, quoth scho, I sall nought spar ; ther is
    no spy neir :
I sall a ragment reveil fra rute of my hert,
A roust that is sa rankild quhill risis my stomok ;
Now sall the byle all out brist, that beild has so
    lang ;
For it to beir one my brist wes berdin our hevy :
I sall the venome devoid with a vent large,

And me assuage of the swalme, that suellit wes
    gret.
  My husband wes a hur maister, the hugeast in
    erd,
Tharfor I hait him with my hert, sa help me our
    Lord !
He is a young man ryght yaip, bot nought in youth
    flouris ;
For he is fadit full far and feblit of strenth :
He wes as flurising fresche within this few yeris,
Bot he is falyeid full far and fulyeid in labour ;
He has bene lychour so lang quhill lost is his
    natur,
His lume is waxit larbar, and lyis in to swonne :
Wes never sugeorne wer set na one that snaill
    tyrit,
For efter vii oulkis rest, it will nought rap anys ;
He has bene waistit apone wemen, or he me wif
    chesit,
And in adultre, in my tyme, I haif him tane oft :
And yit he is als brankand with bonet one syde,
And blenkand to the brichtest that in the burgh
    duellis,
Alse curtly of his clething and kemmyng of his
    hair,
As he that is mare valyeand in Venus chalmer ;
He semys to be sumthing worth, that syphyr in
    bour,
He lukis as he wald luffit be, thocht he be litill of
    valour ;
He dois as dotit dog that damys on all bussis,
And liftis his leg apone loft, thoght he nought list
    pische ;

He has a luke without lust and lif without curage ;
He has a forme without force and fessoun but
    vertu,
And fair wordis but effect, all fruster of dedis ;
He is for ladyis in luf a right lusty schadow,
Bot in to derne, at the deid, he salbe drup
    fundin ;
He ralis, and makis repet with ryatus wordis,
Ay rusing him of his radis and rageing in chalmer ;
Bot God wait quhat I think quhen he so thra
    spekis,
And how it settis him so syde to sege of sic materis.
Bot gif him self, of sum evin, mygth ane say amang
    thaim,
Bot he nought ane is, bot nane of naturis
    possessoris.
  Scho that has ane auld man nought all is
    begylit ;
He is at Venus werkis na war na he semys :
I wend I josit a gem, and I haif geit gottin ;
He had the glemyng of gold, and wes bot glase
    fundin.
Thought men be ferse, wele I fynd, fra falye ther
    curage,
Thar is bot eldnyng or anger ther hertis within.
Ye speik of berdis one bewch : of blise may thai
    sing,
That, one Sanct Valentynis day, ar vacandis ilk
    yer ;
Hed I that plesand prevelege to part quhen me
    likit,
To change, and ay to cheise agane, than, chastite,
    adew !

Than suld I haif a fresch feir to fang in myn
    armes :
To hald a freke, quhill he faynt, may foly be calit.
  Apone sic materis I mus, at mydnyght, full oft,
And murnys so in my mynd I murdris my selfin ;
Than ly I walkand for wa, and walteris about,
Wariand oft my wekit kyn, that me away cast
To sic a craudoune but curage, that knyt my cler
    bewte,
And ther so mony kene knyghtis this kenrik
    within :
Than think I on a semelyar, the suth for to tell,
Na is our syre be sic sevin ; with that I sych
    oft :
Than he ful tenderly dois turne to me his tume
    person,
And with a yoldin yerd dois yolk me in armys,
And sais, " My soverane sueit thing, quhy sleip ye
    no betir ?
Me think ther haldis yow a hete, as ye sum harme
    alyt."
Quoth I, " My hony, hald abak, and handill me
    nought sair ;
A hache is happinit hastely at my hert rut."
With that I seme for to swoune, thought I na swerf
    tak ;
And thus beswik I that swane with my sueit
    wordis :
I cast on him a crabit E, quhen cleir day is
    cummyn,
And lettis it is a luf blenk, quhen he about glemys,
I turne it in a tender luke, that I in tene warit,
And him behaldis hamely with hertly smyling.

I wald a tender peronall, that myght na put
    thole,
That hatit men with hard geir for hurting of
    flesch,
Had my gud man to hir gest ; for I dar God suer,
Scho suld not stert for his straik a stray breid of
    erd.
And syne, I wald that ilk band, that ye so blist call,
Had bund him so to that bryght, quhill his bak
    werkit ;
And I wer in a beid broght with berne that me
    likit,
I trow that bird of my blis suld a bourd want.

Onone, quhen this amyable had endit hir
    speche,
Loudly lauchand the laif allowit hir mekle :
Thir gay Wiffis maid game amang the grene
    leiffis ;
Thai drank and did away dule under derne bewis ;
Thai swapit of the sueit wyne, thai swanquhit of
    hewis,
Bot all the pertlyar in plane thai put out ther
    vocis.

Than said the Weido, I wis ther is no way othir ;
Now tydis me for to talk ; my taill it is nixt :
God my spreit now inspir and my speche quykkin,
And send me sentence to say, substantious and
    noble ;
Sa that my preching may pers your perverst hertis,
And mak yow mekar to men in maneris and
    conditiounis.

I schaw yow, sisteris in schrift, I wes a schrew
    evir,
Bot I wes schene in my schrowd, and schew me
    innocent ;
And thought I dour wes, and dane, dispitous, and
    bald,
I wes dissymblit suttelly in a sanctis liknes :
I semyt sober, and sueit, and sempill without
    fraud,
Bot I couth sexty dissaif that suttillar wer haldin.
  Unto my lesson ye lyth, and leir at me wit,
Gif you nought list be forleit with losingeris un-
    trew :
Be constant in your governance, and counterfeit
    gud maneris,
Thought ye be kene, inconstant, and cruell of
    mynd ;
Thought ye as tygris be terne, be tretable in luf,
And be as turtoris in your talk, thought ye haif
    talis brukill
Be dragonis baith and dowis ay in double forme,
And quhen it nedis yow, onone, note baith ther
    strenthis ;
Be amyable with humble face, as angellis ap-
    perand,
And with a terrebill tail be stangand as edderis ;
Be of your luke like innocentis, thoght ye haif evill
    myndis ;
Be courtly ay in clething and costly arrayit,
That hurtis yow nought worth a hen ; yowr
    husband pays for all.
  Twa husbandis haif I had, thai held me baith
    deir,

Thought I dispytit thaim agane, thai spyit it na
    thing :
Ane wes ane hair hogeart, that hostit out flewme ;
I hatit him like a hund, thought I it hid preve :
With kissing and with clapping I gert the carll
    fone ;
Weil couth I keyth his cruke bak, and kemm his
    cowit noddill,
And with a bukky in my cheik bo on him behind,
And with a bek gang about and bler his ald E,
And with a kynd contynance kys his crynd chekis ;
In to my mynd makand mokis at that mad fader,
Trowand me with trew lufe to treit him so fair.
This cought I do without dule and na dises tak,
Bot ay be mery in my mynd and myrth full of cher.

    I had a lufsummar leid my lust for to slokyn,
That couth be secrete and sure and ay saif my
    honour,
And sew bot at certayne tymes and in sicir placis ;
Ay when the ald did me anger, with akword
    wordis,
Apon the galland for to goif it gladit me agane.
I had sic wit that for wo weipit I litill,
Bot leit the sueit ay the sour to gud sesone bring.
Quhen that the chuf wald me chid, with girnand
    chaftis,
I wald him chuk, cheik and chyn, and cheris him
    so mekill,
That his cheif chymys he had chevist to my sone,
Suppos the churll wes gane chaist, or the child wes
    gottin :
As wis woman ay I wrought and not as wod fule,
For mar with wylis I wan na wichtnes of handis.

Syne maryit I a marchand, myghti of gudis :
He was a man of myd eld and of mene statur ;
Bot we na fallowis wer in frendschip or blud,
In fredome, na furth bering, na fairnes of persoune,
Quhilk ay the fule did foryhet, for febilnes of
    knawlege,
Bot I sa oft thoght him on, quhill angrit his hert,
And quhilum I put furth my voce and Pedder him
    callit :
I wald ryght tuichandly talk be I wes tuyse maryit,
For endit wes my innocence with my ald husband :
I wes apperand to be pert within perfit eild ;
Sa sais the curat of our kirk, that knew me full
    ying :
He is our famous to be fals, that fair worthy prelot ;
I salbe laith to lat him le, quhill I may luke furth.
I gert the buthman obey, ther wes no bute ellis ;
He maid me ryght hie reverens, fra he my rycht
    knew :
For thocht I say it my self, the severance wes
    mekle
Betuix his bastard blude and my birth noble.
That page wes never of sic price for to presome
    anys
Unto my persone to be peir, had pete nought
    grantit.
Bot mercy in to womanheid is a mekle vertu,
For never bot in a gentill hert is generit ony
    ruth.
I held ay grene in to his mynd that I of grace tuk
    him,
And for he couth ken him self I curtasly him
    lerit :

He durst not sit anys my summondis, for, or the
    secund charge,
He was ay redy for to ryn, so rad he wes for blame.
Bot ay my will wes the war of womanly natur ;
The mair he loutit for my luf, the les of him I
    rakit ;
And eik, this is a ferly thing, or I him faith gaif,
I had sic favour to that freke, and feid syne for
    ever.
  Quhen I the cure had all clene and him our-
    cummyn haill,
I crew abone that craudone, as cok that wer
    victour ;
Quhen I him saw subject and sett at myn bydding,
Than I him lichtlyit as a lowne and lathit his
    maneris.
Than woxe I sa unmerciable to martir him I
    thought,
For as a best I broddit him to all boyis laubour :
I wald haif ridden him to Rome with raip in his
    heid,
Wer not ruffill of my renoune and rumour of
    pepill.
And yit hatrent I hid within my hert all ;
Bot quhilis it hepit so huge, quhill it behud out :
Yit tuk I nevir the wosp clene out of my wyde
    throte,
Quhill I ocht wantit of my will or quhat I wald
    desir.
Bot quhen I severit had that syre of substance in
    erd,
And gottin his biggingis to my barne, and hie
    burrow landis,

Than with a stew stert out the stoppell of my hals,
That he all stunyst throu the stound, as of a stele
    wappin.
Than wald I, efter lang, first sa fane haif bene
    wrokin,
That I to flyte wes als fers as a fell dragoun.
I had for flattering of that fule fenyeit so lang,
Mi evidentis of heritagis or thai wer all selit,
My breist, that wes gret beild, bowdyn wes sa
    huge,
That neir my baret out brist or the band makin.
Bot quhen my billis and my bauchles wes all braid
    selit,
I wald na langar beir on bridill, bot braid up my
    heid ;
Thar myght na molet mak me moy, na hald my
    mouth in :
I gert the renyeis rak and rif into sondir ;
I maid that wif carll to werk all womenis werkis,
And laid all manly materis and mensk in this eird.
Than said I to my cumaris in counsall about,
" Se how I cabeld yone cout with a kene brydill !
The cappill, that the crelis kest in the caf mydding,
Sa curtasly the cart drawis, and kennis na
    plungeing,
He is nought skeich, na yit sker, na scippis nought
    one syd " :
And thus the scorne and the scaith scapit he nothir.
    He wes no glaidsum gest for a gay lady,
Tharfor I gat him a game that ganyt him bettir ;
He wes a gret goldit man and of gudis riche ;
I leit him be my lumbart to lous me all misteris,
And he wes fane for to fang fra me that fair office,

And thoght my favoris to fynd through his feill
  giftis.
He grathit me in a gay silk and gudly arrayis,
In gownis of engranyt claith and gret goldin
  chenyeis,
In ringis ryally set with riche ruby stonis,
Quhill hely raise my renoune amang the rude
  peple.
Bot I full craftely did keip thai courtly wedis,
Quhill eftir dede of that drupe, that dotht nought
  in chalmir :
Thought he of all my clathis maid cost and
  expense,
Ane othir sall the worschip haif, that weildis me
  eftir ;
And thoght I likit him bot litill, yit for luf of
  otheris,
I wald me prunya plesandly in precius wedis,
That luffaris myght apone me luke and ying lusty
  gallandis,
That I held more in daynte and derer be ful mekill
Ne him that dressit me so dink : full dotit wes his
  heyd.
Quhen he wes heryit out of hand to hie up my
  honoris,
And payntit me as pako, proudest of fedderis,
I him miskennyt, be Crist, and cukkald him maid ;
I him forleit as a lad and lathlyit him mekle :
I thoght my self a papingay and him a plukit herle ;
All thus enforsit he his fa and fortifyit in strenth,
And maid a stalwart staff to strik him selfe doune.
  Bot of ane bowrd in to bed I sall yow breif
  yit :

Quhen he ane hail year was hanyt, and him be-
huffit rage,
And I wes laith to be loppin with sic a lob avoir,
Alse lang as he wes on loft, I lukit on him never,
Na leit never enter in my thoght that he my thing
persit,
Bot ay in mynd ane other man ymagynit that I
haid ;
Or ellis had I never mery bene at that myrthles
raid.
Quhen I that grome geldit had of gudis and of
natur,
Me thought him graceless one to goif, sa me God
help :
Quhen he had warit all one me his welth and his
substance,
Me thoght his wit wes all went away with the
laif ;
And so I did him despise, I spittit quhen I saw
That super spendit evill spreit, spulyeit of all
vertu.
For, weill ye wait, wiffis, that he that wantis riches
And valyeandnes in Venus play, is ful vile haldin :
Full fruster is his fresch array and fairnes of
persoune,
All is bot frutlese his effeir and falyeis at the up
with.
   I buskit up my barnis like baronis sonnis,
And maid bot fulis of the fry of his first wif.
I banyst fra my boundis his brethir ilkane ;
His frendis as my fais I held at feid evir ;
Be this, ye belief may, I luffit nought him self,
For never I likit a leid that langit till his blude :

And yit thir wisemen, thai wait that all wiffis evill
Ar kend with ther conditionis and knawin with the
    samin.
    Deid is now that dyvour and dollin in erd :
With him deit all my dule and my drery thoghtis ;
Now done is my dolly nyght, my day is up-
    sprungin,
Adew, dolour, adew ! my daynte now begynis :
Now am I a wedow, I wise and weill am at ese ;
I weip as I were woful, but wel is me for ever ;
I busk as I wer bailfull, bot blith is my hert ;
My mouth it makis murnyng, and my mynd
    lauchis ;
My clokis thai ar caerfull in colour of sabill,
Bot courtly and ryght curyus my corse is ther
    undir :
I drup with a ded luke in my dule habit,
As with manis daill (I) had done for dayis of my
    lif.
    Quhen that I go to the kirk, cled in cair weid,
As foxe in a lambis fleise fenye I my cheir ;
Than lay I furght my bright buke one breid one
    my kne,
With mony lusty letter ellummynit with gold ;
And drawis my clok forthwart our my face quhit,
That I may spy, unaspyit, a space me beside :
Full oft I blenk by my buke, and blynis of de-
    votioun,
To se quhat berne is best brand or bredest in
    schulderis,
Or forgeit is maist forcely to furnyse a bancat
In Venus chalmer, valyeandly, withoutin vane
    ruse :

And, as the new mone all pale, oppressit with
    change,
Kythis quhilis her cleir face through cluddis of
    sable,
So keik I through my clokis, and castis kynd
    lukis
To knychtis, and to cleirkis, and cortly personis.
    Quhen frendis of my husbandis behalois me one
      fer,
I haif a watter spunge for wa, within my wyde
    clokis,
Than wring I it full wylely and wetis my chekis,
With that watteris myn ene and welteris doune
    teris.
Than say thai all, that sittis about, " Se ye nought,
    allace !
Yone lustlese led so lelely scho luffit hir husband
Yone is a pete to enprent in a princis hert,
That sic a perle of plesance suld yone pane dre ! "
I sane me as I war ane sanct, and semys ane
    angell ;
At langage of lichory I leit as I war crabit :
I sich, without sair hert or seiknes in body ;
According to my sable weid I mon haif maneris,
Or thai will se all the suth ; for certis, we wemen
We set us all fra the syght to syle men of treuth :
We dule for na evill deid, sa it be derne haldin.
    Wise wemen has wayis and wonderfull gydingis
With gret engyne to bejaip ther jolyus husbandis ;
And quyetly, with sic craft, convoyis our materis
That, under Crist, no creatur kennis of our doingis.
Bot folk a cury may miscuke, that knawledge
    wantis,

And has na colouris for to cover thair awne kindly
    fautis ;
As dois thir damysellis, for derne dotit lufe,
That dogonis haldis in dainte and delis with thaim
    so lang,
Quhill all the cuntre knaw ther kyndes and faith :
Faith has a fair name, bot falsheid faris bettir :
Fy on hir that can nought feyne her fame for to
    saif !
Yit am I wise in sic werk and wes all my tyme ;
Thoght I want wit in warldlynes, I wylis haif in
    luf,
As ony happy woman has that is of hie blude :
Hutit be the halok las a hunder yeir of eild !
    I have ane secrete servand, rycht sobir of his
        toung,
That me supportis of sic nedis, quhen I a syne
    mak :
Thoght he be sympill to the sicht, he has a tong
    sickir ;
Full mony semelyar sege wer service dois mak :
Thought I haif cair, under cloke, the cleir day
    quhill nyght,
Yit haif I solace, under serk, quhill the sone ryse.
    Yit am I haldin a haly wif our all the haill
        schyre,
I am sa peteouse to the pur, quhen ther is personis
    mony.
In passing of pilgrymage I pride me full mekle,
Mair for the prese of peple na ony perdoun
    wynyng.
    Bot yit me think the best bourd, quhen baronis
    and knychtis,

And othir bachilleris, blith blumyng in youth,
And all my luffaris lele, my lugeing persewis,
And fyllis me wyne wantonly with weilfair and
    joy :
Sum rownis ; and sum ralyeis ; and sum redis
    ballatis ;
Sum raiffis furght rudly with riatus speche ;
Sum plenis, and sum prayis ; sum prasis mi bewte,
Sum kissis me ; sum clappis me ; sum kyndnes
    me proferis ;
Sum kerffis to me curtasli ; sum me the cop
    giffis ;
Sum stalwardly steppis ben, with a stout curage,
And a stif standand thing staiffis in my neiff ;
And mony blenkis ben our, that but full fer sittis,
That mai, for the thik thrang, nought thrif as thai
    wald.
Bot, with my fair calling, I comfort thaim all :
For he that sittis me nixt, I nip on his finger ;
I serf him on the tothir syde on the samin fasson ;
And he that behind me sittis, I hard on him lene ;
And him befor, with my fut fast on his I stramp ;
And to the bernis far but sueit blenkis I cast :
To every man in speciall speke I sum wordis
So wisely and so womanly, quhill warmys ther
    hertis.
    Thar is no liffand leid so law of degre
That sall me luf unluffit, I am so loik hertit ;
And gif his lust so be lent into my lyre quhit,
That he be lost or with me lig, his lif sall nocht
    danger.
I am so mercifull in mynd, and menys all wichtis,
My sely saull salbe saif, quhen sa bot all jugis.

Ladyis leir thir lessonis and be no lassis fundin :
This is the legeand of my lif, thought Latyne it be
　　nane.

　Quhen endit had her ornat speche, this eloquent
　　wedow,
Lowd thai lewch all the laif, and loffit hir mekle ;
And said thai suld exampill tak of her soverane
　teching,
And wirk efter hir wordis, that woman wes so
　prudent.
Than culit thai thair mouthis with ·confortable
　drinkis ;
And carpit full cummerlik with cop going round.

　Thus draif thai our that deir nyght with danceis
　　full noble,
Quhill that the day did up daw, and dew donkit
　flouris ;
The morow myld wes and meik, the mavis did sing,
And all remuffit the myst, and the meid smellit ;
Silver schouris doune schuke as the schene
　cristall,
And berdis schoutit in schaw with thair schill
　notis ;
The goldin glitterand gleme so gladit ther hertis,
Thai maid a glorius gle amang the grene bewis.
The soft sowch of the swyr and soune of the
　stremys,
The sueit savour of the sward and singing of foulis,
Myght confort ony creatur of the kyn of Adam,
And kindill agane his curage, thocht it wer cald
　sloknyt.

Than rais thir ryall roisis, in ther riche wedis,
And rakit hame to ther rest through the rise
     blumys ;
And I all prevely past to a plesand arber,
And with my pen did report thair pastance most
     mery.
   Ye auditoris most honorable, that eris has gevin
Oneto this uncouth aventur, quhilk airly me
     happinnit ;
Of thir thre wantoun wiffis, that I haif writtin heir,
Quhilk wald ye waill to your wif, gif ye suld wed
     one ?

William Dunbar.

LXXXI

THE BALLAD OF KYND KITTOK

My gudame wes a gay wif, bot scho wes ryght
     gend,
   Scho duelt furth fer in to France, apon Falkland
     Fell ;
Thay callit her Kynd Kittok, quhasa hir weill
     kend :
   Scho wes like a caldrone cruke cler under kell ;
Thay threpit that scho deit of thrist, and maid a
     gud end.
   Efter hir dede, scho dredit nought in hevin for
     to duell,
And sa to hevin the hieway dreidles scho wend,
   Yit scho wanderit and yeid by to ane elriche well.
     Scho met thar, as I wene,

Ane ask rydand on a snaill,
And cryit, " Ourtane fallow, haill ! "
And raid ane inche behind the taill,
Till it wes neir evin.

Sa scho had hap to be horsit to hir herbry
    Att ane ailhous neir hevin, it nyghttit thaim
        thare ;
Scho deit of thrist in this warld, that gert hir be so
        dry,
    Scho never eit, bot drank our mesur and mair.
Scho slepit quhill the morne at none, and rais
        airly ;
    And to the yettis of hevin fast can the wif fair,
And by Sanct Petir, in at the yet, scho stall
        prevely :
    God lukit and saw hir lattin in and lewch his
        hert sair.
        And thar, yeris sevin
            Scho levit a gud life,
            And wes our Ladyis hen wif :
            And held Sanct Petir at strif
        Ay quhill scho wes in hevin.

Sche lukit out on a day and thoght ryght lang
    To se the ailhous beside, in till ane evill hour ;
And out of hevin the hie gait cought the wif gaing
    For to get hir ane fresche drink, the aill of hevin
        wes sour.
Scho come againe to hevinnis yet, quhen the bell
        rang,
    Saint Petir hat hir with a club, quhill a gret
        clour

Rais in hir heid, becaus the wif yeid wrang.
Than to the ailhous agane scho ran the pycharis
to pour,
And for to brew and baik.
Frendis, I pray yow hertfully,
Gif ye be thristy or dry,
Drink with my Guddame, as ye ga by,
Anys for my saik.

William Dunbar.

LXXXII

[*Heine in Scots*]

LASSIE, WHAT MAIR WAD YOU HAE?

(*Du hast Diamanten und Perlen*)

O, YOU'RE braw wi' your pearls and your diamonds,
You've routh o' a' thing, you may say,
And there's nane has got bonnier een, Kate:
'Od, lassie, what mair wad you hae?

I've written a hantle o' verses,
That'll live till the Hendmost Day;
And they're a' in praise o' your een, Kate:
'Od, lassie, what mair wad you hae?

Your een, sae blue and sae bonny,
Have plagued me till I am fey.
'Deed, I hardly think I can live, Kate:
'Od, lassie, what mair wad you hae?

Alexander Gray.

LXXXIII

THE TESTAMENT OF CRESSEID

ANE doolie sessoun to ane cairfull dyte
 Suld correspond, and be equivalent.
Richt sa it wes quhen I began to wryte
 This tragedie, the wedder richt fervent
 Quhen Aries in middis of the Lent ;
Schouris of haill can fra the north discend,
That scantlie fra the cauld I micht defend.

Yet nevertheles within myne oratur
 I stude, quhen Titan had his bemis bricht
Withdrawin doun, and sylit under cure,
 And fair Venus, the bewtie of the nicht,
 Uprais, and set unto the west full richt
Hir golden face, in oppositioun
Of god Phebus, direct discending doun.

Throwout the glas hir bemis brast sa fair,
 That I micht se on everie syde me by,
The northin wind had purifyit the air,
 And sched the mistie cloudis fra the sky ;
 The froist freisit, the blastis bitterly
Fra Pole Artick come quhisling loud and schill,
And causit me remufe aganis my will.

For I traistit that Venus, luifis quene,
 To quhome sum-tyme I hecht obedience,
My faidit hart of lufe scho wald mak grene ;
 And therupon, with humbill reverence.

I thocht to pray hir hie magnificence ;
Bot for greit cauld as than I lattit was,
And in my chalmer to the fyre can pas.

Thocht lufe be hait, yit in ane man of age
   It kendillis nocht sa sone as in youtheid,
Of quhome the blude is flowing in ane rage,
   And in the auld the curage doif and deid ;
   Of quhilk the fire outward is best remeid,
To help be phisike quhair that nature faillit
I am expert, for baith I have assailit.

I mend the fyre, and beikit me about,
   Than tuik ane drink my spreitis to comfort,
And armit me weill fra the cauld thairout ;
   To cut the winter nicht, and mak it schort,
   I tuik ane quair, and left all uther sport,
Writtin be worthie Chaucier glorious,
Of fair Cresseid and worthie Troylus.

And thair I fand, efter that Diomeid
   Ressavit had that lady bricht of hew,
How Troilus neir out of wit abraid,
   And weipit soir, with visage paill of hew ;
   For quhilk wanhope his teiris can renew,
Quhill Esperus rejoisit him agane :
Thus quhyle in joy he levit, quhile in pane.

Of hir behest he had greit comforting,
   Traisting to Troy that scho suld mak retour,
Quhilk he desyrit maist of eirdly thing ;
   For why ? scho was his only paramour :
   Bot quhen he saw passit baith day and hour

Of hir ganecome, than sorrow can oppres
His wofull hart, in cair and hevines.

Of his distres me neidis nocht reheirs,
    For worthie Chauceir, in the samin buik,
In gudelie termis and in joly veirs
    Compylit hes his cairis, quha will luik.
    To brek my sleip ane uther quair I tuik,
In quhilk I fand the fatall destenie
Of fair Cresseid, that endit wretchitlie.

Quha wait gif all that Chauceir wrait was trew?
    Nor I wait nocht gif this narratioun
Be authoreist, or fenyeit of the new
    Be sum poeit, throw his inventioun
    Maid to report the lamentatioun
And wofull end of this lustie Cresseid;
And quhat distres scho thoillit, and quhat deid.

Quhen Diomed had all his appetyte,
    And mair, fulfillit of this fair ladie,
Upon ane uther he set his haill delyte,
    And send to hir ane lybell of repudie;
    And hir excludit fra his companie.
Than desolait scho walkit up and doun,
And, sum men sayis, in-to the court commoun.

O, fair Cresseid! the floure and *A per se*
    Of Troy and Grece, how was thow fortunait!
To change in filth all thy feminitie,
    And be with fleschelie lust sa maculait,
    And go amang the Greikis air and lait,
Sa giglotlike, takand thy foull plesance!
I have pietie thow suld fall sic mischance.

Yit nevertheles, quhat-ever men deme or say
  In scornefull langage of thy brukkilnes,
I sall excuse, als far furth as I may,
  Thy womanheid, thy wisdome, and fairnes ;
  And quhilk Fortoun hes put to sic distres
As hir pleisit, and na-thing throw the gilt
Of thé, throw wickit langage to be spilt.

This fair lady, in this wyse destitute
  Of all comfort and consolatioun,
Richt privelie, but fellowschip, on fute
  Disagysit passit far out of the toun
  Ane myle or twa, unto ane mansioun,
Beildit full gay, quhair hir father Calchas
Quhilk than amang the Greikis dwelland was.

Quhen he hir saw, the caus he can inquyre
  Of hir cuming ? Scho said, siching full soir,
" Fra Diomeid had gottin his desyre,
  He wox werie, and wald of me no moir ".
  Quod Calchas, " Douchter, weip thow not thairfoir,
Peraventure all cummis for the best,
Welcum to me, thow art full deir ane gest ".

This auld Calchas, efter the law was tho,
  Wes keeper of the tempill, as ane preist,
In quhilk Venus and hir sone Cupido
  War honourit, and his chalmer was thame neist,
  To quhilk Cresseid, with baill aneuch in breist,
Usit to pas, hir prayeris for to say ;
Quhill at the last, upon ane solempne day,

I

As custome was, the pepill far and neir
   Befoir the none unto the tempill went
With sacrifice devoit in thair maneir :
   But still Cresseid, hevie in hir intent,
   In-to the kirk wald not hir-self present,
For givin of the pepill ony deming
Of hir expuls fra Diomeid the king ;

Bot past into ane secreit orature,
   Quhair scho micht weip hir wofull desteny.
Behind hir bak scho cloisit fast the dure,
   And on hir kneis bair fell down in hy ;
   Upon Venus and Cupide angerly
Scho cryit out, and said on this same wyse,
" Allace that ever I maid yow sacrifice !

Ye gave me anis ane devine responsaill,
   That I suld be the flour of luif in Troy,
Now am I maid an unworthie outwaill,
   And all in cair translatit is my joy.
   Quha sall me gyde ? quha sall me now
      convoy,
Sen I fra Diomeid and nobill Troylus
Am clene excludit, as abject odious ?

O fals Cupide, is nane to wyte bot thow,
   And thy mother, of lufe the blind goddess !
Ye causit me alwayis understand and trow
   The seid of lufe was sawin in my face,
   And ay grew grene throw your supplie and
      grace.
Bot now, allace ! that seid with froist is slane,
And I fra luifferis left, and all forlane."

Quhen this was said, doun in ane extasie
  Ravischit in spreit, intill ane dreame scho fell,
And be apperance hard quhair scho did ly
  Cupide the king ringand ane silver bell,
  Quhilk men micht heir fra hevin unto hell ;
At quhais sound befoir Cupide appeiris
The sevin Planetis discending fra their spheiris,

Quhilk hes power of all thing generabill
  To reull and steir, be thair greit influence,
Wedder and wind and coursis variabill.
  And first of all Saturne gave his sentence,
  Quhilk gave to Cupide litill reverence,
Bot as ane busteous churle on his maneir,
Come crabitlie with auster luik and cheir.

His face frosnit, his lyre was lyke the leid,
  His teith chatterit, and cheverit with the chin,
His ene drowpit, how, sonkin in his heid,
  Out of his nois the meldrop fast can rin,
  With lippis bla, and cheikis leine and thin,
The iceschoklis that fra his hair doun hang
Was wonder greit and as ane speir als lang.

Atouir his belt his lyart lokkis lay
  Felterit unfair, ovirfret with froistis hoir,
His garmound and his gyis full gay of gray,
  His widderit weid fra him the wind out woir,
  Ane busteous bow within his hand he boir,
Under his girdill ane flasche of felloun flanis,
Fedderit with ice and heidit with hailstanis.

Than Juppiter richt fair and amiabill,
  God of the starnis in the firmament,

And nureis to all thing generabill,
    Fra his father Saturne far different,
    With burelie face, and browis bricht and brent,
Upon his heid ane garland wonder gay
Of flouris fair, as it had bene in May.

His voice was cleir, as cristall wer his ene,
    As goldin wyre sa glitterand was his hair,
His garmound and his gyis full gay of grene,
    With golden listis gilt on everie gair,
    Ane burelie brand about his middill bair,
In his right hand he had ane groundin speir,
Of his father the wraith fra us to weir.

Nixt efter him come Mars, the god of ire,
    Of strife, debait, and all dissensioun,
To chide and fecht, als feirs as ony fyre,
    In hard harnes, hewmound and habirgeoun,
    And on his hanche ane roustie fell fachioun,
And in his hand he had ane roustie sword,
Wrything his face, with mony angrie word.

Schaikand his sword, befoir Cupide he come
    With reid visage and grislie glowrand ene,
And at his mouth ane bullar stude of fome,
    Lyke to ane bair quhetting his tuskis kene,
    Richt tuilyeour lyke, but temperance in tene ;
Ane horne he blew with mony bosteous brag,
Quhilk all this warld with weir hes maid to wag.

Than fair Phebus, lanterne and lamp of licht
    Of man and beist, baith frute and flourisching
Tender nureis, and banischer of nicht,

And of the warld causing, be his moving
　　And influence, lyfe in all eirdlie thing,
Without comfort of quhome, of force to nocht
Must all ga die that in this warld is wrocht.

As king royall he raid upon his chair,
　　The quhilk Phaeton gydit sum-tyme unricht,
The brichtness of his face, quhen it was bair,
　　Nane micht behald for peirsing of his sicht ;
　　This goldin cart with fyrie bemes bricht
Four yokkit steidis, full different of hew,
Bot bait or tyring throw the spheiris drew.

The first was foyr, with mane als reid as rois,
　　Callit Eoye in-to the Orient ;
The secund steid to name hecht Ethios,
　　Quhitlie and paill, and sum-deill ascendent ;
　　The thrid Peros, right hait and richt fervent ;
The feird was blak, callit Phlegonie,
Quhilk rollis Phebus down in-to the sey.

Venus was thair present, that goddess gay,
　　Her sonnis querrel for to defend, and mak
Hir awin complaint, cled in ane nyce array,
　　The ane half grene, the uther half sabill blak,
　　Quhyte hair as gold, kemmit and sched abak,
Bot in hir face semit greit variance,
Quhyles perfyte treuth, and quhyles inconstance.

Under smyling scho was dissimulait,
　　Provocative with blenkis amorous,
And suddanely changit and alterait,
　　Angrie as ony serpent vennemous,

Richt pungitive with wordis odious.
Thus variant scho was, quha list tak keip,
With ane eye lauch, and with the uther weip.

In taikning that all fleschelie paramour
    Quhilk Venus hes in reull and governance,
Is sum-tyme sweit, sum-tyme bitter and sour,
    Richt unstabill, and full of variance,
    Mingit with cairfull joy, and fals plesance,
Now hait, now cauld, now blyith, now full of wo,
Now grene as leif, now widderit and ago.

With buik in hand than come Mercurius,
    Richt eloquent and full of rethorie,
With polite termis, and delicious,
    With pen and ink to report all reddie,
    Setting sangis, and singand merilie.
His hude was reid, heklit atouir his croun,
Lyke to ane poeit of the auld fassoun.

Boxis he bair with fine electuairis,
    And sugerit syropis for digestioun,
Spycis belangand to the pothecairis,
    With mony hailsum sweit confectioun ;
    Docteur in phisick, cled in skarlot goun,
And furrit weill, as sic ane aucht to be,
Honest and gude, and not ane word culd lie.[1]

Nixt efter him come Lady Cynthia,
    The last of all, and swiftest in hir spheir,
Of colour blak, buskit with hornis twa,

    [1] Mercury was " the god of thieves, pickpockets, and
all dishonest persons ".

And in the nicht scho listis best appeir,
   Har as the leid, of colour na-thing cleir,
For all hir licht scho borrowis at hir brother
Titan, for of hir-self scho hes nane uther.

Hir gyse was gray, and full of spottis blak,
   And on hir breist ane churle paintit full evin,
Beirand ane bunche of thornis on his bak,
   Quhilk for his thift micht clim na nar the hevin.
   Thus quhen thay gadderit war, thir Goddis
     sevin,
Mercurius they cheisit with ane assent
To be foir-speikar in the parliament.

Quha had bene thair, and lyking for to heir
   His facound toung and termis exquisite,
Of rhetorick the prettick he micht leir,
   In brief sermone ane pregnant sentence wryte.
   Before Cupide, veiling his cap alyte,
Speiris [he] the caus of that vocation ;
And he anone schew his intentioun.

" Lo ! " quod Cupide, " quha will blaspheme the
    name
   Of his awin god, outher in word or deid,
To all goddis he dois baith lak and schame,
   And suld have bitter panis to his meid ;
   I say this by yone wretchit Cresseid,
The quhilk throw me was sum-tyme flour of lufe,
Me and my mother starklie can reprufe ;

Saying of hir greit infelicitie
   I was the caus and my mother Venus ;

Ane blind Goddes hir cald that micht not se,
  With sclander and defame injurious.
  Thus hir leving unclene and lecherous
Scho wald returne on me and my mother,
To quhome I schew my grace abone all uther.

And sen ye ar all sevin deificait,
  Participant of devyne sapience,
This greit injurie done to our hie estait,
  Me-think with pane we suld mak recompence ;
  Was never to goddes done sic violence.
As weill for yow as for myself I say,
Thairfoir ga help to revenge, I yow pray."

Mercurius to Cupide gave answeir,
  And said, " Schir King, my counsall is that ye
Refer yow to the hiest planeit heir,
  And tak to him the lawest of degre,
  The pane of Cresseid for to modifie :
As God Saturne, with him tak Cynthia ".
" I am content ", quod he, " to tak thay twa."

Than thus proceidit Saturne and the Mone,
  Quhen thay the mater rypelie had degest ;
For the dispyte to Cupide scho had done,
  And to Venus oppin and manifest,
  In all hir lyfe with pane to be opprest,
And torment sair, with seiknes incurabill,
And to all lovers be abominabill.

This dulefull sentence Saturne tuik on hand,
  And passit doun quhair cairfull Cresseid lay,
And on hir heid he laid ane frostie wand,
  Than lawfullie on this wyse can he say ;

" Thy greit fairnes, and all thy bewtie gay,
Thy wantoun blude, and eik thy goldin hair,
Heir I exclude fra thé for evermair :

" I change thy mirth into melancholy,
   Quhilk is the mother of all pensivenes,
Thy moisture and thy heit in cald and dry,
   Thyne insolence, thy play and wantones
   To greit diseis, thy pomp and thy riches
In mortall neid and greit penuritie ;
Thow suffer sall, and as ane beggar die."

O cruell Saturne ! fraward and angrie.
   Hard is thy dome, and too malitious.
On fair Cresseid quhy hes thow na mercie,
   Quhilk was sa sweit, gentill, and amourous ?
   Withdraw thy sentence, and be gracious,
As thow was never, so schawis thow thy deid,
Ane wraikfull sentence gevin on fair Cresseid.

Than Cynthia, quhen Saturne past away,
   Out of hir sait discendit down belyve,
And red ane bill on Cresseid quhair scho lay,
   Contening this sentence diffinityve,
   " Fra heile of bodie I thé now deprive,
And to thy seiknes sal be na recure,
But in dolour thy dayis to indure.

" Thy cristall ene minglit with blude I mak,
   Thy voice sa cleir unplesand hoir and hace,
Thy lustie lyre ouirspred with spottis blak,
   And lumpis haw appeirand in thy face ;
   Quhair thow cummis ilk man sall fle the place,

1 2

This sall thow go begging fra hous to hous,
With cop and clapper lyke ane lazarous."

This doolie dreame, this uglye visioun
   Brocht to ane end, Cresseid fra it awoik,
And all that court and convocatioun
   Vanischit away.   Than rais scho up and tuik
   Ane poleist glas, and hir schaddow culd luik ;
And quhen scho saw hir face sa deformait,
Gif scho in hart was wa aneuch, God wait !

Weiping full sair, " Lo ! quhat it is," quod sche,
   " With fraward langage for to mufe and steir
Our craibit goddis, and sa is sene on me !
   My blaspheming now have I bocht full deir,
   All eirdly joy and mirth I set areir.
Allace this day ! allace this wofull tyde !
Quhen I began with my goddis for to chyde ! "

Be this was said ane chyld come fra the hall
   To warne Cresseid the supper was reddy ;
First knokkit at the dure, and syne culd call,
   " Madame, your father biddis you cum in hy,
   He has mervell sa lang on grouf ye ly ;
And sayis, Your prayers bene too lang sum-deill,
The goddis wait all your intent full weill."

Quod scho, " Fair chylde, ga to my father deir,
   And pray him cum to speik with me anone ".
And sa he did, and said " Douchter, quhat
     cheir ? "
   " Allace " quod scho, " father, my mirth is
     gone ! "

" How sa ? " quod he ; and scho can all expone,
As I have tauld, the vengeance and the wraik,
For hir trespas, Cupide on hir culd tak.

He luikit on hir uglye lipper face,
  The quhilk befor was quhite as lillie flour ;
Wringand his handis oftymes, he said, Allace,
  That he had levit to se that wofull hour !
  For he knew weill that thair was na succour
To hir seiknes, and that dowblit his pane ;
Thus was thair cair aneuch betuix thame twane.

Quhen thay togidder murnit had full lang,
  Quod Cresseid, " Father, I wald not be kend,
Thairfoir in secreit wyse ye let me gang,
  Unto yone hospitall at the tounis end ;
  And thidder sum meit for cheritie me send
To leif upon ; for all mirth in this eird
Is fra me gane, sic is my wickit weird ".

Than in ane mantill, and ane bavar hat,
  With cop and clapper, wonder prively
He opnit ane secreit yett, and out thairat
  Convoyit hir, that na man suld espy,
  Unto ane village half ane myle thairby,
Delyverit hir in at the spittail hous,
And daylie sent hir part of his almous.

Sum knew hir weill, and sum had na knawledge
  Of hir, becaus scho was sa deformait,
With bylis blak ovirspred in hir visage,
  And hir fair colour faidit and alterait ;
  Yit they presumit for hir hie regrait,

And still murning scho was of nobill kin,
With better will thairfoir they tuik hir in.

The day passit, and Phebus went to rest,
  The cloudis blak ovirquhelmit all the sky,
God wait gif Cresseid was ane sorrowfull gest,
  Seeing that uncouth fair and herbery ;
  But meit or drink scho dressit hir to ly
In ane dark corner of the hous allone,
And on this wyse, weiping, scho maid hir mone.

THE COMPLAINT OF CRESSEID

" O sop of sorrow sonken into cair !
O, cative Cresseid ! now and ever-mair
  Gane is thy joy and all thy mirth in eird,
Of all blyithnes now art thow blaiknit bair.
Thair is na salve may saif thé of thy sair !
  Fell is thy fortoun, wickit is thy weird,
  Thy blys is baneist, and thy baill on breird,
Under the eirth God gif I gravin wer,
  Quhair nane of Grece nor yit of Troy micht
    heird !

" Quhair is thy chalmer wantounlie besene,
With burely bed, and bankouris browderit bene
  Spycis and wyne to thy collatioun,
The cowpis all of gold and silver schene,
The sweit meitis servit in plaittis clene,
  With saipheron sals of ane gude sessoun,
  Thy gay garmentis with mony gudely goun,
Thy plesand lawn pinnit with goldin prene ?
  All is areir, thy greit royall renoun !

" Quhair is thy garding with thir greissis gay,
And fresche flowris, quhilk the Quene Floray
   Had paintit plesandly on everie pane,
Quhair thow was wont full merilye in May
To walk and tak the dew be it was day,
    And heir the merle and mavis mony ane,
    With ladyis fair in carrolling to gane,
And se the royal rinks in thair array,
    In garmentis gay, garnischit on everie grane ?

" Thy greit triumphand fame and hie honour,
Quhair thow was callit of eirdlye wichtis flour,
   All is decayit ; thy weird is welterit so,
Thy hie estait is turnit in darknes dour !
This lipper ludge tak for thy burelie bour,
    And for thy bed tak now ane bunche of stro,
    For waillit wyne and meitis thow had tho,
Tak mowlit breid, peirrie, and ceder sour ;
    Bot cop and clapper now is all ago.

" My cleir voice and courtlie carrolling,
Quhair I was wont with ladyis for to sing,
   Is rawk as ruik, full hiddeous hoir and hace ;
My plesand port all utheris precelling,
Of lustines I was hald maist conding,
    Now is deformit ; the figour of my face
    To luik on it na leid now lyking hes :
Sowpit in syte, I say with sair siching,
    Ludgeit amang the lipper leid, Allace !

" O ladyis fair of Troy and Grece attend
My miserie, quhilk nane may comprehend,
   My frivoll fortoun, my infelicitie,

My greit mischief, quhilk na man can amend.
Be-war in tyme, approchis neir the end,
    And in your mynd ane mirrour mak of me ;
    As I am now, peradventure that ye,
For all your micht, may cum to that same end,
    Or ellis war, gif ony war may be.

" Nocht is your fairnes bot ane faiding flour,
Nocht is your famous laud and hie honour
    Bot wind inflat in uther mennis eiris ;
Your roising reid to rotting sall retour.
Exempill mak of me in your memour,
    Quhilk of sic thingis wofull witnes beiris.
    All welth in eird away as wind it weiris :
Be-war, thairfoir, approchis neir the hour ;
    Fortoun is fikkill quhen scho beginnis and
        steiris."

Thus chydand with her drerie destenye,
    Weiping, scho woik the nicht fra end to end.
Bot all in vane ; hir dule, hir cairfull cry,
    Micht not remeid, nor yit hir murning mend.
    Ane lipper lady rais, and till hir wend,
And said, " Quhy spurnis thow aganis the wall,
To sla thyself, and mend na-thing at all ?

" Sen thy weiping dowbillis bot thy wo,
    I counsall thé mak vertew of ane neid ;
To leir to clap thy clapper to and fro,
    And leir efter the law of lipper leid."
    Thair was na buit, bot furth with thame scho yeid
Fra place to place, quhill cauld and hounger sair
Compellit hir to be ane rank beggair.

That samin tyme of Troy the garnisoun,
   Quhilk had to chiftane worthie Troylus,
Throw jeopardie of weir had strikken down
   Knichtis of Grece in number mervellous.
   With greit tryumphe and laude victorious
Agane to Troy richt royallie they raid
The way quhair Cresseid with the lipper baid.

Seing that companie thai come all with ane
    stevin,
   Thay gaif ane cry, and schuik coppis gude
    speid.
Said, " Worthie lordis, for Goddis lufe of Hevin,
   To us lipper part of your almous deid ".
   Than to thair cry nobill Troylus tuik heid ;
Having pietie, neir by the place can pas
Quhair Cresseid sat, not witting what scho was.

Than upon him scho kest up baith her ene,
   And with ane blenk it come in-to his thocht
That he sum tyme hir face befoir had sene ;
   Bot scho was in sic plye he knew hir nocht.
   Yit than hir luik into his mynd it brocht
The sweit visage and amorous blenking
Of fair Cresseid, sumtyme his awin darling.

Na wonder was, suppois in mynd that he
   Tuik hir figure sa sone, and lo, now, quhy :
The idole of ane thing in cace may be
   Sa deip imprentit in the fantasy
   That it deludis the wittis outwardly,
And sa appeiris in forme and lyke estait
Within the mynd, as it was figurait.

Ane spark of lufe than till his hart culd spring,
　　And kendlit all his bodie in ane fyre
With hait fevir ane sweit and trimbilling
　　Him tuik, quhill he was reddie to expyre ;
　　To beir his scheild his breist began to tyre ;
Within ane quhyle he changit mony hew,
And nevertheless not ane ane-uther knew.

For knichtlie pietie and memoriall
　　Of fair Cresseid ane gyrdill can he tak,
Ane purs of gold, and mony gay jowall,
　　And in the skirt of Cresseid doun can swak :
　　Than raid away, and not ane word he spak,
Pensive in hart, quhill he come to the toun,
And for greit cair oft-syis almaist fell doun.

The lipper folk to Cresseid than can draw,
　　To se the equall distributioun
Of the almous, but quhan the gold they saw
　　Ilk ane to uther prevelie can roun,
　　And said, " Yone lord hes mair affectioun,
How-ever it be, unto yone lazarous,
Than to us all ; we knaw be his almous ".

" Quhat lord is yone," quod scho, " have ye na
　　　　feill,
　　Hes done to us so greit humanitie ? "
" Yes," quod a lipper man, " I knaw him weill :
　　Schir Troylus it is, gentill and fre."
　　Quhen Cresseid understude that it was he
Stiffer than steill thair stert ane bitter stound
Throwout hir hart, and fell doun to the ground.

Quhen scho, ovircome with siching sair and sad,
  With mony cairfull cry and cald " Ochane !
Now is my breist with stormie stoundis stad,
  Wrappit in wo, ane wretch full will of wane ".
  Than swounit scho oft or scho culd refrane,
And ever in hir swouning cryit scho thus :—
" O, fals Cresseid, and trew knicht Troylus !

" Thy lufe, thy lawtie, and thy gentilnes
  I countit small in my prosperitie ;
Sa elevait I was in wantones,
  And clam upon the fickill quheill sa hie ;
  All faith and lufe I promissit to thé
Was in the self fickill and frivolous :
O, fals Cresseid, and trew knicht Troylus !

" For lufe of me thow keipt gude continance,
  Honest and chaist in conversatioun ;
Of all wemen protectour and defence
  Thow was, and helpit thair opinioun.
  My mynd in fleschelie foull affectioun
Was inclynit to lustis lecherous.
Fy, fals Cresseid ! O, trew knicht Troylus !

" Lovers be-war, and tak gude heid about
  Quhome that ye lufe, for quhome ye suffer
    paine,
I lat yow wit, thair is richt few thairout
  Quhome ye may traist to have trew lufe againe :
  Preif quhen ye will, your labour is in vaine.
Thairfoir I reid ye tak thame as ye find,
For thay ar sad as widdercock in wind.

" Becaus I knaw the greit unstabilnes,
    Brukkil as glas, into my-self I say,
Traisting in uther als greit unfaithfulnes,
    Als unconstant, and als untrew of fay.
    Thocht sum be trew, I wait richt few are thay.
Quha findis treuth, lat him his lady ruse ;
Nane but myself, as now, I will accuse."

Quhen this was said, with paper scho sat doun,
    And on this maneir maid hir testament :
" Heir I beteiche my corps and carioun
    With wormis and with taidis to be rent ;
    My cop and clapper, and myne ornament,
And all my gold, the lipper folk sall have,
Quhen I am deid, to burie me in grave.

" This royall ring, set with this rubie reid,
    Quhilk Troylus in drowrie to me send,
To him agane I leif it quhan I am deid,
    To mak my cairfull deid unto him kend :
    Thus I conclude schortlie, and mak ane end
My spreit I leif to Diane, quhair scho dwellis,
To walk with hir in waist woddis and wellis.

" O, Diomeid ! thow hes baith broche and belt
    Quhilk Troylus gave me in takning
Of his trew lufe."—And with that word scho
        swelt.
    And sone ane lipper man tuik of the ring,
    Syne buryit hir withouttin tarying.
To Troylus furthwith the ring he bair,
And of Cresseid the deith he can declair.

Quhen he had hard hir greit infirmitie,
   Hir legacie and lamentatioun,
And how scho endit in sic povertie,
   He swelt for wo, and fell doun in ane swoun,
   For greit sorrow his hart to birst was boun :
Siching full sadlie, said, " I can no moir,
Scho was untrew, and wo is me thairfoir ! "

Sum said he maid ane tomb of merbell gray,
   And wrait hir name and superscriptioun,
And laid it on hir grave, quhair that scho lay,
   In goldin letteris conteining this ressoun :
   " Lo, fair ladyis, Cresseid of Troyis toun,
Sumtyme countit the flour of womanheid,
Under this stane, late lipper, lyis deid ! "

Now, worthie Wemen, in this ballet schort,
   Made for your worschip and instructioun,
Of cheritie I monische and exhort
   Ming not your lufe with fals deceptioun ;
   Beir in your mynd this schort conclusioun
Of fair Cresseid, as I have said befoir.
Sen scho is deid I speik of hir no moir.
                Robert Henryson.

LXXXIV

BONNY KILMENY GAED UP THE GLEN

Bonny Kilmeny gaed up the glen,
But it wasna to meet Duneira's men,
Nor the rosy monk of the isle to see,

For Kilmeny was pure as pure could be.
It was only to hear the yorlin sing,
And pu' the cress-flower round the spring ;
The scarlet hypp and the hindberrye,
And the nut that hung frae the hazel tree ;
For Kilmeny was pure as pure could be.
But lang may her minny look o'er the wa',
And lang may she seek i' the green-wood shaw ;
Lang the laird of Duneira blame,
And lang, lang greet or Kilmeny come hame !

When many a day had come and fled,
When grief grew calm, and hope was dead,
When mass for Kilmeny's soul had been sung,
When the bedes-man had prayed, and the dead
      bell rung,
Late, late in a gloamin' when all was still,
When the fringe was red on the westlin hill,
The wood was sere, the moon i' the wane,
The reek o' the cot hung over the plain,
Like a little wee cloud in the world its lane ;
When the ingle lowed with an eiry leme,
Late, late in the gloamin' Kilmeny came hame !
" Kilmeny, Kilmeny, where have you been ?
Lang hae we sought baith holt and dean ;
By linn, by ford, and green-wood tree,
Yet you are halesome and fair to see.
Where gat you that joup o' the lily schene ?
That bonny snood of the birk sae green ?
And these roses, the fairest that ever were seen ?
Kilmeny, Kilmeny, where have you been ? "

Kilmeny looked up with a lovely grace,

But nae smile was seen on Kilmeny's face ;
As still was her look, and as still was her ee,
As the stillness that lay on the emerant lea,
Or the mist that sleeps on a waveless sea.
For Kilmeny had been she knew not where,
And Kilmeny had seen what she could not declare ;
Kilmeny had been where the cock never crew,
Where the rain never fell, and the wind never
    blew ;
But it seemed as the harp of the sky had rung,
And the airs of heaven played round her tongue,
When she spake of the lovely forms she had seen,
And a land where sin had never been ;
A land of love, and a land of light,
Withouten sun, or moon, or night ;
Where the river swa'd a living stream,
And the light a pure celestial beam :
The land of vision it would seem,
A still, an everlasting dream. . . .
When seven lang years had come and fled ;
When grief was calm, and hope was dead ;
When scarce was remembered Kilmeny's name,
Late, late in a gloamin' Kilmeny came hame !

James Hogg.

LXXXV

A FISHER'S APOLOGY

(Translated from the Latin)

MINISTER, why do you direct your artillery against
my nets ? Why am I forbidden to fish on the
Sabbath Day ?

On Jews alone is this oppressive commandment binding; we, the descendants of Japhet, are a people independent of it.

God's edict is, I acknowledge, just, but it is not intended to be unfair towards anyone—a stain from which the council and hall of Heaven is quite free.

Saturday is a festival day; yet who but a half-wit considers it a time for idling and not tilling the fields?

On that day our Lord himself healed the man with the withered hand, and his disciples, as you may read, did not keep their hands off the corn-ears.

But on the Sabbath it is a sin to break the clods with a harrow or to put a pair of oxen beneath the broad yokes.

These occupations may be resumed on the morrow without regard to wind and rain and without any loss.

But, ah me! how brief is the opportunity *I* have of making profit! Away it flies on wings swifter, East Wind, than thine!

To-day a salmon sports and leaps in my waters; to-morrow it will be off to take up a settled abode in the upper stream.

Why should I be fool enough to let what's mine be taken from me ? What right has another to swallow the sheep I pasture ?

Of their own free will the fish come, asking to be netted. What lunacy it would be to refuse such an offer of a dinner !

Another fact that carries weight is that on the holy mornings the pools abound often more plentifully with fish.

Why does the Sabbath offer such a catch if it forbids the nets to be spread ? Temptation of this sort is but making a fool of mankind.

Moreover, neither is it the case that a fisher is engaged in *work* when he looses the nets—among the ancients this was regarded as pure sport.

After wandering the globe in their traversing of woods, hunter and fowler feel wearied with excessive hard work.

My pursuit causes nothing but delight.—It is *work* that the commandment forbids, but my occupation involves no *work*.

Sitting on a high rock I keep a look-out on the river's transparent waters for the glittering shoal's scaly backs.

The stream is my farm, salmon my yearly crop

—these are the dues that the kindly sea-goddess (Thetis) allots me.

As soon as hope sheds its sunshine, from the rock rings a joyful shout of warning, which the crowd drink in with pricked-up ears.

No delaying or dallying ! The lads quickly get ready their gear and the plying of many an oar makes the water seethe.

Some bend upward the net-edges, others drop in stones, and the rest haul in the linen cavern containing the captured shoal.

Cast ashore out of the boats, the catch dumbly quivers on the sands, and in the open air keeps trying to get back to the waters.

This party kills them ; after the killing that group guts them ; another group removes the scales from their backs, and yet another seasons them in salt.

When the nets lie idle, we hunt the fish with rods and cover the bronze barbs with the treacherous dainties.

Forthwith the tribe, unwitting of the hidden ruse, flies at its prey, and through its undue credulousness perishes.

If bait is not to be got (for who can find bait

enough for so many thousands ?) the hooks are usually hidden in a many-coloured little feather.

At the lure then jumps the raw-recruit salmon, and swallows the hook, and himself gets caught by his catch.

What is he to do ?   He sinks into the water, and, as the line is played out, helplessly drags it in his lacerated mouth as he flees.

Now he rushes downstream, now flies back against the current, now darts through the waters by a cross-path.

Sometimes he whirls round and struggles in the water, making it somewhat turbid.   Sometimes he gapes his mouth, and, too late, shakes his throat vainly.

Worn out by a thousand meanders, he at length leaves the stream, and, on the dry shore, captive, lies dead.

Next, when inclination takes me, I lash the waters with a casting net, or with a leister pierce the gleaming herd.

Now I entangle the hollow river-bed with osier-woven nets ; now, by night, with a torch I let light fall on the stony pools.

Often I depopulate the stream of tributes for

myself with concealed receptacles called in the Scots tongue *cruives*.

These, when the fish are striving towards the upper waters, hinder their efforts and bar their paths.

Not content with suffering this, the herd stupidly makes its way into the open-mouthed wicker-work, and is imprisoned.

A mute company, in a dark gaol, like to the horse that enclosed in its belly the silent Greeks, or Danae's tower, or the labyrinth.

The salmon, thronging, are flustered, dumb-founded, and distressed at being cut off, and rage wildly within the circumscribed water.

Meanwhile a band of youths flies to the rescue, and, swifter than the East Wind, many a boat surrounds the dazed shoal.

This lad shakes out the hollow traps, that fellow bears away the catch in his skiff ; one party counts, another kills, the prisoners.

There is no less delight in playing a trick on the owners of the next fishings—fooling them properly, and snatching their feast from them before they can get it.

It is enjoined that on Saturdays the trellis-work

barriers be removed to let the salmon run freely
into the upper waters.

There is a penalty attached to this law, and it is
necessary to obey ; so a door is opened in the burn
wide enough to let the flock through.

But, to keep them from going through, we put
just there a horse's skull, its bones gleaming whiter
than midwinter snow.

No sooner is their course directed than a panic
possesses the scaly breed, and there is stampede
as if the Gorgon's head lay facing their oncoming.

But, as they flee from Scylla, they enter un-
wittingly into cruel Charybdis's jaws, and come
to a wretched end in the wicker traps I laid.

Thus with a heap of pleasures this *work* is piled,
and with nothing but beguilements and charms.

But if this happy pastime is defiled with sin, or,
rather, with venial failing, there is a crowd left at
home to appease the Powers.

My household utters for my sake prayers to
Heaven. Do you also, for my household's sake,
withhold your imprecations !

My wife and children, flocking to the temples,
will consume much incense, and make presents of
more.

With pious incense the angers of offended Deity are wont to be assuaged, and much fine wood in offerings wins back the propitiousness of Gods.

Do you even as Heaven, minister, and let your wrath abate ; lay aside the roaring thunderbolts of your harshness.

Take my word for it ; the rest of the community is also being struck by these bolts ; a wound in my side draws blood from a whole crowd.

If you mean to ban the fishing-nets, ban also from our land the bounties of Bacchus, for these also we owe to my wares.

I send them over to a foreign nation's shores, and many a ship returns laden with red wine.

I will rise from my chair in honour of my parents, I will dip a sword-point in nobody's blood, nor woo any man's wife.

I will not put my hand into any other person's money-boxes, no one shall raise complaints against me for perjury, no covetousness will take possesion of my soul.

If only religion permits me to yield to this one temptation ! Oh, do let me be privileged to set my lines on the Sunday !

The sin occupies but a short space of time—no

more than a brief summer.   That is all the length
of this harvest-season, I assure you.

I do not even ask for a whole day of it.—Twice
the wave from the neighbouring sea rises with the
tide, twice it ebbs from my waters.

When the waters are high, it is not proper to
use the nets ; thus the Sunday is to be violated
by me but twice.

In one day, a man, otherwise upright and just,
transgresses only as often as the high sea sucks
back the waters it vomits forth.

Pray tell me, why does one failing among the
thousand possible sins—a fault at that but twice
repeated—prove my ruin ?

But there isn't any fault in me if I exert my
energies on this day.— *You* may regard it as a holy
day, but *I* look upon it as a working day.

'Twas on this day that God laid the foundation
of the boundless universe, and the first day of our
week was the first day of the divine toiling.

'Twas on this day that Chaos came into being,
and likewise Daylight, before the sun was yet
created ; and Day too was divided from Night.

If you should count the divisions of the week,

God rested on the day which is believed to be sacred to the scythe-bearing God.

The day whereon you harshly forbid me to use my nets is sacred to Phoebus—and this God is intolerant of idleness.

He never rests ; all day long if I, his worshipper, weary the waters of the rivers, he wearies his steeds.

There is but one slight difference—he is attending to the management of the universe, I am managing my own business.

There is no blame connected with my act.— Who does not attend to finance ? What sin is there in my looking after number one ?

Aye, but, you say, it is contrary to religion.— But no hunter of the waters believes religion to enjoin anything unprofitable.

For profitableness is the standard in reference to which laymen approve of friendship, marriage, the legal system, class distinctions, and even religion itself.

My present attitude to this question in the old days had the assent of the clergy ; how great were the tributes that the Sunday brought in to them !

It was the custom on this day for us to gather

such a catch as we could, whereof they bore off a tythe in their hallowed hands.

When the allotment dissatisfied the fathers, the holy kitchen was enriched with confiscated fish.

God's commandment was altered by the holy Church. Even so, when one God refuses help, another God vouchsafes it.

The only folk whom the clergy invoked this law to oppress were farmers—it was forbidden that the lowing of herds be heard on the Sunday.

But by their express orders, amid the snarling of the rabble, the necks of fishermen were exempt from this yoke.

Whosoever of the fathers authorised the granting of so rare a privilege, O may his bones, I pray, lie lightly.

But ah ! I fear his soul is now deciding points of law by the waters of Styx, if any fish perchance wander in its waters.

But for fishing what would the gay unrespectable young men drink, who have, by day and night, a thirst for Bacchus's juice ?

Or the stern throng of elders, of whom Bacchus is the very life-blood ? What would those great chatterboxes, the old women, do ?

Who would be a worshipper of the muses if you abolished the habit of wine-drinking ? Bah ! the waters of Helicon are tasteless.

When the Sunday comes round, Council and Common folk alike get drunk on wine, nor is there any disgrace in being drunk on the holy day !

Aye, you too, minister, dispense wine in God's honour, and are wont with wine to cut short the lingering day.

If your word were law, no fire would gleam in the house, nor water be fetched from the nearby spring.

No one would stretch out a helping hand to anyone who stumbled, and no one would lift a bleating sheep out of a ditch.

All love-making would be under a ban, and in observance of your Sabbath, a newly-wed wife would flee from her husband's embraces.

The sailors, for want of rowing, and because no one would dare to set sails for the wind, would run aground on rocks.

And when Sunday dawned, the coal-miner would, in the midst of his fires, be drowned in waters welling up from the ground.

Why should I mention the salt-makers ?   Unless their work is perpetually in motion, it goes for nothing and is not made good again.

The forge for glass-making, the forge for smelting the impenetrable iron—either is ruined if the fire slumbers even once.

Oh, me ! why is the seventh day a holy day so far as fishers alone are concerned, but a working day for other people ?

It is a foolish superstition to muffle the mind in numbers—arithmetic of this sort has a bit too much of the magic art in it.

Either blot out the Sabbath days, or postpone them till the idle times of midwinter, when to my disgust rivers are in the grip of lifeless frost.

Then I will keep religious festivals all the week —while winter rules not one working day will there be.

So long as it is mine to enjoy the light of Heaven and the life-giving water, I will obey all the other commandments engraved by God's finger.

To God alone will I pray, I will make no graven image, nor will I take in vain the Lord's name.

However, if you cannot be swayed by this offer, I will submit to your injunctions—only, so far as Sabbath observance is concerned, let me observe the day in my own way !

K

The pious flock of Isaac's sons, by the flowing waters of Babylon, gave countless tears and pious prayers unto God.

Even so, I will perform the rites I deem acceptable regularly each proper day by the waterside, and either bank will hear my prayers.

May it be by that waterside that the Nymphs give me a tomb when I have left the rivers, and may the stone which covers my bones bear this inscription :—

" Here lies a man, owner of the neighbouring pool while he drew breath, but not owner of his own soul.

"Not that he lived unto himself ; he lived for his children ; but his life was nothing but one unconscionable round of work, and not a day nor an hour did he spend at the festivals of religion while alive.

" He took no thought for his future state, and between the palace of Heaven and the halls of the Netherworld, he saw no difference in point of preferableness.

" There are fish in the Heavens ; there are rivers in Hell ; either region affords him, now his day is done, the means of sport."

Arthur Johnstone.

LXXXVI

LAST LEAVE OF THE HILLS

(Cead Deireannach nan Beann)

(Translated from the Gaelic)

I was yesterday in Ben Dorain and in her precincts I was not at a loss.   I saw the glens and the mountains that I knew.   That was the joyous sight, to be walking on the mountains, when the sun was rising and the deer were bellowing.

Joyous was the haughty herd, when they moved noisily, and the hinds on the fountain-green. Handsome were the speckled fawns there, the does and the red bucks, the black cocks and the red. It was the sweetest music ever heard when their noise was heard in the morning twilight.

Keenly would I go to the hunting in the mountain-passes, going out to ascend the rugged places, and late did I come home.   The pure clean water and the atmosphere that are on the tops of the high mountains, they helped me to grow, and gave me health and wholesomeness.

I got a part of my rearing on sheilings that I knew, with sport and mirth and music, sharing in the warm kindness of maidens.   It were a case contrary to nature if that lasted there now.   It was necessary to leave them when the time came.

Now since age has struck me I have got a blemish that I will not get rid of again, that has spoiled my teeth and blinded my eyes. I cannot be strong though I were to need it, and I could not make one step very swiftly even though the pursuit were after me.

Though my head has grown grey and my locks have thinned, often did I let slip the hound against a wild high-headed one.[1]   Though I always loved them, I would not go after them now if I saw them on the mountain, since I have lost the third part of my breath.

In time of going to rutting keenly I used to follow them, and the people of the country had a time making new songs and rhymings for them ; and hearty were we when we were in the camps and the dram was not a rarity.

When I was in my early youth it was folly that kept me empty-handed.   It is fortune that gives us each good thing promised us.   Though I am scant of store my mind is full of joy since I am hoping that George's daughter will make bread for me.

I was in the mountain yesterday and my mind was full of the thought that the beloved ones, who were wont to be traversing the wilderness with me, were not there.   And the Ben—it's little I thought that she would change !   Since she is now under sheep, the world has deceived me !

[1] The deer.

When I looked on each side of me, I could not
but be sorrowful, since wood and heather are spent
there, and the men that were live no more.   There
is not a deer to hunt there, there is not a bird or
roe there.   The few that are not dead of them are
now departed wholly from it.

My farewell to the forests !   Oh, marvellous
mountains they are, with green cress, and spring-
water, a drink noble, splendid and pleasing.   The
pastures that are precious, and the wastes that are
many, gratefully I left them.   Forever, my thou-
sand blessings be with them !

> *Duncan Ban MacIntyre.*
> *(Donnchadh Ban Mac an-t-saoir.)*

LXXXVII

REQUIEM

Under the wide and starry sky
Dig the grave and let me lie :
Glad did I live and gladly die,
   And I laid me down with a will.

This be the verse you grave for me :
Here he lies where he long'd to be ;
Home is the sailor, home from sea,
   And the hunter home from the hill.

> *Robert Louis Stevenson.*

LXXXVIII

THE SEED-SHOP

Here in a quiet and dusty room they lie,
    Faded as crumbled stone or shifting sand,
Forlorn as ashes, shrivelled, scentless, dry,
    Meadows and gardens running through my
      hand.

In this brown husk a dale of hawthorn dreams,
    A cedar in this narrow cell is thrust
That will drink deeply of a century's streams ;
    These lilies shall make Summer on my dust.

Here in their safe and simple house of death,
    Sealed in their shells a million roses leap ;
Here I can blow a garden with my breath,
    And in my hand a forest lies asleep.
Muriel Stuart.

LXXXIX

THE MAID OF NEIDPATH

Earl March look'd on his dying child,
    And, smit with grief to view her—
" The youth ", he cried, " whom I exiled
    Shall be restored to woo her."

She's at the window many an hour
    His coming to discover :

And he look'd up to Ellen's bower
   And she look'd on her lover—

But ah ! so pale, he knew her not,
   Though her smile on him was dwelling—
" And am I then forgot—forgot ? "
   It broke the heart of Ellen.

In vain he weeps, in vain he sighs,
   Her cheek is cold as ashes ;
Nor love's own kiss shall wake those eyes
   To lift their silken lashes.

               Thomas Campbell.

XC

THE TWA CORBIES

I

As I was walking all alane,
I heard twa corbies making a mane :
The tane unto the tither did say,
" Whar sall we gang and dine the day ? "

II

" —In behint yon auld fail dyke
I wot there lies a new-slain knight ;
And naebody kens that he lies there
But his hawk, his hound, and his lady fair.

III

" His hound is to the hunting gane,
His hawk to fetch the wild-fowl hame,

His lady's ta'en anither mate,
So we may mak' our dinner sweet.

IV

" Ye'll sit on his white hause-bane,
And I'll pike out his bonny blue e'en :
Wi' ae lock o' his gowden hair
We'll theek our nest when it grows bare.

V

" Mony a one for him maks mane,
But nane sall ken whar he is gane :
O'er his white banes, when they are bare,
The wind sall blaw for evermair."

Anonymous.

XCI

THE DOWIE HOUMS O' YARROW

I

LATE at een, drinkin' the wine,
　　And ere they paid the lawin',
They set a combat them between,
　　To fight it in the dawin'.

II

" O stay at hame, my noble lord !
　　O stay at hame, my marrow !
My cruel brother will you betray,
　　On the dowie houms o' Yarrow."—

III

" O fare ye weel, my lady gay !
    O fare ye weel, my Sarah !
For I maun gae, tho' I ne'er return
    Frae the dowie banks o' Yarrow."

IV

She kiss'd his cheek, she kamed his hair,
    As she had done before, O ;
She belted on his noble brand,
    An' he's awa to Yarrow.

V

O he's gane up yon high, high hill—
    I wat he gaed wi' sorrow—
An' in a den spied nine arm'd men,
    I' the dowie houms o' Yarrow.

VI

" O are ye come to drink the wine,
    As ye hae done before, O ?
Or are ye come to wield the brand,
    On the dowie houms o' Yarrow ? "—

VII

" I am no come to drink the wine,
    As I hae done before, O,
But I am come to wield the brand,
    On the dowie houms o' Yarrow."

VIII

Four he hurt an' five he slew,
    On the dowie houms o' Yarrow

Till that stubborn knight came him behind,
    An' ran his body thorrow.

IX

" Gae hame, gae hame, good brother John,
    An' tell your sister Sarah
To come an' lift her noble lord,
    Who's sleepin' sound on Yarrow."

X

" Yestreen I dream'd a dolefu' dream ;
    I ken'd there wad be sorrow ;
I dream'd I pu'd the heather green,
    On the dowie banks o' Yarrow."

XI

She gaed up yon high, high hill—
    I wat she gaed wi' sorrow—
An' in a den spied nine dead men,
    On the dowie houms o' Yarrow.

XII

She kiss'd his cheek, she kamed his hair,
    As oft she did before, O ;
She drank the red blood frae him ran,
    On the dowie houms o' Yarrow.

XIII

" O haud your tongue, my douchter dear,
    For what needs a' this sorrow ?
I'll wed you on a better lord
    Than him you lost on Yarrow."—

XIV

"O haud your tongue, my father dear,
   An' dinna grieve your Sarah ;
A better lord was never born
   Than him I lost on Yarrow.

XV

"Tak hame your ousen, tak hame your kye,
   For they hae bred our sorrow ;
I wiss that they had a' gane mad
   Whan they cam' first to Yarrow."

Anonymous.

XCII

RARE WILLY DROWNED IN YARROW

I

"WILLY's rare, and Willy's fair,
   And Willy's wondrous bonny ;
And Willy heght to marry me,
   Gin e'er he marryd ony.

II

"Yestreen I made my bed fu' braid
   The night I'll make it narrow,
For a' the live-long winter's night
   I lie twin'd of my marrow.

III

"O came you by yon water-side ?
   Pu'd you the rose or lily ?

Or came you by yon meadow green ?
  Or saw you my sweet Willy ? "

IV

She sought him east, she sought him west,
  She sought him braid and narrow ;
Sine, in the clifting of a craig,
  She found him drown'd in Yarrow.
                                    Anonymous.

XCIII

THOMAS THE RHYMER

I

TRUE Thomas lay on Huntlie bank ;
  A ferlie he spied wi' his e'e ;
And there he saw a ladye bright
  Come riding down by the Eildon Tree.

II

Her skirt was o' the grass-green silk,
  Her mantle o' the velvet fyne ;
At ilka tett o' her horse's mane
  Hung fifty siller bells and nine.

III

True Thomas he pu'd aff his cap,
  And louted low down on his knee :
" Hail to thee, Mary, Queen of Heaven !
  For thy peer on earth could never be."

IV

" O no, O no, Thomas," she said,
  " That name does not belang to me ;
I'm but the Queen o' fair Elfland,
  That am hither come to visit thee.

V

" Harp and carp, Thomas," she said ;
  " Harp and carp along wi' me ;
And if ye dare to kiss my lips,
  Sure of your bodie I will be."

VI

" Betide me weal, betide me woe,
  That weird shall never daunten me."
Syne he has kiss'd her rosy lips,
  All underneath the Eildon Tree.

VII

" Now ye maun go wi' me," she said,
  " True Thomas, ye maun go wi' me ;
And ye maun serve me seven years,
  Thro' weal or woe as may chance to be."

VIII

She's mounted on her milk-white steed,
  She's ta'en true Thomas up behind ;
And aye, whene'er her bridle rang,
  The steed gaed swifter than the wind.

IX

O they rade on, and farther on,
  The steed gaed swifter than the wind ;

Until they reach'd a desert wide,
    And living land was left behind.

X

" Light down, light down now, true Thomas,
    And lean your head upon my knee ;
Abide ye there a little space,
    And I will show you ferlies three.

XI

" O see ye not yon narrow road,
    So thick beset wi' thorns and briers ?
That is the Path of Righteousness,
    Though after it but few inquires.

XII

" And see ye not yon braid, braid road,
    That lies across the lily leven ?
That is the Path of Wickedness,
    Though some call it the Road to Heaven.

XIII

" And see ye not yon bonny road
    That winds about the fernie brae ?
That is the road to fair Elfland,
    Where thou and I this night maun gae.

XIV

" But, Thomas, ye sall haud your tongue,
    Whatever ye may hear or see ;
For speak ye word in Elfyn-land,
    Ye'll ne'er win back to your ain countrie."

XV

O they rade on, and farther on,
    And they waded rivers abune the knee ;
And they saw neither sun nor moon,
    But they heard the roaring of the sea.

XVI

It was mirk, mirk night, there was nae starlight,
    They waded thro' red blude to the knee ;
For a' the blude that's shed on the earth
    Rins through the springs o' that countrie.

XVII

Syne they came to a garden green,
    And she pu'd an apple frae a tree :
" Take this for thy wages, true Thomas ;
    It will give thee the tongue that can never lee."

XVIII

" My tongue is my ain," true Thomas he said ;
    " A gudely gift ye wad gie to me !
I neither dought to buy or sell
    At fair or tryst where I might be.

XIX

" I dought neither speak to prince or peer,
    Nor ask of grace from fair ladye ! "—
" Now haud thy peace, Thomas," she said,
    " For as I say, so must it be."

XX

He has gotten a coat of the even cloth,
    And a pair o' shoon of the velvet green ;

And till seven years were gane and past,
　　True Thomas on earth was never seen.
　　　　　　　　　　　Anonymous.

XCIV

THE WIFE OF USHER'S WELL

I

THERE lived a wife at Usher's well,
　　And a wealthy wife was she ;
She had three stout and stalwart sons,
　　And sent them o'er the sea.

II

They hadna been a week from her,
　　A week but barely ane,
When word came to the carline wife
　　That her three sons were gane.

III

They hadna been a week from her,
　　A week but barely three,
When word came to the carline wife
　　That her sons she'd never see.

IV

" I wish the wind may never cease,
　　Nor fashes in the flood,
Till my three sons come hame to me
　　In earthly flesh and blood ! "

V

It fell about the Martinmas,
    When nights are lang and mirk,
The carline wife's three sons came hame,
    And their hats were o' the birk.

VI

It neither grew in syke nor ditch,
    Nor yet in ony sheugh ;
But at the gates o' Paradise
    That birk grew fair eneugh.

VII

" Blow up the fire, my maidens !
    Bring water from the well !
For a' my house shall feast this night,
    Since my three sons are well."

VIII

And she has made to them a bed,
    She's made it large and wide ;
And she's ta'en her mantle her about,
    Sat down at the bedside.

IX

Up then crew the red, red cock,
    And up and crew the gray ;
The eldest to the youngest said,
    " 'Tis time we were away."

X

The cock he hadna craw'd but once,
    And clapp'd his wings at a',

When the youngest to the eldest said,
  " Brother, we must awa'.

XI

" The cock doth craw, the day doth daw,
  The channerin' worm doth chide ;
Gin we be miss'd out o' our place,
  A sair pain we maun bide."—

XII

" Lie still, lie still but a little wee while,
  Lie still but if we may ;
Gin my mother should miss us when she wakes
  She'll go mad ere it be day."—

XIII

" Fare ye weel, my mother dear !
  Fareweel to barn and byre !
And fare ye weel, the bonny lass
  That kindles my mother's fire ! "

               Anonymous.

XCV

GET UP AND BAR THE DOOR

I

It fell about the Martinmas time,
  And a gay time it was then,
When our goodwife got puddings to make,
  And she's boil'd them in the pan.

II

The wind sae cauld blew south and north,
   And blew into the floor ;
Quoth our goodman to our goodwife,
   " Gae out and bar the door ".—

III

" My hand is in my hussyfskap,
   Goodman, as ye may see ;
An' it shou'dna be barr'd this hundred year,
   It's no be barr'd for me."

IV

They made a paction 'tween them twa,
   They made it firm and sure,
That the first word whae'er shou'd speak,
   Shou'd rise and bar the door.

V

Then by there came two gentlemen,
   At twelve o'clock at night,
And they could neither see house nor hall,
   Nor coal nor candle-light.

VI

" Now whether is this a rich man's house,
   Or whether is it a poor ? "
But ne'er a word wad ane o' them speak,
   For barring of the door.

VII

And first they ate the white puddings,
   And then they ate the black.

Tho' muckle thought the goodwife to hersel'
    Yet ne'er a word she spake.

VIII

Then said the one unto the other,
    " Here, man, tak ye my knife ;
Do ye tak aff the auld man's beard,
    And I'll kiss the goodwife ".—

IX

" But there's nae water in the house
    And what shall we do than ? "—
" What ails ye at the pudding-broo,
    That boils into the pan ? "

X

O up then started our goodman,
    An angry man was he :
" Will ye kiss my wife before my een,
    And sca'd me wi' pudding-bree ? "

XI

Then up and started our goodwife,
    Gied three skips on the floor :
" Goodman, you've spoken the foremost word !
    Get up and bar the door."

Anonymous.

XCVI

LOCK THE DOOR, LARISTON

" LOCK the door, Lariston, lion of Liddesdale ;
Lock the door, Lariston, Lowther comes on ;

The Armstrongs are flying,
The widows are crying,
The Castletown's burning, and Oliver's gone !

" Lock the door, Lariston—high on the weather-
        gleam
See how the Saxon plumes bob on the sky—
        Yeomen and carbineer,
        Billman and halberdier,
Fierce is the foray, and far is the cry !

" Bewcastle brandishes high his broad scimitar ;
Ridley is riding his fleet-footed grey ;
        Hidley and Howard there,
        Wandale and Windermere ;
Lock the door, Lariston ; hold them at bay.

" Why dost thou smile, noble Elliot of Lariston ?
Why does the joy-candle gleam in thine eye ?
        Thou bold Border ranger,
        Beware of thy danger ;
Thy foes are relentless, determined, and nigh."

Jack Elliot raised up his steel bonnet and lookit,
His hand grasp'd the sword with a nervous
        embrace ;
        " Ah, welcome, brave foemen,
        On earth there are no men
More gallant to meet in the foray or chase !

" Little know you of the hearts I have hidden here ;
Little know you of our moss-troopers' might—

Linhope and Sorbie true,
Sundhope and Milburn too,
Gentle in manner, but lions in fight !

" I have Mangerton, Ogilvie, Raeburn, and
Netherbie,
Old Sim of Whitram, and all his array ;
Come all Northumberland,
Teesdale and Cumberland,
Here at the Breaken tower end shall the fray ! "

Scowled the broad sun o'er the links of green
Liddesdale,
Red as the beacon-light tipped he the wold ;
Many a bold martial eye
Mirror'd that morning sky,
Never more oped on his orbit of gold.

Shrill was the bugle's note, dreadful the warrior's
shout,
Lances and halberds in splinters were borne ;
Helmet and hauberk then
Braved the claymore in vain,
Buckler and armlet in shivers were shorn.

See how they wane—the proud files of the
Windermere !
Howard ! ah, woe to thy hopes of the day !
Hear the wide welkin rend,
While the Scots' shouts ascend—
" Elliot of Lariston, Elliot for aye ! "

James Hogg.

XCVII

HELEN OF KIRKCONNELL

I

I wish I were where Helen lies,
Night and day on me she cries ;
O that I were where Helen lies,
  On fair Kirkconnell lea !

II

Curst be the heart that thought the thought,
And curst the hand that fired the shot,
When in my arms burd Helen dropt,
  And died to succour me !

III

O think na ye my heart was sair,
When my Love dropp'd and spak nae mair !
There did she swoon wi' meikle care,
  On fair Kirkconnell lea.

IV

As I went down the water side,
None but my foe to be my guide,
None but my foe to be my guide,
  On fair Kirkconnell lea ;

V

I lighted down my sword to draw,
I hackèd him in pieces sma',

I hackèd him in pieces sma',
  For her sake that died for me.

VI

O Helen fair, beyond compare !
I'll mak a garland o' thy hair,
Shall bind my heart for evermair,
  Until the day I dee !

VII

O that I were where Helen lies !
Night and day on me she cries ;
Out of my bed she bids me rise,
  Says, " Haste, and come to me ! "

VIII

O Helen fair ! O Helen chaste !
If I were with thee, I'd be blest,
Where thou lies low an' taks thy rest,
  On fair Kirkconnell lea.

IX

I wish my grave were growing green,
A winding-sheet drawn owre my een,
And I in Helen's arms lying,
  On fair Kirkconnell lea.

X

I wish I were where Helen lies !
Night and day on me she cries ;
And I am weary of the skies,
  For her sake that died for me.

                    Anonymous.

XCVIII

PROUD MAISIE

PROUD Maisie is in the wood,
 Walking so early ;
Sweet Robin sits on the bush,
 Singing so rarely.

" Tell me, thou bonny bird,
 When shall I marry me ? '
" When six braw gentlemen
 Kirkward shall carry ye."

" Who makes the bridal bed,
 Birdie, say truly ? "
" The grey-headed sexton
 That delves the grave duly.

" The glow-worm o'er grave and stone
 Shall light thee steady ;
The owl from the steeple sing,
 ' Welcome, proud lady ' ! "
 Sir Walter Scott.

XCIX

LUCY ASHTON'S SONG

LOOK not thou on beauty's charming,
Sit thou still when kings are arming,
Taste not when the wine-cup glistens,
Speak not when the people listens,

Stop thine ear against the singer,
From the red gold keep thy finger ;
Vacant heart and hand and eye,
Easy live and quiet die.
                    Sir Walter Scott.

c

SONG

WHAUR yon broken brig hings owre ;
Whaur yon water maks nae soun' ;
Babylon blaws by in stour :
Gang doun wi' a sang, gang doun.

Deep, owre deep, for onie drouth :
Wan eneuch an ye wud droun :
Saut, or seelfu', for the mouth ;
Gang doun wi' a sang, gang doun.

Babylon blaws by in stour
Whaur yon water maks nae soun' :
Darkness is your only door ;
Gang doun wi' a sang, gang doun.
                    William Soutar

CI

THE GOWK

HALF doun the hill, whaur fa's the linn
Far frae the flaught o' fowk,
I saw upon a lanely whin
A lanely singin' gowk :

Cuckoo, cuckoo ;
And at my back
The howie hill stude up and spak :
Cuckoo, cuckoo.

There was nae soun' : the loupin' linn
Hung frostit in its fa' :
Nae bird was on the lanely whin
Sae white wi' fleurs o' snaw :
Cuckoo, cuckoo ;
I stude stane still ;
And saftly spak the howie hill :
Cuckoo, cuckoo.

William Soutar.

CII

CATTLE SHOW

I SHALL go among red faces and virile voices,
See stylish sheep, with fine heads and well-woolled,
And great bulls mellow to the touch,
Brood mares of marvellous approach, and geldings
With sharp and flinty bones and silken hair.

And through th' enclosure draped in red and
       gold
I shall pass on to spheres more vivid yet
Where countesses' coque feathers gleam and glow
And, swathed in silks, the painted ladies are
Whose laughter plays like summer lightning there.

Hugh MacDiarmid.

CIII

TO A MOUSE

*(On turning her up in her nest with the plough,
November 1785)*

Wee, sleekit, cow'rin', tim'rous beastie,
O, what a panic's in thy breastie !
Thou need na start awa sae hasty,
  Wi' bickering brattle !
I wad be laith to rin an' chase thee
  Wi' murd'ring pattle !

I'm truly sorry man's dominion
Has broken nature's social union,
An' justifies that ill opinion,
  Which makes thee startle
At me, thy poor, earth-born companion
  An' fellow-mortal !

I doubt na, whiles, but thou may thieve ;
What then ? poor beastie, thou maun live !
A daimen-icker in a thrave
  'S a sma' request ;
I'll get a blessin' wi' the lave,
  An' never miss't !

Thy wee bit housie, too, in ruin !
It's silly wa's the win's are strewin' !
An' naething, now, to big a new ane,
  O' foggage green !

An' bleak December's winds ensuin,
    Baith snell an' keen !

Thou saw the fields laid bare an' waste,
An' weary winter comin fast,
An' cozie here, beneath the blast,
    Thou thought to dwell—
Till crash ! the cruel coulter past
    Out thro' thy cell.

That wee bit heap o' leaves an' stibble,
Has cost thee mony a weary nibble !
Now thou's turned out, for a' thy trouble,
    But house or hald,
To thole the winter's sleety dribble,
    An' cranreuch cauld !

But, Mousie, thou art no thy lane,
In proving foresight may be vain ;
The best-laid schemes o' mice an' men
    Gang aft agley,
An' lea'e us nought but grief an' pain
    For promis'd joy !

Still thou art blest, compar'd wi' me ;
The present only toucheth thee :
But och ! I backward cast my e'e,
    On prospects drear !
An' forward, tho' I canna see,
    I guess an' fear !

                Robert Burns.

THE AULD MAN'S MEAR'S DEAD

The auld man's mear's dead ;
The puir body's mear's dead ;
The auld man's mear's dead,
   A mile aboon Dundee.

There was hay to ca', and lint to lead,
A hunner hotts o' muck to spread,
And peats and truffs and a' to lead—
   And yet the jaud to dee !

CHORUS
The auld man's mear's dead, etc.

She had the fiercie and the fleuk,
The wheezloch and the wanton yeuk ;
On ilka knee she had a breuk—
   What ail'd the beast to dee ?

He's thinkin' on the by-gane days,
And a' her douce and canny ways ;
And how his ain gude-wife, auld Bess,
   Micht maist as weel been spared.
           Patrick Birnie.

CV

MOLECATCHER

STRAMPIN' the bent, like the Angel o' Daith,
  The mowdie-man staves by ;
Alang his pad the mowdie-worps
  Like sma' Assyrians lie.

And where the Angel o' Daith has been
  Yirked oot o' their yirdy hames,
Lie Sennacherib's blasted hosts
  Wi' guts dung oot o' wames.

Sma' black tramorts wi' gruntles grey,
  Sma' weak weemin's hands,
Sma' bead-een that wid touch ilk hert
  Binnae the mowdie-man's.

                          Albert D. Mackie.

CVI

AULD ROBIN GRAY

WHEN the sheep are in the fauld, and the kye at
      hame,
And a' the warld to rest are gane,
The waes o' my heart fa' in showers frae my e'e,
While my gudeman lies sound by me.

Young Jamie lo'ed me weel, and sought me for
      his bride ;

But saving a croun he had naething else beside :
To make the croun a pund, young Jamie gaed to
    sea ;
And the croun and the pund were baith for me.

He hadna been awa' a week but only twa,
When my father brak his arm, and the cow was
    stown awa' ;
My mother she fell sick,—and my Jamie at the
    sea—
And auld Robin Gray came a-courtin' me.

My father couldna work, and my mother couldna
    spin ;
I toil'd day and night, but their bread I couldna
    win ;
Auld Rob maintain'd them baith, and wi' tears in
    his e'e
Said, " Jennie, for their sakes, O, marry me ! "

My heart it said nay ; I look'd for Jamie back ;
But the wind it blew high, and the ship it was a
    wrack ;
His ship it was a wrack—Why didna Jamie dee ?
Or why do I live to cry, Wae's me !

My father urged me sair : my mother didna
    speak ;
But she look'd in my face till my heart was like to
    break :
They gi'ed him my hand, tho' my heart was in
    the sea ;
Sae auld Robin Gray he was gudeman to me.

I hadna been a wife a week but only four,
When mournfu' as I sat on the stane at the door,
I saw my Jamie's wraith,—for I couldna think
    it he,
Till he said, " I'm come hame to marry thee ".

O sair, sair did we greet, and muckle did we say ;
We took but ae kiss, and we tore ourselves away :
I wish that I were dead, but I'm no like to dee ;
And why was I born to say, Wae's me !

I gang like a ghaist, and I carena to spin ;
I daurna think on Jamie, for that wad be a sin ;
But I'll do my best a gude wife aye to be,
For auld Robin Gray he is kind unto me.
               Lady Anne Lindsay.

CVII

O WALY, WALY

O WALY, waly up the bank,
   And waly, waly down the brae,
And waly, waly by yon burnside
   Where I and my Love wont to gae.
I leant my back against an aik,
   I thought it was a trusty tree ;
But first it bow'd and syne it brak :
   Sae my true Love did lichtly me.

O wally, waly, but love is bonny
   A little time while it is new ;

L

But when 'tis auld, it waxeth cauld
    And fades awa' like morning dew.
O wherefore should I busk my head ?
    O wherefore should I kame my hair ?
For my true Love has me forsook,
    And says he'll never lo'e me mair.

Now Arthur's Seat sall be my bed,
    The sheets sall ne'er be prest by me ;
Saint Anton's Well sall be my drink,
    Since my true Love's forsaken me.
Mart'mas wind, when wilt thou blaw
    And shake the green leaves aff the tree ?
O gentle Death, when wilt thou come ?
    For of my life I am wearie.

'Tis not the frost, that freezes fell,
    Nor blawing snaw's inclemencie,
'Tis not sic cauld that makes me cry,
    But my Love's heart grown cauld to me.
When we came in by Glasgow town
    We were a comely sight to see :
My Love was clad in the black velvet,
    And I myself in cramasie.

But had I wist, before I kist,
    That love had been sae ill to win,
I had lockt my heart in a case of gowd
    And pinn'd it with a siller pin.
And O ! if my young babe were born,
    And set upon the nurse's knee,
And I myself were dead and gane,
    And the green grass growing over me.

Anonymous.

CVIII

LOW DOUN IN THE BROOM

My daddie is a cankert carle,
  He'll no twine wi' his gear ;
My minnie she's a scauldin' wife,
  Hauds a' the house asteer.
      But let them say, or let them do,
        It's a' ane to me,
      For he's low doun, he's in the broom,
        That's waitin' on me :
    Waitin' on me, my love,
      He's waitin' on me :
      For he's low doun, he's in the broom,
        That's waitin' on me.

My auntie Kate sits at her wheel,
  And sair she lightlies me ;
But weel I ken it's a' envy,
  For ne'er a joe has she.

My cousin Kate was sair beguiled
  Wi' Johnnie o' the Glen ;
And aye sinsyne she cries, Beware
  O' fause deluding men.

Gleed Sandy he cam west yestreen,
  And speired when I saw Pate ;
And aye sinsyne the neebors round
  They jeer me air and late.

But let them say, or let them do,
   It's a' ane to me,
For he's low doun, he's in the broom,
   That's waitin' on me :
Waitin' on me, my love,
   He's waitin' on me :
For he's low doun, he's in the broom,
   That's waitin' on me.

Anonymous.

CIX

AYE WAUKIN' O !

O SPRING's a pleasant time,
   Flowers o' every colour—
The sweet bird builds her nest,
   And I long for my lover.
     Aye waukin' O,
       Waukin' aye, and weary,
     Sleep can I get nane,
       For thinkin' o' my dearie.

O I'm wat, wat,
   O I'm wat and weary ;
Yet fain I'd rise and run
   If I thought to meet my dearie

When I sleep I dream,
   When I wauk I'm eerie ;
Sleep can I get nane,
   For thinkin' o' my dearie.

Lanely night comes on ;
  A' the lave are sleeping ;
I think on my love,
  And blear my een wi' greeting.

Feather-beds are soft,
  Painted rooms are bonnie ;
But a kiss o' my dear love
  Is better far than ony.

O for Friday's night,
  Friday at the gloaming !
O for Friday's night !
  Friday's lang o' coming.
    Aye waukin' O,
      Waukin' aye, and weary,
    Sleep can I get nane,
      For thinkin' o' my dearie.
                Anonymous.

CX

THE WHISTLE

HE cut a sappy sucker from the muckle rodden-
    tree,
He trimmed it, an' he wet it, an' he thumped it on
    his knee ;
He never heard the teuchat when the harrow broke
    her eggs,
He missed the craggit heron nabbin' puddocks in
    the seggs,

He forgot to hound the collie at the cattle when
    they strayed,
But you should hae seen the whistle that the wee
    herd made !

He wheepled on't at mornin' an' he tweetled on't
    at nicht,
He puffed his freckled cheeks until his nose sank
    oot o' sicht,
The kye were late for milkin' when he piped them
    up the closs,
The kitlins got his supper syne, an' he was beddit
    boss ;
But he cared na doit nor docken what they did or
    thocht or said,
There was comfort in the whistle that the wee
    herd made.

For lyin' lang o' mornin's he had clawed the caup
    for weeks,
But noo he had his bonnet on afore the lave had
    breeks ;
He was whistlin' to the porridge that were hott'rin'
    on the fire,
He was whistlin' ower the travise to the baillie in
    the byre ;
Nae a blackbird nor a mavis, that hae pipin' for
    their trade,
Was a marrow for the whistle that the wee herd
    made.

He played a march to battle. It cam' dirlin'
    through the mist.

Till the halflin' squared his shou'ders an' made up
    his mind to 'list ;
He tried a spring for wooers, though he wistna
    what it meant,
But the kitchen-lass was lauchin' an' he thocht she
    maybe kent ;
He got ream an' buttered bannocks for the lovin'
    lilt he played.
Wasna that a cheery whistle that the wee herd
    made ?

He blew them rants sae lively, schottisches, reels,
    an' jigs,
The foalie flang his muckle legs an' capered ower
    the rigs,
The grey-tailed futt'rat bobbit oot to hear his ain
    strathspey,
The bawd cam' loupin' through the corn to " Clean
    Pease Strae ",
The feet o' ilka man an' beast gat youkie when he
    played—
Hae ye ever hear o' whistle like the wee herd
    made ?

But the snaw it stopped the herdin' an' the winter
    brocht him dool,
When in spite o' hacks and chilblains he was shod
    again for school ;
He couldna sough the Catechis nor pipe the rule o'
    three,
He was keepit in an' lickit when the ither loons got
    free ;

But he aften played the truant—'twas the only
    thing he played,
For the maister brunt the whistle that the wee herd
    made !

                   Charles Murray.

CXI

THE GABERLUNZIE MAN

THE pawky auld carle cam owre the lea
Wi' mony good-e'ens and days to me,
Saying, " Gudewife, for your courtesie,
    Will you lodge a silly poor man ? "
The night was cauld, the carle was wat,
And down ayont the ingle he sat ;
My dochter's shoulders he 'gan to clap,
    And cadgily ranted and sang.

" O wow ! " quo' he, " were I as free
As first when I saw this countrie,
How blyth and merry wad I be !
    And I wad nevir think lang."
He grew canty, and she grew fain,
But little did her auld minny ken
What thir twa togither were say'n
    When wooing they were sa thrang.

" An' O ! " quo' he, " an' ye were as black
As e'er the crown of your daddy's hat,
'Tis I wad lay thee by my back,
    And awa' wi' me thou sould gang."

" An' O ! " quo' she, " an' I were as white
As e'er the snaw lay on the dike,
I'd clead me braw and lady-like,
   And awa' wi' thee I would gang."

Between the twa was made a plot ;
They raise a wee before the cock,
And wilily they shot the lock,
   And fast to the bent are gane.
Up in the morn the auld wife raise,
And at her leisure put on her claiths
Syne to the servant's bed she gaes,
   To speir for the silly poor man.

She gaed to the bed where the beggar lay,
The strae was cauld, he was away ;
She clapt her hand, cried " Waladay !
   For some of our gear will be gane ".
Some ran to coffers and some to kist,
But nought was stown, that could be mist ;
She danced her lane, cried " Praise be blest,
   I have lodg'd a leal poor man.

" Since naething's awa' as we can learn,
The kirn's to kirn and milk to earn ;
Gae but the house, lass, and waken my bairn,
   And bid her come quickly ben."
The servant gaed where the dochter lay,
The sheets were cauld, she was away,
And fast to her goodwife did say,
   " She's aff with the gaberlunzie man ".

" O fy gar ride and fy gar rin,
And haste ye find these traitors again ;

For she's be burnt, and he's be slain,
    The wearifu' gaberlunzie man."
Some rade upo' horse, some ran afit,
The wife was wud, and out of her wit :
She could na gang, nor yet could she sit,
    But ay she curs'd and she bann'd.

Meantime far 'hind out o'er the lea,
Fu' snug in a glen, where nane could see,
The twa, with kindly sport and glee,
    Cut frae a new cheese a whang :
The priving was gude, it pleas'd them baith,
To lo'e her for ay, he ga'e her his aith.
Quo' she, " To leave thee I will be laith,
    My winsome gaberlunzie man.

" O kend my minny I were wi' you,
Ill-fardly wad she crook her mou' ;
Sic a poor man she'd never trow,
    After the gaberlunzie man."
" My dear," quo' he, " ye're yet owre young
And ha'e na learn'd the beggar's tongue,
To follow me frae toun to toun
    And carry the gaberlunzie on.

" Wi' cauk and keel I'll win your bread,
And spindles and whorles for them wha need,
Whilk is a gentle trade indeed,
    The gaberlunzie to carry, O.
I'll bow my leg, and crook my knee,
And draw a black clout owre my e'e ;
A cripple or blind they will ca' me
    While we sall sing and be merry, O."

                                        Anonymous.

CXII

THE BEWTEIS OF THE FUTE-BALL

Brissit brawnis and broken banis,
Strife, discord, and waistis wanis,
Crookit in eild, syne halt withal—
Thir are the bewteis of the fute-ball.

Anonymous.

CXIII

PEBLIS TO THE PLAY

At Beltane, when ilk body bownis
To Peblis to the play,
To hear the singin' and the soundis,
The solace, sooth to say ;
Be firth and forest furth they found ;
They graithit them full gay ;
God wait that wald they do, that stound,
For it was their feast day,
                        They said,
Of Peblis to the play.

All the wenches of the west
Were up or the cock crew ;
For reiling there micht na man rest,
For garray and for glew.
And said, " My curches are not prest ! "
Than answerit Meg full blue,

" To get an hude, I hald it best ! "
" Be Goddis saul that is true ",
Quod she,

Of Peblis to the play.

She tuk the tippet be the end,
To lat it hing she let not.
Quod he, " Thy back sall bear ane bend ";
" In faith," quod she, " we meit not ! "
She was so guckit, and so gend,
That day ane bite she eat nocht ;
Than spak her fellowis that her kend,
" Be still, my joy, and greet not,
Now,

Of Peblis to the play.

" Ever, alas ! " than said she,
" Am I nocht clearly tynt ?
I dar nocht come yon merkat to,
I am so evil sun-brint.
Amang you merchants my erandis do,
Marie ; I sall anis mynt
Stand off far, and keik them to,
As I at hame was wont ",
Quod she,

Of Peblis to the play.

Hopcalyo and Cardronow
Gadderit out thick-fauld,
With " hey and how rolumbelow "
The young folk were full bauld.
The bagpipe blew, and they out-threw
–Out of the townis untauld.

Lord, sic ane shout was them amang,
When they were owre the wald,
                    There west,
Of Peblis to the play.

Ane young man start into that steid
As cant as ony colt,
Ane birken hat upon his heid,
With ane bow and ane bolt ;
Said, " Merrie maidenis, think not lang ;
The weddir is fair and smolt ".
He cleikit up ane hie rough sang,
There fure ane man to the holt,
                    Quod he,
Of Peblis to the play.

They had nocht gane half of the gate
When the maidenia come upon them,
Ilk ane man gaif his conceit,
How at they wald dispone them.
Ane said, " The fairest fallis to me ;
Tak ye the laif and fone them ".
Ane other said, " Wys lat me be !
On, Twedel-side, and on them
                    Swyth !
Of Peblis to the play."

Than he to-ga, and she to-ga,
And never ane bade abide you.
Ane winklot fell, and her tail up ;
" Wow," quod Malkin, " Hide you !
What needis you to make it swa ?
Yon man will not our-ride you."

" Are ye owre gude," quod she, " I say,
To lat them gang beside you,
                    Yonder,
Of Peblis to the play ? "

Than they come to the townis end
Withouttin more delay,
He before, and she before,
To see wha was maist gay.
All that lukit them upon
Leuch fast at their array ;
Some said that they were merkat folk ;
Some said the Queen of May
                    Was comit
Of Peblis to the play.

Than they to the tavern-house
With meikle olyprance ;
And spak wi' wordis wonder crouse,
" A done with ane mischance !
Braid up the burde," he hydis tyt,
" We are all in ane trance :
See that our nap'ry be white,
For we will dine and dance,
                    There out.
Of Peblis to the play ".

Ay as the gudewife brocht in,
Ane scorit upon the wauch,
Ane bade pay, ane other said, " Nay,
Bide whill we reckon our lauch ".
The gudewife said, " Have ye na dreid ;
Ye sall pay at ye auch ".

Ane young man start upon his feet,
And he began to lauche,
                        For heydin,
Of Peblis to the play.

He gat ane trencheour in his hand
And he began to compt :
" Ilk man twa and ane ha'penny !
To pay thus we were wont ".
Ane other start upon his feet,
And said, " Thou art owre blunt
To tak sic office upon hand !
Be God thou 'servit ane dunt
                        Of me,
Of Peblis to the play."

" Ane dunt," quod he, " what devil is that ?
Be God, you dar not do't ! "
He start till ane broggit staff,
Winceand as he were wood.
All that house was in ane reird :
And cryit, " The haly rude !
Help us, Lord, upon this erd,
That there be spilt na blude
                        Herein,
Of Peblis to the play ! "

They thrang out at the door at anis
Withouttin ony reddin' ;
Gilbert in ane gutter glade,
He gat na better beddin'.
There was not ane of them that day
Wald do ane otheris biddin'.

Thereby lay three and thretty-some
Thrimland in ane middin'
                    Of draff,
Of Peblis to the play.

Ane cadger on the merkat gate
Heard them bargane begin ;
He gaif ane shout, his wife came out ;
Scantly she micht ourhye him :
He held, she drew, for dust that day
Micht na man see ane styme
                    To red them.
Of Peblis to the play.

He start to his great grey mare,
And off he tumblit the creelis.
" Alas ! " quod she, " Hald our gudeman ! "
And on her knees she kneelis.
" Abide," quod she ; " Why, nay," quod he ;
In-till his stirrupis he lap ;
The girdin brak, and he flew off,
And upstart baith his heelis,
                    At anis,
Of Peblis to the play.

His wife came out, and gaif ane shout,
And be the fit she gat him ;
All bedirtin drew him out ;
" Lord God ! richt weil that sat him ! "
He said, " Where is yon culroun knave ? "
Quod she, " I rede ye, lat him
Gang hame his gates ".   " Be God," quod
    he,

" I sall anis have at him
Yit,
Of Peblis to the play."

" Ye 'filed me, fy for shame ! " quod she ;
" See as ye have drest me !
How feel ye, sir ? "   " As my girdin brak,
What meikle devil may lest me.
I wait weil what ; it was
My awn grey mare that kest me :
Or gif I was forfochtin faint,
And syne lay doun to rest me,
Yonder,
Of Peblis to the play."

Be that the bargane was all playit,
The stringis start out of their nocks ;
Seven-some that the tulzie made,
Lay gruffiling in the stocks.
John Nikson of the nether ward
Had lever have giffin an ox
Or he had comin in that company,
He sware be Goddis locks,
And manis baith,
Of Peblis to the play.

With that Will Swane come sweatand out,
Ane meikle miller man ;
" Gif I sall dance have done, lat see,
Blaw up the bagpipe than !
The schamous dance I maun begin ;
I trow it sall not pane."
So heavily he hochit about,

To see him, Lord, as they ran,
                    That tide,
Of Peblis to the play !

They gadderit out of the toun,
And nearer him they dreuch ;
And bade gife the danceris room ;
Will Swane makis wonder teuch.
Than all the wenches Te he ! they playit ;
Bot Lord, as Will Young leuch !
" Gude gossip, come hyne yon gatis,
For we have dansit aneuch,
                    At anis,
At Peblis to the play."

Sa fiercely fire-het was the day
His face began to frekill.
Than Tisbe tuk him by the hand,
Was new comen fra the heckill.
" Alas," quod she, " what sall I do ?
And our door has na stekill ! "
And she to-ga as her tail brint,
And all the carlis to ceckle
                    At her,
Of Peblis to the play.

The piper said, " Now I begin
To tire for playing to you ;
Bot yit I have gotten naething
For all my piping to you.
Three ha'pennies for half ane day
And that will not undo you ;
And gif ye will gife me richt nocht,

The meikle Devil gang wi' you ! "
                          Quod he,
Of Peblis to the play.

Baith the dancing was all done,
Their leif tuk less and mair ;
When the winklottis and the wooeris twinit
To see it was hairt sair.
Wat Atkin said to fair Ales,
" My bird, now will I fare ".
The devil a word that she might speak
Bot swoonit that sweet of swair
                          For kindness.
Of Peblis to the play.

He fippilit like ane faderless fole ;
" And be still, my sweet thing ! "
" Be the haly rude of Peblis
I may nocht rest for greeting."
He whissillit and he pipit baith,
To mak her blyth that meeting :
" My honey hairt, how sayis the sang,
There sall be mirth at our meeting
                          Yit,
Of Peblis to the play ".

Be that the sun was settand shaftis ;
And near done was the day :
There men micht hear schukin of schaftis
When that they went their way.
Had there been mair made of this sang,
Mair suld I to you say.

At Beltane ilka body bown'd
To Peblis to the play.

Anonymous.

CXIV

TAM O' SHANTER

(" Of Brownis and of Bogillis full is this Buke."
GAVIN DOUGLAS)

WHEN chapmen billies leave the street,
And drouthy neibors, neibors meet ;
As market-days are wearing late,
And folk begin to tak the gate,
While we sit bousing at the nappy,
An' getting fou and unco happy,
We think na on the lang Scots miles,
The mosses, waters, slaps and stiles,
That lie between us and our hame,
Where sits our sulky, sullen dame,
Gathering her brows like gathering storm,
Nursing her wrath to keep it warm.

This truth fand honest Tam o' Shanter,
As he frae Ayr ae night did canter ;
(Auld Ayr, wham ne'er a town surpasses
For honest men and bonnie lasses.)

O Tam ! hadst thou but been sae wise,
As taen thy ain wife Kate's advice !
She tauld thee weel thou was a skellum,
A blethering, blustering, drunken blellum ;
That frae November till October,

Ae market-day thou was na sober ;
That ilka melder wi' the miller,
Thou sat as lang as thou had siller ;
That ev'ry naig was ca'd a shoe on,
The Smith and thee gat roarin' fou on ;
That at the Lord's house, ev'n on Sunday,
Thou drank wi' Kirkton Jean till Monday ;
She prophesied that late or soon,
Thou wad be found, deep drown'd in Doon,
Or catch'd wi' warlocks in the mirk,
By Alloway's auld haunted kirk.

Ah, gentle dames ! it gars me greet,
To think how mony counsels sweet,
How mony lengthen'd, sage advices,
The husband frae the wife despises !

But to our tale :—Ae market night,
Tam had got planted unco right,
Fast by an ingle, bleezing finely,
Wi' reaming swats that drank divinely ;
And at his elbow, Souter Johnie,
His ancient, trusty, drouthy crony :
Tam lo'ed him like a very brither ;
They had been fou for weeks thegither.
The night drave on wi' sangs an' clatter ;
And aye the ale was growing better :
The landlady and Tam grew gracious,
Wi' favours secret, sweet and precious :
The Souter tauld his queerest stories ;
The landlord's laugh was ready chorus :
The storm without might rair and rustle,
Tam did na mind the storm a whistle.

Care, mad to see a man sae happy,
E'en drown'd himsel' amang the nappy.
As bees flee hame wi' lades o' treasure,
The minutes wing'd their way wi' pleasure :
Kings may be blest, but Tam was glorious,
O'er a' the ills o' life victorious !

But pleasures are like poppies spread,
You seize the flow'r, its bloom is shed ;
Or like the snow falls in the river,
A moment white—then melts for ever ;
Or like the borealis race,
That flit ere you can point their place ;
Or like the rainbow's lovely form
Evanishing amid the storm.—
Nae man can tether Time nor Tide,
The hour approaches Tam maun ride ;
That hour, o' night's black arch the key-stane,
That dreary hour he mounts his beast in ;
And sic a night he taks the road in,
As ne'er poor sinner was abroad in.

The wind blew as 'twad blawn its last ;
The rattling showers rose on the blast ;
The speedy gleams the darkness swallow'd ;
Loud, deep, and lang the thunder bellow'd :
That night, a child might understand,
The deil had business on his hand.

Weel-mounted on his grey mare, Meg,
A better never lifted leg,
Tam skelpit on thro' dub and mire,
Despising wind, and rain, and fire ;

Whiles holding fast his gude blue bonnet ;
Whiles crooning o'er some auld Scots sonnet ;
Whiles glow'ring round wi' prudent cares,
Lest bogles catch him unawares ;
Kirk-Alloway was drawing nigh,
Where ghaists and houlets nightly cry.

By this time he was cross the ford,
Where in the snaw the chapman smoor'd ;
And past the birks and meikle stane,
Where drunken Charlie brak's neck-bane ;
And thro' the whins, and by the cairn,
Where hunters fand the murder'd bairn ;
And near the thorn, aboon the well,
Where Mungo's mither hang'd hersel'.
Before him Doon pours all his floods,
The doubling storm roars thro' the woods,
The lightnings flash from pole to pole,
Near and more near the thunders roll,
When, glimmering thro' the groaning trees,
Kirk-Alloway seem'd in a bleeze,
Thro' ilka bore the beams were glancing,
And loud resounded mirth and dancing.

Inspiring bold John Barleycorn !
What dangers thou canst make us scorn !
Wi' tippeny, we fear nae evil ;
Wi' usquabae, we'll face the devil !
The swats sae reamed in Tammie's noddle,
Fair play, he car'd na deils a boddle,
But Maggie stood, right sair astonish'd,
Till, by the heel and hand admonish'd,
She ventur'd forward on the light ;

And, wow ! Tam saw an unco sight !
Warlocks and witches in a dance :
Nae cotillon, brent new frae France,
But hornpipes, jigs, strathspeys, and reels,
Put life and mettle in their heels.
A winnock-bunker in the east,
There sat auld Nick, in shape o' beast ;
A tousie tyke, black, grim, and large,
To gie them music was his charge :
He screw'd the pipes and gart them skirl,
Till roof and rafters a' did dirl.—
Coffins stood round, like open presses,
That shaw'd the dead in their last dresses ;
And (by some devilish cantraip sleight)
Each in its cauld hand held a light.
By which heroic Tam was able
To note upon the haly table,
A murderer's banes, in gibbet-airns ;
Twa span-lang, wee, unchristened bairns ;
A thief, new-cutted frae a rape,
Wi' his last gasp his gab did gape ;
Five tomahawks, wi' blude red-rusted ;
Five scimitars, wi' murder crusted ;
A garter which a babe had strangled ;
A knife, a father's throat had mangled,
Whom his ain son of life bereft,
The grey hairs yet stuck to the heft ;
Wi' mair of horrible and awfu',
Which even to name wad be unlawfu'.

As Tammie glowr'd, amaz'd and curious,
The mirth and fun grew fast and furious ;
The piper loud and louder blew

The dancers quick and quicker flew,
They reel'd, they set, they cross'd, they cleekit,
Till ilka carlin swat and reekit,
And coost her duddies to the wark,
And linkit at it in her sark !

Now Tam, O Tam ! had they been queans,
A' plump and strapping in their teens !
Their sarks, instead o' creeshie flannen,
Been snaw-white seventeen-hunder linen !—
Thir breeks o' mine, my only pair,
That aince were plush, o' guid blue hair,
I wad hae gien them off my hurdies,
For ae blink o' the bonnie burdies !
But wither'd beldams, auld and droll,
Rigwoodie hags wad spean a foal,
Louping an' flinging on a crummock,
I wonder did na turn thy stomach.

But Tam kent what was what fu' brawlie :
There was ae winsome wench and waulie
That night enlisted in the core,
Lang after ken'd on Carrick shore
(For mony a beast to dead she shot,
And perish'd mony a bonie boat,
An' shook baith meikle corn and bear,
And kept the country-side in fear) ;
Her cutty sark, o' Paisley harn,
That while a lassie she had worn,
In longitude tho' sorely scanty,
It was her best, and she was vauntie.
Ah ! little ken'd thy reverend grannie,
That sark she coft for her wee Nannie,

Wi' twa pund Scots ('twas a' her riches),
Wad ever grac'd a dance of witches !

But here my Muse her wing maun cour,
Sic flights are far beyond her power ;
To sing how Nannie lap and flang
(A souple jade she was and strang),
And how Tam stood, like ane bewitch'd,
And thought his very een enrich'd :
Even Satan glowr'd, and fidg'd fu' fain,
And hotch'd and blew wi' might and main :
Till first ae caper, syne anither,
Tam tint his reason a' thegither,
And roars out, " Weel done, Cutty-sark ! "
And in an instant all was dark :
And scarcely had he Maggie rallied,
When out the hellish legion sallied.

As bees bizz out wi' angry fyke,
When plundering herds assail their byke ;
As open pussie's mortal foes,
When, pop ! she starts before their nose ;
As eager runs the market-crowd,
When " Catch the thief ! " resounds aloud ;
So Maggie runs, the witches follow,
Wi' mony an eldritch skreich and hollo.

Ah, Tam !   Ah, Tam ! thou'll get thy fairin',
In hell they'll roast thee like a herrin' !
In vain thy Kate awaits thy comin' !
Kate soon will be a woefu' woman !
Now, do thy speedy utmost, Meg,
And win the key-stane o' the brig ;

There, at them thou thy tail may toss,
A running stream they dare na cross ;
But ere the key-stane she could make,
The fient a tail she had to shake !
For Nannie, far before the rest,
Hard upon noble Maggie prest,
And flew at Tam wi' furious ettle ;
But little wist she Maggie's mettle !
Ae spring brought off her master hale,
But left behind her ain grey tail :
The carlin claught her by the rump,
And left poor Maggie scarce a stump.

Now, wha this tale o' truth shall read,
Ilk man and mother's son take heed :
Whene'er to drink you are inclin'd,
Or cutty-sarks rin in your mind,
Think, ye may buy the joys o'er dear ;
Remember Tam o' Shanter's mare.

Robert Burns.

CXV

FROM " THE JOLLY BEGGARS "

SEE the smoking bowl before us,
    Mark our jovial ragged ring !
Round and round take up the chorus,
    And in raptures let us sing—

CHORUS

A fig for those by law protected !
    Liberty's a glorious feast !

Courts for cowards were erected,
  Churches built to please the priest.

What is title, what is treasure,
  What is reputation's care ?
If we lead a life of pleasure,
  'Tis no matter how or where !

        A fig for, etc.

With the ready trick and fable,
  Round we wander all the day ;
And at night in barn or stable,
  Hug our doxies on the hay.

        A fig for, etc.

Does the train-attended carriage
  Thro' the country lighter rove ?
Does the sober bed of marriage
  Witness brighter scenes of love ?

        A fig for, etc.

Life is all a variorum,
  We regard not how it goes ;
Let them cant about decorum,
  Who have character to lose.

        A fig for, etc.

Here's to budgets, bags and wallets !
  Here's to all the wandering train.
Here's our ragged brats and callets,
  One and all cry out, Amen !

CHORUS

A fig for those by law protected !
   Liberty's a glorious feast !
Courts for cowards were erected,
   Churches built to please the priest.
                 Robert Burns.

CXVI

THE EXCISEMAN

(AIR : " The de'il cam' fiddling through the town ")

THE de'il cam' fiddling through the town,
   An' danced awa' wi' the Exciseman,
And ilka wife cries—" Auld Mahoun,
   I wish you luck o' the prize, man ! "
     The de'il's awa', the de'il's awa',
       The de'il's awa' wi' the Exciseman ;
     He's danc'd awa', he's danc'd awa',
       He's danc'd awa' wi' the Exciseman !

We'll mak' our maut, we'll brew our drink,
   We'll dance, an' sing, an' rejoice, man ;
And mony braw thanks to the meikle black de'il
   That danc'd awa' wi' the Exciseman.
     The de'il's awa', the de'il's awa',
       The de'il's awa' wi' the Exciseman ;
     He's danc'd awa', he's danc'd awa',
       He's danc'd awa' wi' the Exciseman.

There's threesome reels, there's foursome reels,
   There's hornpipes and strathspeys, man ;

But the ae best dance e'er cam' to the land
   Was—the de'il's awa' wi' the Exciseman.
   The de'il's awa', the de'il's awa',
     The de'il's awa' wi' the Exciseman ;
   He's danc'd awa', he's danc'd awa',
     He's danc'd awa' wi' the Exciseman.
                    Robert Burns.

CXVII

AGANIS THE THIEVIS OF LIDDISDALE

Of Liddisdale the common thievis
Sa pertlie stealis now and reivis,
   That nane may keep
   Horse, nolt, nor sheep,
Nor yit dar sleep for their mischiefis.

They plainlie through the countrie ridis ;
I trow the meikle devil them guidis ;
   Where they onset
   Ay in their gate
There is na yett nor door them bidis.

They leif richt nocht ; wherever they gae
There can na thing be hid them frae ;
   For, gif men wald
   Their houses hald,
Then wax they bauld to burn and slay.

Thae thievis have nearhand herreit haill
Ettrick Forest and Lauderdale ;

Now are they gane
In Lothiane,
And sparis nane that they will wale.

Thae landis are with stouth sa socht,
To extreme povertie are brocht ;
Thae wicked shrewis
Has laid the plowis,
That nane or few is that are left oucht.

By common taking of black-mail,
They that had flesh and bread and ale,
Now are sa wraikit,
Made pure and naikit,
Fain to be slaikit with water-kail.

Thae thievis that stealis and tursis hame,
Ilk ane of them has ane to-name :
Will of the Lawis,
Hab of the Shawis ;
To mak bare wa'is, they think na shame.

They spuilye puir men of their packis ;
They leave them nocht on bed nor backis ;
Baith hen and cock,
With reel and rock,
The Lairdis Jock, all with him takis.

They leave not spindle, spoon, nor spit,
Bed, bowster, blanket, serk, nor sheet :
John of the Park
Ripes kist and ark ;
For all sic wark he is richt meet.

He is weil kend, John of the Side ;
A greater thief did never ride :
    He never tires
    For to break byres ;
Owre muir and mires owre gude ane guide.

There is ane, callit Clement's Hob,
Fa ilk puir wife reivis her wob,
    And all the lave,
    Whatever they have :
The devil resave therefor his gob !

To see sa great stouth wha wald trow it,
Bot gif some great man it allowit ?
    Richt sair I rue,
    Though it be true,
There is sa few that dar avow it.

Of some great men they have sic gate,
That ready are them to debate
    And will up-wear
    Their stolen gear,
That nane dar steir them, air nor late.

What causes thievis us our-gang
Bot want of justice us amang ?
    Nane takis care
    Though all forfare :
Na man will spare now to do wrang.

Of stouth thoch now they come gude speed
That neither of men nor God has dreid,

Yet, or I die,
  Some sall them see
Hing on a tree whill they be deid.
                 Sir Richard Maitland.

CXVIII

ANE SUPPLICATION IN CONTEMPTIOUN OF SYDE TAILLIS

SCHIR, though your grace has put great order
Baith in the Hieland and the Border,
Yet make I supplicatioun
Till have some reformatioun
Of ane small fault whilk is nocht treason,
Though it be contrary to reason.
Because the matter been so vile
It may nocht have an ornate style :
Wharefore I pray your excellence
To hear me with great patience :
Of stinkand weedis maculate
No man may make a rose chaplet.
Soverane, I mean of thir syde taillis
Whilk through the dust and dubbis traillis
Three quarteris lang behind their heelis,
Express agane all Commoun weillis.
Though bishopis in their pontificalis
Have men for to bear up their tailis
For dignity of their office,
Richt so ane queen or ane Emprice,
Howbeit they use sic gravity
Conformand to their majesty ;

M

Though their robe royalis be upborne,
I think it is ane very scorn
That every lady of the land
Suld have her tail so syde trailand,
Howbeit they bene of hie estate,
The Queen they suld nocht counterfait.
Wharever they go it may be seen
How kirk and causay they soup clean.
The imagis into the kirk
May think of their syde taillis irk,
For when the wedder bene most fair,
The dust flies highest in the air
And all their faces dois begarie.
Gif they culd speak, they wald them warie.
To see I think ane pleasant sicht
Of Italy the ladyis bricht,
In their clothing maist triumphand
Above all other Christian land.
Yet when they travel through the townes
Men seis their feet beneath their gownis,
Four inch abune their proper heelis,
Circulate about as round as wheelis,
Whare through there dois na poulder rise
There fair white limbis to supprise.
Bot I have most into despite
Puir claggokis clad in raploch white
Whilk has scant twa merkis for their fees
Will have twa ellis beneath their knees.
Kittok that clekkit was yestreen,
The morn will counterfeit the Queen.
Ane muirland Meg that milkis the yowis
Claggit with clay abune the howis,
In barn nor byre she will nocht bide

Without her kirtle tail be syde.
In boroughis wanton burgess wivis
Wha may have sidest taillis strivis,
Weill borderit with velvet fine :
Bot following them it is ane pyne ;
In summer when the streetis dryis
They raise the dust abune the skyis :
None may go near them at their ease
Without they cover mouth and neis,
I think maist pain after ane rain
To see them tuckit up again ;
Then when they step furth through the street
Thare faldingis flappis about their feet,
Their laithlie lining furthward flypit
Whilk has the muck and midding wypit.

.   .   .   .   .

Bot wald your grace my counsel tak
Ane proclamation ye suld mak,
Baith through the land and borrowstounis
To shaw their face and cut their gownis.
Nane suld fra that exemptit be
Except the Queenis Majesty.
                              Sir David Lyndsay.

THE PAWKY DUKE

THERE aince was a very pawky duke,
    Far kent for his joukery-pawkery,

Wha owned a hoose wi' a grand outlook,
    A gairden and a rockery.
Hech mon ! The pawky duke !
    Hoot ay ! An' a rockery !
For a bonnet-laird wi' a sma' kailyard
    Is naethin' but a mockery !

He lived far up a Heelant glen,
    Where the foamin' flood an' the crag is,
An' he dined each day on the usquebae
    An' he washed it doon wi' haggis.
Hech mon ! The pawky duke !
    Hoot ay ! An' a haggis !
For that's the way the Heelanters dae,
    Where the foamin' flood an' the crag is !

He wore a sporran and a dirk
    An' a beard like besom bristles,
He was an elder o' the kirk
    An' he hated kists o' whistles.
Hech mon ! The pawky duke !
    An' doon on kists o' whistles !
They're a reid-heidit fowk up North
    Wi' beards like besom bristles !

Then ilka four hoors through the day
    He took a muckle jorum,
An' when the gloamin' gathered grey
    Got fou' wi' great decorum.
Hech mon ! The pawky duke !
    Blin' fou' wi' great decorum !
There ne'er were males among the Gaels
    But loo'ed a muckle jorum !

His hair was reid as ony rose,
   His legs were lang an' bony,
He keepit a hoast an' a rubbin'-post
   An' a buskit cockernony.
Hech mon ! The pawky duke !
   Wi' a buskit cockernony !
Ye ne'er will ken true Heelant men
   Who'll own they hadna ony !

An' if he met a Sassenach loon
   Attour in Caledonia,
He gar'd him lilt in a cotton kilt
   Till he had an acute pneumonia.
Hech mon ! The pawky duke !
   An' a Sassenach wi' pneumonia !
He lat him feel that the land o' the leal
   Is gey near Caledonia !

He never went awa' doon Sooth
   To mell wi' legislation,
For weel he kent sic things to be
   Unfitted for his station.
Hech mon ! The pawky duke !
   An' weel he kent his station,
For dustmen noo we a' alloo
   Are best at legislation !

Then aye afore he socht his bed,
   He danced the Ghillie-Callum,
An' wi's Kilmarnock owre his neb
   What evil could befall 'im ?
Hech mon ! The pawky duke !
   What evil could befall 'im,

When he casts his buits and soupled his cuits
    With a gude-gaun Ghillie-Callum ?

But they brocht ae day a muckle joke
    For his ducal eedification,
An' they needit to trephine his heid,
    An' he dee'd o' the operation !
Hech mon !   The pawky duke !
    Wae's me for the operation !
For weel I wot this typical Scot
    Was a michty loss to the nation !
                                          David Rorie.

CXX

ADDRESS TO THE DEIL

(" O Prince ! O chief of many thronèd pow'rs
    That led th' embattl'd seraphim to war— "
                                          MILTON)

O Thou ! whatever title suit thee—
Auld Hornie, Satan, Nick, or Clootie,
Wha in yon cavern grim an' sootie,
                    Clos'd under hatches,
Spairges about the brunstane cootie,
                    To scaud poor wretches !

Hear me, auld Hangie, for a wee,
An' let poor damnèd bodies be ;
I'm sure sma' pleasure it can gie,
                    Ev'n to a deil,
To skelp an' scaud poor dogs like me,
                    An' hear us squeel !

Great is thy pow'r an' great thy fame ;
Far ken'd an' noted is thy name ;
An' tho' yon lowin' heuch's thy hame,
        · Thou travels far ;
An' faith ! thou's neither lag nor lame,
          Nor blate, nor scaur.

Whiles, ranging like a roarin lion,
For prey, a' holes and corners tryin ;
Whiles, on the strong-wing'd tempest flyin,
          Tirlin the kirks ;
Whiles, in the human bosom pryin,
          Unseen thou lurks.

I've heard my rev'rend graunie say,
In lanely glens ye like to stray ;
Or where auld ruin'd castles grey
          Nod to the moon,
Ye fright the nightly wand'rer's way,
          Wi' eldritch croon.

When twilight did my graunie summon,
To say her pray'rs, douse, honest woman !
Aft 'yont the dyke she's heard you bummin,
          Wi' eerie drone ;
Or, rustlin, thro' the boortrees comin,
          Wi' heavy groan.

Ae dreary, windy, winter night,
The stars shot down wi' sklentin light,
Wi' you mysel' I gat a fright,
          Ayont the lough ;
Ye, like a rash-buss, stood in sight,
          Wi' wavin sough.

The cudgel in my nieve did shake,
Each bristl'd hair stood like a stake,
When wi' an eldritch, stoor " quaick, quaick ",
    Amang the springs,
Awa ye squatter'd like a drake,
    On whistling wings.

Let warlocks grim, an' wither'd hags,
Tell how wi' you, on ragweed nags,
They skim the muirs an' dizzy crags,
    Wi' wicked speed;
And in kirk-yards renew their leagues,
    Owre howkit dead.

Thence countra wives, wi' toil and pain,
May plunge an' plunge the kirn in vain;
For oh! the yellow treasure's ta'en
    By witchin skill;
An' dawtit, twal-pint hawkie's gane
    As yell's the bill.

Thence mystic knots mak great abuse
On young guidmen, fond, keen an' crouse
When the best wark-lume i' the house,
    By cantrip wit,
Is instant made no worth a louse,
    Just at the bit.

When thowes dissolve the snawy hoord,
An' float the jinglin icy boord,
Then water-kelpies haunt the foord,
    By your direction,
And 'nighted trav'lers are allur'd
    To their destruction.

And aft your moss-traversin Spunkies
Decoy the wight that late an' drunk is :
The bleezin, curst, mischievous monkies
    Delude his eyes,
Till in some miry slough he sunk is,
     Ne'er mair to rise.

When masons' mystic word an' grip
In storms an' tempest raise you up,
Some cock or cat your rage maun stop,
     Or, strange to tell !
The youngest brither ye wad whip
    Aff straught to hell.

Lang syne in Eden's bonie yard,
When youthfu' lovers first were pair'd,
An' all the soul of love they shar'd,
    The raptur'd hour,
Sweet on the fragrant flow'ry swaird,
    In shady bower ;

Then you, ye auld, snick-drawing dog !
Ye cam to Paradise incog,
An' play'd on man a cursèd brogue,
    (Black be your fa' !)
An' gied the infant warld a shog,
    'Maist ruin'd a'.

D'ye mind that day when in a bizz
Wi' reekit duds, an' reestit gizz,
Ye did present your smoutie phiz
    'Mang better folk

An' sklented on the man of Uzz
                    Your spitefu' joke ?

An' how ye gat him i' your thrall,
An' brak him out o' house an' hal',
While scabs and botches did him gall,
                    Wi' bitter claw ;
An' lows'd his ill-tongu'd wicked scaul',
                    Was warst ava ?

But a' your doings to rehearse,
Your wily snares an' fechtin fierce,
Sin' that day Michael did you pierce,
                    Down to this time,
Wad ding a Lallan tongue, or Erse,
                    In prose or rhyme.

   An' now, auld Cloots, I ken ye're thinkin,
A certain bardie's rantin, drinkin,
Some luckless hour will send him linkin
                    To your black pit ;
But faith ! he'll turn a corner jinkin,
                    An' cheat you yet.

But fare-you-weel, auld Nickie-ben !
O wad ye tak a thought an' men' !
Ye aiblins might—I dinna ken—
                    Still hae a stake :
I'm wae to think upo' yon den,
                    Ev'n for your sake !
                            Robert Burns.

CXXI

[*Virgil in Scots*]

THE ENTRANCE TO HELL

(*Aeneid*, vi. 268-84)

THAY walkit furth so derk oneith they wist
Whidder thay went amyddis dim schaddois thare,
Whare ever is nicht, and never licht doth repare,
Throwout the waste dungeoun of Pluto king,
Thay roid boundis and the gousty ring ;
Siklyke as wha wald throw thick woodis wend,
In obscure light whare none may not be kend,
As Jupiter the king etherial
With erdis skug hydis the hevynnys al,
And the mirk nicht with her vysage gray
From every thing has reft the hew away.

Before the portis and first jawis of hel
Lamentacioun and wraikful Thochtis fel
Thare loging had, and thereat dwellis eik
Pale Maledyis that causis man be seik,
The fereful Drede and als unweildy Age,
The felone Hunger with her undantit rage :
There was also the laithly Indigence,
Terribil of schape and schameful her presence ;
The grisly Dede that mony ane has slane,
The hard Laubour and diseisful Pane,
The slottry Slepe Dedis cousin of kynd,
Inordinat Blithnes of perversit mind :
And in the yett, forganis thaym did stand

The mortal Battel with his dedely brand,
The irne chalmeris of hellis Furies fel,
Witles Discord, that woundring maist cruel.
Womplit and buskit in ane bludy bend,
With snakis hung at every haris end.
And in the myddis of the uttir ward,
With brade branchis sprede over al the sward,
Ane rank eleme tre stude, huge, grete and stok
    auld.
The vulgar pepil in that samyn hauld
Belevis thare vane Dremes makis thare dwelling,
Under ilk leif ful thik they stik and hing.

                        Gavin Douglas.

CXXII

THE DAY OF JUDGMENT

(Translated from the Gaelic)

ASUNDER shall the clouds be rolled,
Like to God's golden palace gate.
Then shall our eyes the Judge behold
In glorious and solemn state.

The rainbow's splendour for His crown :
His voice like torrents in the glen :
His glance like lightning flashing down
From dark clouds to affrighted men.

The sun, that bright torch of the sky,
Shall pale before such radiant light ;
The blinding flashes from His eye
Shall hide its brilliance from our sight.

Thus mournfully its light shall fade :
And red with blood shall be the moon.
The stars in heaven shall be swayed,
And totter at the knell of doom.

Like fruit-buds on a wind-swept plain
The stars shall scatter through the skies,
And drop down to the earth like rain,
With vanished light like dead men's eyes.
Dugald Buchanan.

CXXIII

THE SOLSEQUIUM

LIKE as the dumb solsequium, with care ourcome
  Dois sorrow, when the sun goes out of sicht,
Hings doun his head, and droops as dead, nor will
    not spread,
  Bot locks his leavis through languor all the
    nicht,
      Till foolish Phaeton rise
        With whip in hand,
      To purge the crystal skyis
        And licht the land.
Birds in their bour waitis for that hour
  And to their prince ane glaid good-morrow givis ;
Fra then, that flour list not till lour,
  Bot laughis on Phoebus loosing out his leavis.

So standis with me, except I be where I may see
  My lamp of licht, my lady and my luve ;

Fra she depairts, ane thousand dairts, in sundry
    airts
    Thirlis through my heavy hairt but rest or rove ;
        My countenance declares
          My inward grief,
        And hope almaist despairs
          To find relief.
I die, I dwine, play dois me pyne,
    I loathe on every thing I look, alace !
Till Titan mine upon me shine
    That I revive through favour of her face.

Fra she appear into her sphere begins to clear
    The dawing of my long desirit day :
Then Courage cryis on Hope to rise, when he espyis
    My noysome nicht of absence went away.
        No woe, fra I awauk,
          May me empesh ;
        Bot on my stately stalk
          I flourish fresh.
I spring, I sprout, my leavis lie out,
    My colour changes in ane heartsome hue.
No more I lout, bot stand up stout,
    As glad of her for whom I only grew.

O happy day ! go not away, Apollo ! stay
    Thy chair from going doun into the west :
Of me thou mak thy zodiac, that I may tak
    My pleasure to behold whom I luve best.
        Thy presence me restores
          To life from death ;
        Thy absence likewayis schores
          To cut my breath.

I wish, in vain, thee to remain,
　Sen primum mobile sayis me alwayis nay ;
At least, thy wain turn soon again,
　Fareweill, with patience perforce till day.
Alexander Montgomerie.

CXXIV

HOLY WILLIE'S PRAYER

("And send the godly in a pet to pray."
POPE)

O THOU, that in the heavens does dwell,
Wha, as it pleases best Thysel',
Sends ane to heaven an' ten to hell,
　　　A' for thy glory,
And no for onie guid or ill
　　　They've done afore Thee !

I bless and praise Thy matchless might,
When thousands Thou hast left in night
That I am here afore Thy sight,
　　　For gifts an' grace
A burning and a shining light
　　　To a' this place.

What was I, or my generation,
That I should get sic exaltation,
I wha deserv'd most just damnation
　　　For broken laws,
Sax thousand years ere my creation,
　　　Thro' Adam's cause.

When from my mither's womb I fell,
Thou might hae plung'd me deep in hell,
To gnash my gooms, and weep and wail,
   In burnin lakes,
Where damnèd devils roar and yell,
    Chain'd to their stakes.

Yet I am here a chosen sample,
To show thy grace is great and ample ;
I'm here a pillar o' Thy temple,
   Strong as a rock,
A guide, a buckler, and example,
   To a' Thy flock.

O Lord, Thou kens what zeal I bear,
When drinkers drink, an' swearers swear,
An' singing here, an' dancin' there,
   Wi' great and sma' ;
For I am keepit by Thy fear
   Free frae them a'.

But yet, O Lord ! confess I must,
At times I'm fash'd wi' fleshly lust :
An' sometimes, too, in warldly trust,
   Vile self gets in ;
But Thou remembers we are dust,
   Defil'd wi' sin.

O Lord ! yestreen, Thou kens, wi' Meg—
Thy pardon I sincerely beg ;
O ! may't ne'er be a livin plague
   To my dishonour,
An' I'll ne'er lift a lawless leg
   Again upon her.

Besides, I farther maun allow,
Wi' Leezie's lass, three times I trow—
But Lord, that Friday I was fou,
      When I cam near her ;
Or else, Thou kens, Thy servant true
      Wad never steer her.

Maybe Thou lets this fleshly thorn
Buffet Thy servant e'en and morn,
Lest he owre proud and high shou'd turn,
      That he's sae gifted :
If sae, Thy han' maun e'en be borne,
      Until Thou lift it.

Lord, bless Thy chosen in this place,
For here Thou has a chosen race :
But God confound their stubborn face,
      An' blast their name,
Wha bring Thy elders to disgrace
      An' public shame.

Lord, mind Gaw'n Hamilton's deserts ;
He drinks, an' swears, an' plays at cartes,
Yet has sae mony takin arts,
      Wi' great and sma',
Frae God's ain priest the people's hearts
      He steals awa.

An' when we chasten'd him therefor,
Thou kens how he bred sic a splore,
An' set the warld in a roar
      O' laughing at us ;—

Curse Thou his basket and his store,
   Kail an' potatoes.

Lord, hear my earnest cry and pray'r,
Against that Presbyt'ry o' Ayr ;
Thy strong right hand, Lord, make it bare
   Upo' their heads ;
Lord, visit them, an' dinna spare,
   For their misdeeds.

O Lord, my God ! that glib-tongu'd Aiken,
My vera heart and flesh are quakin,
To think how we stood sweatin, shakin,
   An' p—'d wi' dread,
While he, wi' hingin lip an' snakin,
   Held up his head.

Lord, in Thy day o' vengeance try him,
Lord, visit them wha did employ him,
And pass not in Thy mercy by them,
   Nor hear their pray'r,
But for thy people's sake destroy them,
   An' dinna spare.

But, Lord, remember me an' mine
Wi' mercies temporal and divine,
That I for grace an' gear may shine,
   Excell'd by nane,
And a' the glory shall be thine,
   Amen, Amen !
      Robert Burns.

CXXV

THE DANCE OF THE SEVIN DEIDLY SYNNIS

OFF Februar the fyiftene nycht,
Full lang befoir the dayis lycht,
I lay in till a trance ;
And then I saw baith hevin and hell :
Me thocht, amangis the feyndis fell,
Mahoun gart cry ane dance
Off schrewis that wer nevir schrevin,
Aganis the feist of Fasternis evin
To mak thair observance ;
He bad gallandis ga graith a gyis,
And kast up gamountis in the skyis,
That last came out of France.

" Lat se," quod he, " Now quha begynnis ? " ;
With that the fowll Sevin Deidly Synnis
Begowth to leip at anis.
And first of all in dance wes Pryd,
With hair wyld bak and bonet on syd,
Lyk to mak waistie wanis ;
And round abowt him, as a quheill,
Hang all in rumpillis to the heill
His kethat for the nanis :
Mony prowd trumpour with him trippit,
Throw skaldand fyre ay as thay skippit
Thay gyrnd with hiddous granis.

Heilie harlottis on hawtane wyis

Come in with mony sindrie gyis,
Bot yit luche nevir Mahoun,
Quhill preistis come in with bair schevin nekkis,
Than all the feyndis lewche and maid gekkis,
Blak Belly and Bawsy Brown.

Than Yre come in with sturt and stryfe ;
His hand wes ay upoun his knyfe,
He brandeist lyk a beir :
Bostaris, braggaris, and barganeris,
Eftir him passit in to pairis,
All bodin in feir of weir ;
In jakkis, and stryppis and bonettis of steill,
Thair leggis wer chenyeit to the heill,
Frawart wes thair affeir :
Sum upoun udir with brandis beft,
Sum jaggit uthiris to the heft,
With knyvis that scherp cowd scheir.

Nixt in the dance followit Invy,
Fild full of feid and fellony,
Hid malyce and dispyte ;
For pryvie hatrent that tratour trymlit
Him followit mony freik dissymlit,
With fenyeit wirdis quhyte ;
And flattereris in to menis facis ;
And bakbyttaris in secreit places,
To ley that had delyte ;
And rownaris of fals lesingis ;
Allace ! that courtis of noble kingis
Of thame can nevir be quyte.

Nixt him in dans come Cuvatyce,

Rute of all evill and grund of vyce,
That nevir cowd be content ;
Catyvis, wrechis, and ockeraris,
Hud-pykis, hurdaris, and gadderaris,
All with that warlo went :
Out of thair throttis thay schot on udder
Hett moltin gold, me thocht a fudder,
As fyreflawcht maist fervent ;
Ay as thay tomit thame of schot,
Feyndis fild thame new up to the thrott
With gold of allkin prent.

Syne Sweirnes, at the secound bidding,
Come lyk a sow out of a midding,
Full slepy wes his grunyie :
Mony sweir bumbard-belly huddroun,
Mony slute daw and slepy duddroun,
Him servit ay with sounyie ;
He drew thame furth in till a chenyie,
And Belliall, with a brydill renyie,
Evir lascht thame on the lunyie :
In dance thay war so slaw of feit,
Thay gaif thame in the fyre a heit,
And maid thame quicker of counyie.

Than Lichery, that lathly cors,
Come berand lyk a bagit hors,
And Ydilnes did him leid ;
Thair wes with him ane ugly sort,
And mony stynkand fowll tramort,
That had in syn bene deid.
Quhen thay wer entrit in the dance,
Thay wer full strenge of countenance,

Lyk turkas birnand reid ;
All led thay uthir by the tersis,
Suppois thay fyllt with their ersis,
It mycht be na remeid.

Than the fowll monstir Glutteny,
Off wame unsasiable and gredy,
To dance he did him dres :
Him followit mony fowll drunckart
With can and collep, cop and quart,
In surffet and exces ;
Full mony a waistles wallydrag,
With wamis unweildable, did furth wag,
In creische that did incres ;
" Drynk ! " ay thay cryit, with mony a gaip,
The feyndis gaif thame hait leid to laip,
Thair lovery wes na les.

Na menstrallis playit to thame but dowt,
For glemen thair wer haldin owt,
Be day and eik by nycht ;
Except a menstrall that slew a man,
Swa till his heretage he wan,
And entirt be breif of richt.

Than cryd Mahoun for a Heleand padyane ;
Syne ran a feynd to feche Makfadyane,
Far northwart in a nuke ;
Be he the correnoch had done schout,
Erschemen so gadderit him abowt,
In Hell grit rowme thay take.
Thae tarmegantis, with tag and tatter,
Full lowd in Ersche begowth to clatter,

And rowp lyk revin and ruke :
The Devill sa devit wes with thair yell,
That in the depest pot of hell
He smorit thame with smuke.

William Dunbar.

THE CITY OF DREADFUL NIGHT

Proem

Lo, thus, as prostrate, " In the dust I write
   My heart's deep languor and my soul's sad
      tears ".
Yet why evoke the spectres of black night
   To blot the sunshine of exultant years ?
Why disinter dead faith from mouldering hidden ?
Why break the seals of mute despair unbidden,
   And wail life's discords into careless ears ?

Because a cold rage seizes one at whiles
   To show the bitter old and wrinkled truth
Stripped naked of all vesture that beguiles,
   False dreams, false hopes, false masks and modes
      of youth ;
Because it gives some sense of power and passion
In helpless impotence to try to fashion
   Our woe in living words howe'er uncouth.

Surely I write not for the hopeful young,
   Or those who deem their happiness of worth,

Or such as pasture and grow fat among
   The shows of life and feel nor doubt nor dearth,
Or pious spirits with a God above them
To sanctify and glorify and love them,
   Or sages who foresee a heaven on earth.

For none of these I write, and none of these
   Could read the writing if they deigned to try :
So may they flourish, in their due degrees,
   On our sweet earth and in their unplaced sky.
If any cares for the weak words here written,
It must be some one desolate, Fate-smitten,
   Whose faith and hope are dead, and who would
      die.

Yes, here and there some weary wanderer
   In that same city of tremendous night,
Will understand the speech, and feel a stir
   Of fellowship in all-disastrous fight ;
" I suffer mute and lonely, yet another
Uplifts his voice to let me know a brother
   Travels the same wild paths though out of
      sight ".

O sad Fraternity, do I unfold
   Your dolorous mysteries shrouded from of yore ?
Nay, be assured ; no secret can be told
   To any who divined it not before :
None uninitiate by many a presage
Will comprehend the language of the message,
   Although proclaimed aloud for evermore.
                  James Thomson.

CXXVII

TO OUR LADIES OF DEATH

Tired with all these, for restful death I cry.

WEARY of erring in this Desert Life,
  Weary of hoping hopes for ever vain,
Weary of struggling in all-sterile strife,
  Weary of thought which maketh nothing plain,
I close my eyes and calm my panting breath,
  And pray to Thee, O ever-quiet Death !
  To come and soothe away my bitter pain.

The strong still strive,—may they be victors
    crowned ;
  The wise still seek,—may they at length find
    truth ;
The young still hope,—may purest love be found
  To make their age more glorious than their
    youth.
For me ; my brain is weak, my heart is cold . .
My hope and faith long dead ; my life but bold
  In jest and laugh to parry hateful ruth.

Over me pass the days and months and years
  Like squadrons and battalions of the foe
Trampling with thoughtless thrusts and alien
    jeers
  Over a wounded soldier lying low :
He grips his teeth, or flings them words of scorn
To mar their triumph : but the while, outworn,
  Inwardly craves for death to end his woe.

Thus I in secret call, O Death ! to Thee,
   Thou Youngest of the solemn Sisterhood,
Thou Gentlest of the mighty Sisters Three
   Whom I have known so well since first endued
By Love and Grief with vision to discern
What spiritual life doth throb and burn
    Through all our world, with evil powers and
     good.

The Three whom I have known so long, so well,
   By intimate communion, face to face,
In every mood, of Earth, of Heaven, of Hell,
   In every season and in every place,
That joy of life has ceased to visit me,
As one estranged by powerful witchery,
   Infatuate in a Siren's weird embrace.

First Thou, O priestess, prophetess, and queen,
   Our Lady of Beatitudes, first Thou :
Of mighty stature, of seraphic mien,
   Upon the tablet of whose broad white brow
Unvanquishable Truth is written clear,
The secret of the mystery of our sphere,
   The regnant word of the Eternal Now.

Thou standest garmented in purest white ;
   But from thy shoulders wings of power half-
    spread
Invest thy form with such miraculous light
   As dawn may clothe the earth with : and instead
Of any jewel-kindled golden crown,
The glory of thy long hair flowing down
   Is dazzling noonday sunshine round thy head.

Upon a sword thy left hand resteth calm,
　　A naked sword, two-edged and long and straight;
A branch of olive with a branch of palm
　　Thy right hand proffereth to hostile Fate.
Thy shining plumes that clothe thy feet are bound
By knotted strings, as if to tread the ground
　　With weary steps when thou wouldst soar elate.

Twin heavens uplifted to the heavens, thine eyes
　　Are solemn with unutterable thought
And love and aspiration ; yet there lies
　　Within their light eternal sadness, wrought
By hope deferred and baffled tenderness :
Of all the souls whom thou dost love and bless,
　　How few revere and love thee as they ought !

Thou leadest heroes from their warfare here
　　To nobler fields where grander crowns are
　　　won ;
Thou leadest sages from this twilight sphere
　　To cloudless heavens and an unsetting sun ;
Thou leadest saints into that purer air
Whose breath is spiritual life and prayer :
　　Yet, lo ! they seek thee not, but fear and
　　　shun !

Thou takest to thy most maternal breast
　　Young children from the desert of this earth,
Ere sin hath stained their souls, or grief opprest,
　　And bearest them unto an heavenly birth,
To be the Vestals of God's Fane above :
And yet their kindred moan against thy love,
　　With wild and selfish moans in bitter dearth.

Most holy Spirit, first Self-conqueror ;
   Thou victress over Time and Destiny
And Evil, in the all-deciding war
    So fierce, so long, so dreadful !—Would that
       me
Thou hadst upgathered in my life's pure
      morn !
Unworthy then, less worthy now, forlorn,
   I dare not, Gracious Mother, call on Thee.

Next Thou, O Sibyl, sorceress and queen,
   Our Lady of Annihilation, Thou !
Of mighty stature, of demoniac mien ;
   Upon whose swarthy face and livid brow
Are graven deeply anguish, malice, scorn,
Strength ravaged by unrest, resolve forlorn
   Of any hope, dazed pride that will not bow.

Thy form is clothed with wings of iron gloom ;
   But round about thee, like a chain, is rolled,
Cramping the sway of every mighty plume,
   A stark constringent serpent, fold on fold :
Of its two heads, one sting is in thy brain,
The other in thy heart ; their venom-pain
   Like fire distilling through thee uncontrolled.

A rod of serpents wieldeth thy right hand ;
   Thy left a cup of raging fire, whose light
Burns lurid on thyself as thou dost stand ;
   Thy lidless eyes tenebriously bright ;
Thy wings, thy vesture, thy dishevelled hair
Dark as the Grave ; thou statue of Despair,
   Thou Night essential radiating night.

Thus have I seen thee in thine actual form ;
    Not thus can see thee those whom thou dost
        sway,
Inscrutable Enchantress ; young and warm,
    Pard-beautiful and brilliant, ever gay ;
Thy cup the very Wine of Life, thy rod
The wand of more voluptuous spells than God
    Can wield in Heaven ; thus charmest thou thy
        prey.

The selfish, fatuous, proud, and pitiless,
    All who have falsified life's royal trust ;
The strong whose strength hath basked in idleness,
    The great heart given up to worldly lust,
The great mind destitute of moral faith,
Thou scourgest down to Night and utter Death,
    Or penal spheres of retribution just.

O mighty Spirit, fraudful and malign,
    Demon of madness and perversity !
The evil passions which may make me thine
    Are not yet irrepressible in me ;
And I have pierced thy mask of riant youth,
And seen thy form in all its hideous truth :
    I will not, Dreadful Mother, call on Thee.

Last Thou, retirèd nun and throneless queen,
    Our Lady of Oblivion, last Thou :
Of human stature, of abstracted mien ;
    Upon whose pallid face and drooping brow
Are shadowed melancholy dreams of Doom,
And deep absorption into silent gloom,
    And weary bearing of the heavy Now.

Thou art all shrouded in a gauzy veil,
   Sombrous and cloudlike ; all, except that face
Of subtle loveliness though weirdly pale.
   Thy soft, slow-gliding footsteps leave no trace,
And stir no sound. Thy drooping hands·infold
Their frail white fingers ; and, unconscious, hold
   A poppy-wreath, thine anodyne of grace.

Thy hair is like a twilight round thy head ;
   Thine eyes are shadowed wells, from Lethe-
      stream
With drowsy subterranean waters fed ;
   Obscurely deep, without a stir or gleam ;
The gazer drinks in from them with his gaze
An opiate charm to curtain all his days,
   A passive languor of oblivious dream.

Thou hauntest twilight regions, and the trance
   Of moonless nights when stars are few and wan :
Within black woods ; or over the expanse
   Of desert seas abysmal ; or upon
Old solitary shores whose populous graves
Are rocked in rest by ever-moaning waves ;
   Or through vast ruined cities still and lone.

The weak, the weary, and the desolate,
   The poor, the mean, the outcast, the opprest,
All trodden down beneath the march of Fate,
   Thou gatherest, loving Sister, to thy breast,
Soothing their pain and weariness asleep ;
Then in thy hidden Dreamland hushed and
      deep
   Dost lay them, shrouded in eternal rest.

O sweetest Sister, and sole Patron Saint
  Of all the humble eremites who flee
From out life's crowded tumult, stunned and
    faint,
  To seek a stern and lone tranquillity
In Libyan wastes of time : my hopeless life
With famished yearning craveth rest from strife ;
  Therefore, thou Restful One, I call on Thee !

Take me, and lull me into perfect sleep ;
  Down, down, far-hidden in thy duskiest cave ;
While all the clamorous years above me sweep
  Unheard, or, like the voice of seas that rave
On far-off coasts, but murmuring o'er my trance,
A dim, vast monotone, that shall enhance
  The restful rapture of the inviolate grave.

Upgathered thus in thy divine embrace,
  Upon mine eyes thy soft mesmeric hand,
While wreaths of opiate odour interlace
  About my pulseless brow; babe-pure and
    bland,
Passionless, senseless, thoughtless, let me dream
Some ever-slumbrous, never-varying theme,
  Within the shadow of thy Timeless Land.

That when I thus have drunk my inmost fill
  Of perfect peace, I may arise renewed ;
In soul and body, intellect and will,
  Equal to cope with Life whate'er its mood ;
To sway its storm and energise its calm ;
Through rhythmic years evolving like a psalm
  Of infinite love and faith and sanctitude.

But if this cannot be, no less I cry,
  Come, lead me with thy terrorless control
Down to our Mother's bosom, there to die
  By abdication of my separate soul:
So shall this single, self-impelling piece
Of mechanism from lone labour cease,
  Resolving into union with the whole.

Our Mother feedeth thus our little life,
  That we in turn may feed her with our death:
The great Sea sways, one interwoven strife,
  Wherefrom the sun exhales a subtle breath,
To float the heavens sublime in form and hue,
Then turning dark and cold in order due
  Rain weeping back to swell the Sea beneath,

One part of me shall feed a little worm,
  And it a bird on which a man may feed;
One lime the mould, one nourish insect-sperm;
  One thrill sweet grass, one pulse in bitter
    weed;
This swell a fruit, and that evolve in air;
Another trickle to a springlet's lair,
  Another paint a daisy on the mead:

With cosmic interchange of parts for all,
  Through all the modes of being numberless
Of every element, as may befall.
  And if earth's general soul hath consciousness,
Their new life must with strange new joy be
    thrilled,
Of perfect law all perfectly fulfilled;
  No sin, no fear, no failure, no excess.

Weary of living isolated life,
   Weary of hoping hopes for ever vain,
Weary of struggling in all-sterile strife,
   Weary of thought which maketh nothing plain,
I close my eyes and hush my panting breath,
And yearn for Thee, divinely tranquil Death,
   To come and soothe away my bitter pain.

James Thomson.

CXXVIII

WELCOME EILD

WHEN Phoebus in the rainy cloud
   Oursylit had the bemis bricht,
And all was lowne before was loude,
   Causit be silence of the nicht,
I saw sittand ane weary wicht
   Mourning and making ane dreary moan,
Whilk full soberly sat and sicht,
   " Welcome eild, for youth is gone.

" The gayness of my yearis gent,
   The flouris of my fresh youthheid,
I wat not how, away is went,
   And wallowit as the winter weed.
My courage waxis deaf and deid,
   My ruby cheekis was red as rone
Are lean and lauchtane as the leid :
   Welcome eild, for youth is gone.

" As shadow in the sonnis beam,
   Or primrose in the winter shower,

N

So all my dayis is bot ane dream,
　　And half the sleeping of an hour.
For my pleasance of paramour
　　This proverb now I mon propone,
Exempill is said as sweet as sour.
　　Welcome eild, for youth is gone.

" Ane nap is nurissand after noon,
　　Ane fire is fosterand for my feet,
With double sockis for my shoon,
　　And mittanis for my handis meet.
At luvis lair I list nocht leit,
　　I like best when I lie alone,
Now all is sour before was sweet :
　　Welcome eild, for youth is gone.

" My curland hair, my crystal een
　　Are bald and bleared as all may see ;
My back, that sometime brent has been,
　　Now crookis like ane camok tree.
By me your sample ye may see,
　　For as said worthy Solomon,
Elding is end of earthly glee :
　　Welcome eild, for youth is gone.

" O fresh youthhead of flouris green !
　　O tender plant of high courage !
Now as you art so have I been
　　As plesand and of high parage.
Youthhead have mind on age,
　　And death that closis all in stone :
Sen here lastis none heritage ;
　　Welcome eild, for youth is gone."

Anonymous.

CXXIX

[*Heine in Scots*]

THE KINGS FROM THE EAST

(*Die heil'gen drei Kön'ge aus Morgenland*)

THERE were three kings cam frae the East ;
  They spiered in ilka clachan :
" O, which is the wey to Bethlehem,
  My bairns, sae bonnily lachin' ? "

O neither young nor auld could tell ;
  They trailed till their feet were weary.
They followed a bonny gowden starn,
  That shone in the lift sae cheery.

The starn stüde ower the ale-hoose byre
  Whaur the stable gear was hingin'.
The owsen mooed, the bairnie grat,
  The kings begoud their singin'.

Alexander Gray.

CXXX

MESSAGE TO THE BARD

(*Fiosdhun a' Bhaird*)

(Translated from the Gaelic)

THE morning is bright and sunlit, and the west
wind running smoothly. The sea-sound is
slippery, tranquil, since the strife of the skies has

calmed. The ship is in her beautiful clothing and weariness will not put her to seek rest. As I found and as I saw, bring this message to the poet.

This is the crowning of that month's goodliness in which herds of cattle go to the wilderness, to the glens of the lonely hollows in which no corn is sown or reaped, meadow-bed of lowing cattle. My quota did not go up with the others yesterday. As I found and as I saw, bring this message to the poet.

Thousands of cattle are on the fields there, and white sheep on the heathery hill-tops and the deer on the barren peaks, where the floor of the wind is undefiled, their wild strong progeny wet with the dew of the moist warm breeze. As I found and as I saw, bring this message to the poet.

The plain and the rugged corries, the sea-shore and every smooth corn-land, have the virtues of the sky's warmth, as we should all wish. The wild shamrock and the daisy are on the grassy meads in bloom. As I found and as I saw, bring this message to the poet.

The swift brooks of spring-water come down from behind the hills, from clean lochs free from red scum, set on eminences far from the shore, where the deer drinks his abundance, and where beautiful is the covey of wild-ducks swimming. As I found and as I saw, bring this message to the poet.

The great reef of the sea, as ordained by ever-lasting law, is in the greatness of nature's majesty, his high head to the waves of the ocean, and with his white halo extending for seven miles of sand cast up from the mouth of the flood-tide. As I found and as I saw, bring this message to the poet.

The elements, the foundation of creation, warmth and streams and the breath of clouds are cherishing fresh herbs on which the dew lies gently when the shade of night falls as if mourning for what is no more. As I found and as I saw, bring this message to the poet.

Although the beams of the sun impart the mild-ness of the skies to the bloom of the meads, and though there is seen stock on the sheilings and folds full of the young of cattle, Islay is today without people. The sheep have put her town-ships to desolation. As I found and as I saw, bring this message to the poet.

Though the distressed and stranger wanderer came here, and he were beset in mist, he would not see a glimmer from any hearth on this shore for evermore. The venomed hate of the Saxons has exiled those who have gone from us and will never return. As I found and as I saw, bring this message to the poet.

Though there be raised Alba's army of famous repute on the field of strife, the heather banner of the men of Islay will not take its place along with the rest. Malice has scattered them over the ocean and there are only dumb brutes left in their place. As I found and as I saw, bring this message to the poet.

The inherited houses of those who have left us are cold cairns throughout the land. Gone are the Gaels and they shall not return. The cultivation has ceased ; there is no more sowing and reaping. The stones of the melancholy larochs bear witness and say : " As I found and as I saw, bring this message to the poet ".

There will not be heard the maiden's ditty, the chorus of songs at the waulking-board, nor will stalwart fellows be seen as was their wont playing the game on an even field. The unjust violence of exile took them from us, and gave the strangers the victory they desired. As I found and as I saw, bring this message to the poet.

The needy will not get shelter, nor the wayfarer a rest from weariness, nor the evangelist an audience. Injustice, Rent Exactions, and the Saxons have triumphed, and the speckled serpent lies in folds on the floors where the fine folk I knew of old were nurtured. Bring this message to the poet.

The land of Oa has been made desolate, beautiful Lanndaidh and Roinn Mhic Aoidh. And sunny valleyed Learga has only a woeful remnant on her side. The glen is a green lea land held by

men who hate, without tenantry or crop. As I
found and as I saw, bring this message to the poet.
William Livingston.

CXXXI

THE DIFFICULTIES OF TRANSLATION

(From the Prologue to the First Book of
the *Aeneid*)

LAUDE, honor, praisingis, thankis infinite
To thee, and thy dulce ornate fresh indite,
Maist reverend Virgil, of Latin poetis prince,
Gem of ingine and flood of eloquence.

.   .   .   .   .

In every volume whilk thee list do write
Surmounting far all other manner indite,
Like as the rose in June with her sweet smell
The marigold or daisy doth excel.
Why suld I then, with dull forheid and vain,
With rude ingine and barren emptive brain,
With bad harsh speech and lewit barbour tongue,
Presume to write whare thy sweet bell is rung,
Or counterfeit sa precious wordis dear ?
Na, na, nocht swa, bot kneel when I them hear.

.   .   .   .   .

And natheless with support and correctioun
For natural love and friendful affectioun,
Whilkis I bear to thy warkis and indite,
Although, God wat, tharein I knaw full lyte,
And that thy facund sentence mycht be sung

In our language as weill as Latin tongue ;
As weill, na, na, impossible were, per de,
Yet with thy leave, Virgil, to follow thee,
I wald into my rural vulgar gross
Write some savouring of thyne Eneados.
Bot sair I dread for to distene thee quite
Through my corruptit cadence imperfyte ;
Distene thee, nay forsooth, that may I nocht,
Weill may I shaw my burell, busteous thocht,
Bot thy work sal endure in laud and glory,
But spot or fault, condign, eterne memory.
Though I offend unwemmyt is thy fame,
Thine is the thank, and mine sall be the shame.
Wha may thy versis follow in all degree,
In beauty, sentence and in gravity ?
None is, nor was, nor yet sall be, trow I,
Had, has, or sall have, sic craft in poetry.

. . . . .

And thus I make my protestatioun.
First I protest, beau schiris, by your leif
Beis weill advisit my werk or ye reprief ;
Consider it warely, read ofter than anis,
Weill, at ane blenk, slee poetry nocht ta'en is.
And yet forsooth I set my busy pain,
As that I couth, to make it braid and plain,
Kepand na Sudroun bot our own langage,
And speakis as I lernit when I was page.
Nor yet sa clean all Sudroun I refuse
Bot some word I pronounce as nychbour dois.
Like as in Latin bene Greek termis some,
So me behuvit whilom, or than be dumb,
Some bastard Latin, French or Inglis use,

Where scant were Scottis ; I had na other choiss.
Nocht for our tongue is in the selvin scant,
Bot for that I the fouth of langage want,
Where as the colour of his propertie
To keep the sentence, thereto constrainit me,
Or than to mak my saying short sometime,
Mair compendious, or to likely my ryme.
Therefore, guid friendis, for ane gymp or a bourd,
I pray you, note me not at every word.

.   .   .   .   .

Adherand to my protestatioun
Though William Caxton, of Inglis natioun,
In prose has prent ane buik of Inglis gross
Clepand it Virgil in Eneados,
Whilk that, he says, of French he did translate,
It has na thing ado therewith, God wait,
Nor na mair like than the devil and Sanct Austyne ;
Have he na thank therefor bot lose his pyne,
So shamefully that story did pervert ;
I read his werk with harmis at my hert,
That sic ane book, but sentence or ingyne,
Suld be intitillit efter the poet divine.

.   .   .   .   .

Traist on na wise at this my work be sic,
Whilk did my best, as my wit mycht attain
Virgilis versis to follow, and nathing feign.
Ye worthy nobillis readis my werkis forthy
And cast this other book on side far by,
Whilk, under colour of some French strange wicht
So Frenchly leis, uneth two wordis gais richt.
I nald ye traist I said this for despite,
For me list with na Inglis bookis flyte,

Na with na bogil na browny to debate,
Noder auld ghaistis nor spreitis deid of late.
Nor na man wil I lakkin or despise
My werkis till authoreis be sic wise.

. . . . .

Bot touching Virgilis honour and reverence,
Wha ever contrarie, I mon stand at defence,
And bot my book be fundin worth sic three
When it is read, do warp it in the sea,
Thraw it in the fire, or rent it every crum.
Touchand that part, lo ! here is all and sum.
Syne I defend and forbiddis every wicht
That can nocht spell their Pater Noster richt
For till correct or yet amend Virgil,
Or the translator blame in his vulgar style.
I knaw what pain is to follow him foot hait,
Albeit thou think my saying intricate.
Traist weill, to follow ane fixt sentence or matter
Is mair practic, difficil, and mair straiter,
Though thine ingyne be elevate and hie,
Than for to write all ways at libertie.
Gif I had nocht bene to ane boundis constrainit,
Of my bad wit, perchance, I culd have feignit
In ryme ane ragmen twice as curious,
Bot nocht by twenty part, sa sententious.
Wha is attachit ontil a stake, we see,
May go no farrer, bot wrele about that tree ;
Richt so am I to Virgilis text ybound,
I may nocht flee, les than ane fault be found,
For though I wald transcend and go beside
His werk remanis, my shame I can nocht hide ;
And thus I am constrainit, als near I may,

To hald his verse and go no other way,
Les some history, subtle word, or the ryme
Causis me mak digressioun some time.

. . . . .

Beside Latin our language is imperfite,
Whilk in some part is the cause and wyte
Why that of Virgilis verse the ornate beauty
Intill our tongue may nocht observit be ;
For there be Latin wordis many ane
That in our leid ganand translatioun has nane
Les than we mynis thar sentence and gravity ;
And yet scant weill exponit ; wha trowis nocht me
Lat them interpret animal and homo
With mony hundred other termis mo
Whilkis in our language soothly, as I ween,
Few men can tell me clearly what they mean.
Betwixt genus, sexus and species
Diversity to seek in our leid I ceis.
For objectum and subjectum alswa
He war expert culd find me termis twa.

. . . . .

Bot yet touchand our tongis penuritie,—
I mean unto compare of fair Latin
That knawin is maist perfyte language fyne.

. . . . .

God wat, in Virgil are termis mony ane hunder
For to expone made me ane felloun blunder,
To follow alanerlie Virgilis wordis, I ween,
There suld few understand me what they mean
The beauty of his ornate eloquence
May nocht all time be kepit with the sentence.

Sanct Gregor eik forbiddis us to translate
Word after word, bot sentence follow allgait.
Wha haldis, quod he, of wordis the properteis
Full oft the verity of the sentence fleeis.
And to the samin purpose may apply
Horatius in his Art of Poetry.
Press nocht, says he, thou traist interpreter,
Word after word to translate thy matter.
Lo ! he repreifis, and haldis mis-seeming
Aye word by word to reduce ony thing.

.   .   .   .   .

Forgive me Virgil, gif I thee offend,
Pardon thy scholar, suffer him to ryme
Sen thou was bot a mortal man sometime.
In case I fail have me nocht at disdain,
Though I be lewit, my leil heart can nocht feign,
I sall thee follow, suld I tharefor have blame ?
Wha can do better, say furth in Goddis name.
I shrink not anis correckit for to be
With ony wicht groundit on charity,
And gladly wald I baith inquire and leir,
And to ilk cunnand wicht lay to my ear ;
Bot laith me were, but other offence or crime,
Ane burell body suld intertrike my ryme ;
Though some wald swear that I the text have
        wareit
Or that I have this volume quite miscareit,
Or threip plainlie that I com never near hand it,
Or that the werk is werse than ever I fand it,
Or yet argue Virgil stude weill before,
As now were time to shift the verse ourscore ;
Ellis have I said, there may be na compare

Betwix his versis and my style vulgair.
Although he stand in Latyn maist perfite,
Yet stude he never weill in our tongue indite,
Les than it be by me now at this time ;
Gif I have failit, baldly reprove my ryme,
Bot first I pray you, grape the matter clean,
Reproach me nocht whill the work be ourseen.
Beis nocht ourstudious to spy a mote in my ee
That in your own a ferry-boat cannot see !
And do to me as ye would be done to.

                                   Gavin Douglas.

BRAID CLAITH

Ye wha are fain to hae your name
Wrote i' the bonny book o' Fame,
Let merit nae pretension claim
            To laurell'd wreath,
But hap ye weel, baith back and wame,
            In gude Braid Claith.

He that some ells o' this may fa',
And slae-black hat on pow like snaw,
Bids bauld to bear the gree awa,
            Wi' a' this graith,
Whan bienly clad wi' shell fu' braw
            O' gude Braid Claith.

Waesuck for him wha has nae feck o't !
For he's a gowk they're sure to geck at,

A chiel that ne'er will be respeckit
              While he draws breath
Till his four quarters are bedeckit
              Wi' gude Braid Claith.

On Sabbath-days the barber spark,
Whan he has done wi' scrapin' wark,
Wi' siller broachie in his sark,
              Gangs trigly, faith !
Or to the Meadow, or the Park,
              In gude Braid Claith.

Weel might ye trow, to see them there,
That they to shave your haffits bare,
Or curl and sleek a pickle hair,
              Wad be right laith,
Whan pacing wi' a gawsy air
              In gude Braid Claith.

If ony mettl'd sturrah green
For favour frae a lady's een,
He maunna care for being seen
              Before he sheath
His body in a scabbard clean
              O' gude Braid Claith.

For, gin he come wi' coat thread-bare,
A feg for him she winna care,
But crook her bonny mou' fu' sair,
              And scald him baith.
Wooers should ay their travel spare
              Without Braid Claith.

Braid Claith lends fouk an unco heese,
Maks mony kail-worms butterflies,
Gives mony a doctor his degrees
      For little skaith :
In short, you may be what you please
        Wi' gude Braid Claith.

For thof ye had as wise a snout on
As Shakespeare or Sir Isaac Newton,
Your judgment fouk wad hae a doubt on,
      I'll tak my aith,
Till they cou'd see ye wi' a suit on
        O' gude Braid Claith.
                Robert Fergusson.

CXXXIII

IN MEMORIAM : JOHN DAVIDSON

WE watched thy spirit flickering in the dark,
Like a phantasmal lark
Fluttering on the moon ;
We knew thine ire
Like lightning on a lyre,
Like thunder in the lily throat of June.
We saw thy discontent like lambent fire,
Purple and red,
Smoking and smouldering beneath the pyre
Of Beauty widowed, and of Joyance dead.
Thou with a rapier didst reap the rose
That on Parnassus grows ;
Thou the white brow of Poesie didst scar,

Lopping her laurels with a scimitar.
So strange, so fierce, so various, so bright,
Thy wrath, thy woe, thy melody, thy light.

Sweet-bitter was thy life, and bitter-sweet,
Blown with success, and bloody with defeat,
Beloved by beauty, and oppressed with care,
Fevered by passion, frozen by despair.
Thy fervour would not wait
The seed within the sod,
The ripening of Fate,
The harvesting of God.
Thy zeal to right the wrong,
Both right and wrong down-hurled,
Wert fain by dint of song
To build a better world.

But mortised well, and founded deep,
The world's divine foundations are ;
The briny tears that mortals weep
May water lilies on a star,
And what we sow our souls may reap
Eternities afar.
To none our final doom is known,
As none our primal birth foresaw ;
Yet all things would be overthrown
By any fault, by any flaw,
By loosening of a little stone
In the great Temple of the Law.
We cannot guess, who cannot see
The meanings of Eternity ;
And all thy discontent and wrath
Were but a cobweb in God's path ;

Still moves the Mighty Purpose on
Through pain to joy, through dusk to dawn.

Wert thou a rebel grappling with the stars
That swing their swords before the Gate of
    God ;
How clashed and clanged the bolts and bars,
With hurtling of thy shoulders broad !
The round sky shuddered, and the sea
Plangent reverberated thee !
Nay, but a bird,
With futile rage,
Shrilling a tune,
Upon the moon.
Bruising thy wings against a cage,
Or a wild moth,
Most vainly wroth,
That war against the world would wage.

Life took some dust within his hands,
And made it hear and made it see ;
Love rent thy narrow swaddling-bands,
And bore thee over seas and lands
To the Pisgah of Infinity ;
Yet thou art but putrescent dust,
Blown in creation's frolic breath—
The fool of love, the toy of lust,
The dupe of Death.
Dust on a bit of spinning slag,
Belched from the furnace of the sun,
Wouldst dare to raise a rebel flag
Against the Wise and Mighty One !
Why doubtest what He has decreed ?

What man can know
What He can sow
Who brings a forest from a seed ?

Or soon or late the fiercest rebel breath
Is subjugate to Death.
Although we would escape
The grisly shape,
The visage proud and pale,
The grey forefinger with the purple nail
Pointing into the darkness, gross and thick,
Making the senses sick
And the courage quail,
Yet, be we foolish, be we wise,
Death in the end will look us in the eyes.
This is the test
Of triumph or defeat,
Of worst and best,
Of bitter and of sweet ;
This is God's arbiter we all must meet.

And yet, perchance, it was this thought, like flame,
Moved thee too soon to call upon Death's name,
To call upon his might to save or slay ;
When thou with load of glory and of shame,
With crowns of rankling thorn, and withered bay,
Thou with half-finished work, half-ripened fame,
Went forth and cursed and called him, till he
        came
In a swirl of surging waves, in a cloud of spray,
And in the deep
Gave thy hot sorrow sleep,
And in his arms carried thy soul away.

Who, who will blame thee for thy broken sword,
Or scorn thee for the discords of thy lyre ?
Thou wert a noble singer, and the Lord,
For a reward,
Filled thy wild heart with fire.
It was not strange the cold world should discord
With thy desire ;
It was not strange a soul so full of woes
Should seek repose.
We blame thee not, thy failures we forget,
Forget the seeming-weak, the seeming-wrong ;
But in our hearts there blooms and blossoms yet
The sweet, wild, poignant passion of thy song.

Ronald Campbell Macfie.

CXXXIV

LIKE THE IDALIAN QUEEN

LIKE the Idalian queen,
Her hair about her eyne,
With neck and breast's ripe apples to be seen,
At first glance of the morn,
In Cyprus' gardens gathering those fair flow'rs
Which of her blood were born,
I saw, but fainting saw, my paramours.
The Graces naked danc'd about the place,
The winds and trees amaz'd
With silence on her gaz'd ;
The flow'rs did smile, like those upon her
    face,
And as their aspen stalks those fingers band,

That she might read my case,
A hyacinth I wish'd me in her hand.
        William Drummond of Hawthornden.

CXXXV

PHOEBUS, ARISE

PHOEBUS, arise,
And paint the sable skies
With azure, white, and red ;
Rouse Memnon's mother from her Tithon's bed,
That she thy career may with roses spread ;
The nightingales thy coming eachwhere sing ;
Make an eternal spring,
Give life to this dark world which lieth dead ;
Spread forth thy golden hair
In larger locks than thou wast wont before,
And, emperor-like, decore
With diadem of pearl thy temples fair :
Chase hence the ugly night,
Which serves but to make dear thy glorious light.
This is that happy morn,
That day, long-wishèd day,
Of all my life so dark
(If cruel stars have not my ruin sworn,
And fates not hope betray),
Which, only white, deserves
A diamond for ever should it mark :
This is the morn should bring unto this grove
My love, to hear and recompense my love.
Fair king, who all preserves,

But show thy blushing beams,
And thou two sweeter eyes
Shalt see, than those which by Peneus' streams
Did once thy heart surprise ;
Nay, suns, which shine as clear
As thou when two thou did to Rome appear.
Now, Flora, deck thyself in fairest guise ;
If that ye, winds, would bear
A voice surpassing far Amphion's lyre,
Your stormy chiding stay ;
Let zephyr only breathe,
And with her tresses play,
Kissing sometimes those purple ports of death.
The winds all silent are,
And Phoebus in his chair,
Ensaffroning sea and air,
Makes vanish every star :
Night like a drunkard reels
Beyond the hills to shun his flaming wheels ;
The fields with flow'rs are deck'd in every hue,
The clouds bespangle with bright gold their blue ;
Here is the pleasant place,
And ev'ry thing, save her, who all should grace.
          William Drummond of Hawthornden.

CXXXVI

FOR THE BAPTIST

THE last and greatest herald of heaven's King,
Girt with rough skins, hies to the deserts wild,
Among that savage brood the woods forth bring,

Which he than man more harmless found and
        mild :
His food was locusts, and what young doth
        spring,
With honey that from virgin hives distill'd ;
Parch'd body, hollow eyes, some uncouth thing
Made him appear, long since from earth exil'd.
There burst he forth : " All ye, whose hopes rely
On God, with me amidst these deserts mourn ;
Repent, repent, and from old errors turn ".
Who listen'd to his voice, obey'd his cry ?
    Only the echoes, which he made relent,
    Rung from their marble caves, " Repent,
        repent ! "
                William Drummond of Hawthornden.

CXXXVII

THE LAST JOURNEY

(From *The Testament of John Davidson*)

I FELT the world a-spinning on its nave,
    I felt it sheering blindly round the sun ;
I felt the time had come to find a grave :
    I knew it in my heart my days were done.
I took my staff in hand ; I took the road,
And wandered out to seek my last abode.
            Hearts of gold and hearts of lead
                Sing it yet in sun and rain,
            " Heel and toe from dawn to dusk,
                Round the world and home again ".

O long before the bere was steeped for malt,
   And long before the grape was crushed for wine,
The glory of the march without a halt,
   The triumph of a stride like yours and mine
Was known to folk like us, who walked about,
To be the sprightliest cordial out and out !
      Folk like us, with hearts that beat,
        Sang it too in sun and rain—
      " Heel and toe from dawn to dusk,
        Round the world and home again ".

My feet are heavy now, but on I go,
   My head erect beneath the tragic years.
The way is steep, but I would have it so ;
   And dusty, but I lay the dust with tears,
Though none can see me weep : alone I climb
The rugged path that leads me out of time—
      Out of time and out of all,
        Singing yet in sun and rain,
      " Heel and toe from dawn to dusk,
        Round the world and home again ".

Farewell the hope that mocked, farewell despair
   That went before me still and made the pace.
The earth is full of graves, and mine was there
   Before my life began, my resting-place ;
And I shall find it out and with the dead
Lie down for ever, all my sayings said—
      Deeds all done and songs all sung,
        While others chant in sun and rain,
      " Heel and toe from dawn to dusk,
        Round the world and home again ".
                     John Davidson.

THE SKELETON OF THE FUTURE

(At Lenin's Tomb)

RED granite and black diorite, with the blue
Of the labradorite crystals gleaming like precious
    stones
In the light reflected from the snow : and behind
    them
The eternal lightning of Lenin's bones.

Hugh MacDiarmid.

NOTES

SUMMARY.—This, being not a complete collection of, but a selection from, the best work of the poets of Scotland, whether in Scots, English, Gaelic, or Latin, is necessarily in some degree a personal and arbitrary choice. At the same time the size of the selection has been determined by the series in which it appears, and the compiler has had to omit many poems he would have liked to include. If, however, he has only been able to draw to a very small extent on the great treasury of Gaelic song, happily, in *The Owl Remembers* (1933), the Rev. John MacKechnie and Dr. Patrick McGlynn have met the long-felt need for a better introduction to Scottish Gaelic poetry, and given, alongside the Gaelic texts, English renderings of John Mac-Codrum, Ewen Maclachlan, Cathal Macvurich, and about a score of other poets, without, albeit, over-lapping on the Gaelic poems given in the present book ; Mr. John Lorne Campbell in his *Highland Songs of the Forty-Five* (1933) has given non-Gaelic readers much useful information about the great volume of Gaelic political poetry composed between the years 1640 and 1750, along with English translations of many of these poems by Alexander MacDonald, John Roy Stewart, Rob Donn, John MacCodrum, William Ross, Duncan Ban Mac-Intyre, and others, while the Scottish Gaelic Texts Society have published (1937) Professor W. J. Watson's text, with translations, of thirty-eight of the poems in *The Book of the Dean of Lismore* and (1940) Dr. Neil Ross's *Heroic Poetry from the Book of the Dean of Lismore*, a manuscript which contains about 11,000 lines of Gaelic verse by Scottish and Irish poets, written between 1310 and 1500. It is a sign of the change that has come over the Scottish literary outlook in recent years that Mr. William Power in his admirable survey of Scottish literature, *Literature and Oatmeal* (1935), gives a full account of " the Gaelic centuries ", and that Mr. Aodh de Blácam in *Gaelic Literature Surveyed* (1929) devotes a chapter to Scottish Gaelic Literature, in which, incidentally, he does a measure of justice, in reviewing the Ossian controversy, to the European significance and great, if oblique, service to Irish and Scottish literature of James Macpherson.

If I have been unable to include more of Burns's less well known but to my mind better (since livelier and more *sui generis*) poems (all of which, and most of the kindred lyrics in the Scottish corpus, have been set to music by Mr. Francis George Scott in the five volumes of his *Scottish Lyrics*, published by Messrs. Bayley & Ferguson, Glasgow), at least I have published elsewhere (Augustan Poets' Series, 1930) a tendentious selection of Burns's poems, with a prefatory essay, showing the lines along which I think the long overdue critical revaluation of Burns's work must proceed.

In the same way, if it has been impossible to include here all the poems by the Auld Makars that might be desired, all these are happily accessible enough now in other quarters. Other landmarks in this recent process of recovery, revaluation, and reorientation of Scottish literary interest are the new editions of *The Poems and Fables of Robert Henryson* and *The Cherrie and Slae of Alexander Montgomerie*, by Dr. H. Harvey Wood ; *The Poems of William Dunbar* and *The Kingis Quhair*, by

Dr. W. Mackay Mackenzie; Miss M. M. Gray's *Scottish Poetry from Barbour to James VI* (1935); *Sir David Lyndsay, Poet—and Satirist of the Old Church in Scotland*, by W. Murison (1938), and the excellent chapter on an all-too-little-known poet, Sir William Mure of Rowallan, in Dr. Mary P. Ramsay's *Calvin and Art, Considered in Relation to Scotland* (1938). Mure is of special interest to us at this moment, when the talents of Mr. Ian White have so lately been applied to the orchestration of the lovely tunes collected by Mure in his *Lute Book*, till recently lying unpublished in the University Library in Edinburgh. Under the auspices of the Saltire Society have recently appeared, at popular prices (over 400 sets being subscribed in advance), *The Gude and Godlie Ballatis*, edited by Iain Ross, *John Knox's Historie of the Reformation in Scotland*, edited by Ralph S. Walker, *Selected Poems by James Hogg*, edited by J. W. Oliver, and *Selected Poems by Allan Ramsay*, edited by H. Harvey Wood, to be followed by *Scott's Songs*, edited by Sir Herbert Grierson, *Fergusson's Poems*, edited by A. Law, *Selections from Urquhart*, edited by Dr. Purves, and *The Complaynt of Scotland*, edited by Dr. Sharp.

While the work of the early poets, alike in Scots and Gaelic, is thus becoming readily accessible in excellent editions at popular prices, this is not the case with the work of many recent or still living poets, and the present editor would specially mention two very remarkable young Gaelic poets, George Campbell Hay and Somhairle MacGill-Eathain, neither of whom have yet published in volume form, though in a privately printed brochure, *17 Poems for 6d.* (1940), Somhairle MacGill-Eathain gives, alongside Scots poems by Robert Garioch, the opening part of his " An Cuilthionn ", a long poem (of some 2000 lines) not yet published, which is probably the greatest " poem of some length " in Scots Gaelic poetry since William Livingston's " Blar Shunadail " or the same poet's " Driod-fhortan Imhir an Racain " (both published in *The Gael* after Livingston's death in 1870), or since Donald Sinclair's (Dómhnull Mac-na-Ceardaich's) " Lá Nan Seachd ", and several times longer than any of these three considerable pieces. MacGill-Eathain gives in the same brochure several of his " Dain do Eimhir ", a sequence of some forty love-lyrics, which is also as yet unpublished. These facts are mentioned to show that Scottish poetry today, both in Scots and Gaelic, is not only in a very active state, but that big developments are imminent.

The work of these two young poets, alike in quality and quantity, perhaps heralds a new efflorescence of Scottish Gaelic poetry similar to that which marked the period of the '45. Students of Scottish poetry should also note Mr. George Campbell Hay's important essay on " Gaelic and Literary Form " which appeared in the quarterly *The Voice of Scotland*, June–August 1939, and is one of the many signs in recent years that the most significant of the younger Scottish writers today— the Scottish Vernacular Revival having been only a stage in the break-away from English, preliminary to the greater task of recapturing and developing our great Gaelic heritage—are bent upon realising William Livingston's objective which he himself defined in the following Scots quatrain :

> We see the buckles glancin'
> On his *fraochan* shoon.
> *He'll mak' the Lowlands Hielan'*
> Ere he'll lea' the toun.

The wider setting of all this is expressed by Mr. Arthur Donaldson in his *Scottish News and Comment* (February 1940) when he says : " To find a parallel to present world conditions, it is necessary to go back to that great period of the 15th to 17th centuries commonly known as the Renaissance-Reformation period. The parallels are so close that they can easily be pursued dangerously—history does repeat itself in a measure but never as a whole. Yet the conditions out of which that revolution arose were strikingly similar to the present ones. The Scotland of those centuries participated in those great events and was moved to its core. National and international changes were made which reversed the whole direction of Scottish purpose. Scotland moved into England's orbit, turned her back on Europe, threw her whole energies into the creation of England's empire. Today we stand at another like point in Scottish history, and it is more than likely that once again Scotland will reverse her course. This time she will return in large measure to her ancient policies. She will become more and more Scotland—but she will also resume her place as a European nation, contributing to and drawing upon the great stream of European thought and action."

This is the *Kulturkampf* that has been prophesied and advocated in Scottish literature in the past twenty years, as I have shown in my Introduction and Notes and exemplified in this anthology. I have written above mainly of some of our poets in Scots and in Gaelic, but our Latin poets have not been neglected in this national stock-taking and re-orientation either, and we find Dr. James M. Aitken in his *The Trial of George Buchanan before the Lisbon Inquisition* (1940) rightly claiming that " in reviewing his life and opinions from 1538 to 1550 Buchanan presents an illuminating self-revelation of the reaction of an educated and cultured mind to the conflicting ideologies of sixteenth-century Europe. His endeavours to attain a balanced judgment on disputed questions of his day in a Europe rapidly approaching the era of the Wars of Religion are not devoid of topical interest for the student of historical parallels.''

In her *John Davidson und sein geistiges Werden unter dem Einfluss Nietzsches* (Leipzig, 1928), Dr. Gertrud von Petzold, referring to one of Davidson's stories, expresses regret that he had not given us '' more Jenny Macintoshes and fewer Earl Lavenders, more Scottish heart-notes of so full and deep a resonance, and fewer super-clever London extravagances ''. And in the same way Professor B. Ifor Evans in his *English Poetry in the Later Nineteenth Century* (1933)—a volume incidentally which may be recommended specially to students of Scottish poetry, since it contains excellent essays on such Scottish poets as James Thomson (1834–1882), Robert Louis Stevenson, John Davidson, George MacDonald, Robert Buchanan, David Gray, and others—wishes, in George MacDonald's case, '' that the Jacobite ancestor could have dominated him more often and allowed him, in writing more Scottish ballads, to have grown into a greater poet '' ; '' like Stevenson, he seems, in his own tongue, to penetrate to some parts of his nature, humorous, satiric, which he can never release in English ''. And very valuable, too, is Professor Evans's demolition of the Stevenson myth : '' The reader of Stevenson's poetry before 1916 could not have guessed how much had been closed out of view. It cannot be claimed that the poems issued in 1916 and 1921 by George S. Hellman convert Stevenson into a great poet, but they show that he attempted to express many phases of his experience. An important group of poems dates from his Edinburgh days, particularly from 1871 to 1875 ; many moods arise, and in keen self-revelatory poems he explores them. . . . The unpublished work reveals, then, a poet who treated poetry much more seriously than the published work would suggest. Only a limited number of these pieces exceed in technical accomplishment the ' official ' pieces ; many of them fall below. Stevenson had to pay the price of every busy prose-writer who puts poetry on ' half-pay '. But the image of Stevenson as a poet demands that these pieces should be considered. We need not doubt that the optimistic, open-road mood was one which he sincerely felt, but it is elevated in the official poetry into a dominant, almost an all-prevailing, mood. Distress, self-reproach, poignancy, such are the themes which intrude from the unpublished work, and present us with a fuller and more human Stevenson.''

What is that but a parable of what is being done today for Scottish life and literature as a whole ? The official versions will no longer do ; our younger writers and critics and historians are at last presenting us with a fuller and more human picture,— hitherto denied us for much the same reasons that Stevenson was falsified.

P. xv. Roger O'Connor (1762–1834) was, like his brother Arthur O'Connor (afterwards one of Napoleon's generals), a member of the " United Irishmen ", and was imprisoned for several years for sedition. *The Chronicles of Eri*, his rendering of which he completed while a prisoner at Fort George in Scotland, was first published in 1822. Practically all this edition speedily disappeared, however, and may have been suppressed by the English Government.

P. xxii. '' Facts are chiels that winna ding '' and the facts are unaltered though the critic has changed his opinion, so it is worth while here to quote this passage in full : " Since English became the literary language of Scotland there has been no Scots imaginative writer who has attained greatness in the first or even second rank through the medium of English. Scott achieved classical prose, prose with the classical qualities of solidity, force, and measure, only when he wrote in the Scottish dialect ; his Scottish dialogue is great prose, and his one essay in Scottish imaginative literature, ' Wandering Willie's Tale ', is a masterpiece of prose, of prose which one must go back to the seventeenth century to parallel. The style of Carlyle, on the other hand, was taken bodily from the Scots pulpit ; he was a parish minister of genius, and his English was not great English but great Scots English ; the most hybrid of all styles, with some of the virtues of the English Bible and many of the vices of the Scottish version of the Psalms of David ; a style whose real model may be seen in Scott's anticipatory parody of it in *Old Mortality*. He took the most difficult qualities of the English language and the worst of the Scots, and through them attained a sort of absurd, patchwork greatness. But—this can be said for him—his style expressed, in spite of its overstrain, and even through it, something real, the struggle of a Scots peasant, born to other habits of speech and of thought, with the English language. Stevenson—and it was the sign of his inferiority, his lack of fundamental merit—never had this struggle, nor realised that it was necessary that he should have it. . . . The other two Scots-English writers of the last half-century, John Davidson and James Thomson (the author of *The City of Dreadful Night*), were greater men than Stevenson, less affected and more fundamental ; but fundamental as they were, they lacked something which in English prose is fundamental, and the oblivion into which they are fallen, undeserved as it seems when we consider their great talents, is yet, on some ground not easy to state, just. The thing I am examining here, superficial in appearance, goes deep."

A much more important book than Mr. Muir's, dealing with substantially the same issues, has just appeared as this anthology goes to press, viz. *The Scots Literary Tradition* (1940), by John Speirs. This is " an attempt to focus as a whole, and with regard to our present problems . . . the literary tradition in Scots ". In subject it ranges from fifteenth-century Scots poetry—the period of Henryson, Dunbar, Douglas, etc.—through the work of the sixteenth and seventeenth centuries to Allan Ramsay, Robert Fergusson, and Burns. There are chapters on the Scottish Ballads, the Nineteenth Century, and, finally, the present position. " It has seemed for long urgent ", says the Introduction, " that the cultivated, whether Scottish or English, should become more sufficiently cognisant of this tradition as being a whole, and as being something distinct from the southern. Realised as such, its powers might have a chance to become effective both as an enrichment and as a corrective."

It is a pity that Mr. Speirs, while attributing the failure of Scots as a literary medium to the absence of prose works, does not deal with the prose that has actually been written in Scots, not only in former centuries but recently. It is by no means as negligible as is generally assumed. Mr. Speirs confines himself to a chapter on George Douglas Brown's *House with the Green Shutters*. But he ought to have followed this with another chapter on the late Lewis Grassic Gibbon's (James Leslie Mitchell's) trilogy (*Sunset Song*, *Cloud Howe*, and *Grey Granite*, forming *A Scots Quair*), which is one of the memorable novels of our generation. The author used for narrative as well as dialogue a lowland Scots literary dialect which may not help the reader-over-the-Border through three volumes, and, as an English critic said, " it is at least arguable that his Joycean technique is not best suited to *our* purpose, though it worked out so well for *his* ".

Even more essential to the full story which Mr. Speirs fails to tell would have been a chapter on that Aberdeenshire classic, William Alexander's *Johnny Gibb of Gushetneuk*, which has gone through a score or so of editions since it first appeared in 1871. None of the arguments of critics like Messrs. Muir and Speirs on the alleged desuetude of the Scots vernacular prevail against the great argument for its continuance which Mr. James Leathem, in his centenary pamphlet on Dr. Alexander (re-printed from the *Transactions of the Buchan Club*, 1926), expresses when he says : " The captains and the kings depart ; but the blind beggar of Chios still sings to us in *Odyssey* and *Iliad* ; and relatively humble as William Alexander's themes and medium may both be, his work has the stamp of permanence. We still read Barbour, despite the unfamiliarity of his language, as chief authority on the Bruce ; and William Alexander will be to future centuries not less a standard of the speech and manners of the same shire when that speech and those manners will have changed even more than they have changed since Barbour's time."

This argument is put even more forcibly by Mr. W. Cumming in his preface to the Third (1923) Series of that remarkable repository of con-temporary Scots prose and verse in the Buchan dialect, *Swatches o' Hamespun*, when he says : " When we wish to soar, we mount another steed altogether, very often with disastrous results. When we wish to be impressive, we drop the couthy ' mither ' tongue, and adopt our very best English. When the point is made that no great theme can be handled in the dialect, we admit at once that it never is so used. When it is further pressed that the dialect should therefore be dropped, we demur immediately, unless our critic is prepared to urge the scrapping of all writings that do not reach the standard of great literature. And what a hole that would make in most libraries, even in yours, dear critic ! Some of our greatest favourites would go, it is feared, for do we not love some books not because they inculcate high ideals, not because the most charming language is employed, but because they portray ordinary, everyday life, ordinary, everyday men and women, truthfully and artistically ? ''

So far from Scots being dead or dying, the raciest passages in the vernacular writings of James Hogg or the writers of the chap-books can be found equalled any day in the Glasgow police courts, Aberdeen Fish Market, and elsewhere all over Scotland. It is still true of the whole of Scotland, as one of the Stewart Kings is said to have remarked —that there was a town in his realm, so large that the inhabitants in one end of it spoke a language different from the inhabitants in the other end. The pleasantry referred to Nairn. The folk of the Fishertown spoke English, or at least a variety of it. The people in the west end spoke Gaelic. That wise, if ponderous, man (as Mr. Thomas Henderson reminds us in his book *The Findhorn*, 1932) Dr. Johnson noted the same phenomenon long after the Stewarts had lost crown and fortune : '' In Nairn we may fix the verge of the Highlands ; for here I first saw peat fires and first heard the Erse language ''.

The division today is a class division. Scots is the speech of the vast majority of the working class. There has been a great loss of vocabulary, of course, but on the staple of the speech the attritions of B.B.C. English, American slang *via* the cinemas, and the influence of the educational system and the press alike, have had little effect. As Mr. George Watson, the compiler of *The Roxburghshire Word-Book* (1923), says, the really astonishing thing about Scots is not the extent of its decline but the amazing tenacity with which—and high degree to which—it retains its hold on the masses of our people.

If Scots were half as dead as is usually pretended, instead of being a singularly lively corpse and a source of extreme and endless difficulty to those charged with the task of imposing a uniform English upon us, the Research Committee of the Glasgow Local Association of the Educational In-stitute of Scotland would hardly have had to make an extensive inquiry into Glasgow speech and issue a long printed report of their findings in 1933–1934, in the course of which they say : " Too often censure was founded on the assumption that ' Proper English ' is the language spoken by Englishmen, whereas the ' bairn from Falkirk ' and the ' Glesca keelie ', on finding themselves in the same pen at Wembley with a Cockney, a Tyke, a Lancashire lad, a Stafford potter, and a Durham miner, might wonder if they had not been misdirected to the Tower of Babel. . . . In most cases Glasgow pupils enter the schools with one language only, the Central Scottish dialect, and they proceed to learn to write Standard English. As the result of education the vernacular is gradually eliminated from written work, but it persists in colloquial use." *Q.E.D.* Messrs. Muir and Speirs are wrong.

Apart from the large amount of published work in Scots in prose and verse during recent years, and the activities of the Vernacular Circles associated with the Federation of Burns Clubs, another con-clusive indication of the survival of, and unabated interest in, Scots is the great number of lexico-graphical works issued during the past few years.

These indicate no little measure of public approval and support. They include Sir William A. Craigie's *Dictionary of the Older Scottish Tongue*, the *Scottish National Dictionary*, edited by Dr. William Grant, Sir James Wilson's *The Dialects of Central Scotland* and *The Dialect of Robert Burns*. A full list would run to several scores of titles. The same tale is told by the numerous recent anthologies like the late Lord Tweedsmuir's (John Buchan's) *The Northern Muse*, Thomas Henderson's *A Scots Garland ; an Anthology of Scottish Vernacular Verse*, and Ninian MacWhannell's *Oor Mither Tongue*. The fact of the matter is that Scots is just as strong today as the dialects spoken in Northumberland, Yorkshire, Dorset, Somerset, and elsewhere, and if it fails like these to find expression in literature, literature is to that extent divorced from the life of the people. Scots still has an ample spoken basis and there is little work in Scots to-day which contains any higher proportion of little known, obsolete, or technical words than are to be found in the language written by Thomas Hardy, George Meredith, and other English writers. Writing in Scots is thus far from being an artificial literary exercise but has profound social and political bearings, and if " Synthetic Scots " is condemned today those who condemn it should remember that Burns also wrote a synthetic Scots, spoken nowhere, but drawn from divers dialects and periods of history.

Not only does Mr. Speirs give a wrong impression altogether by leaving out of account the Scots prose of Lewis Grassic Gibbon, John Galt, and many others, but so far as poetry, his main concern, goes, the picture is hopelessly defective through his failure to provide a Scots equivalent of such a book as D. Emrys James's *Odl A Chynghanedd* (Llundain, 1938), an account of the poetry columns which have always been popular in Welsh newspapers, as a means for ordinary talent to get into print. This is a kind of literary activity widespread in Scotland as in Wales, and the underground life of the Scots language in modern times and the source of its occasional upspringing into higher literary forms cannot be understood unless due account is taken of this obscure nourishing process in the popular local press and in wide sections of the working-class reading public. This is a source of the keenest interest too, and serves to maintain old ties unbroken, among many thousands of Scots abroad in America and throughout the Empire.

Among the indispensable earlier books heralding the current developments in Scottish literature are W. P. Ker's (1855–1923) *Epic and Romance, The Dark Ages, Essays on Medieval Literature,* etc.; G. Gregory Smith's *Scottish Literature* (1919), J. H. Millar's *Literary History of Scotland* (1903), and T. F. Henderson's *Scottish Vernacular Literature* (1898 ; third edition, revised, 1910).

P. xxvii. With regard to this vexed question of thinking in Scots and writing in English, Mr. Leathem, in his pamphlet on the *Centenary of William Alexander* (1926), says of Alexander: " The dialect invades his purely descriptive writing, the Aberdeenshire words being given within inverted commas, often where an English word would have served fully as well. This just means that the writer *thought* in the Doric, and found it hard to accept the terms of what was to him, after all his journalising, an alien tongue. Those who met him could see how anodyne to his nature the native words were." Mr. William Will, the late Dr. J. M. Bulloch, and, in regard to Gaelic, the late Sir Donald McAlister of Tarbert and many others, have testified to like effect, while the Research

Committee of the Glasgow Local Association of the Educational Institute of Scotland in its report on Glasgow speech (1933–1934) says : " The Central Scottish dialect is the medium of expression naturally employed by the Glasgow child, who may interrogate the teacher during a Dictation with such a question as ' Whit cums efter " after " ? ' In the playground children who try to speak Standard English are generally laughed at, whilst in the class-room a lapse into the mother-tongue is greeted with hilarity." Mrs. Virginia Woolf in her essay " Gas at Abbotsford " has fully shown the necessity and complete justification of the Vernacular Revival Movement when, writing of the Scott and the anti-Scott parties, she asks, " Is it not the combination in the Waverley novels of gas and daylight, ventriloquy and truth, that separates the two parties ? ", and tells how, in the course of one of those ghastly nights at Abbotsford, " There is Lady Scott gossiping with kind Mrs. Hughes ; there is Scott himself, prosing and pompous, grumbling about his son Charles and his passion for sport. To complete the horror, the German Baron D'Este strums on the guitar. He is showing ' how in Germany they introduced into guitar performances of martial music the imitation of the beating of drums '. Miss Scott—or is she Miss Wardour or another of the vapid and vacant Waverley novel heroines ?—hangs over him entranced. Then, suddenly, the whole scene changed. Scott began in a low, mournful voice to recite the ballad of Sir Patrick Spens :

> Oh lang, lang may their ladies sit
> With their fans in their hands
> Or e'er they see Sir Patrick Spens
> Come sailing to the land.

The guitar stopped ; Sir Walter's lips trembled as

he came to an end. So it happens, too, in the novels . . . the lifeless English turns to living Scots." This was the first objective of the new Scottish Movement—to break into real life again, and to get rid of all the false values of the pro-English " courtier school ", represented in our time by such people as the late Lord Tweedsmuir, Professor Sir Herbert Grierson, Mr. Edwin Muir, and Dr. Agnes Mure Mackenzie. The way in which critics who contend that there is no basis in speech today for literary work in Scots disregard the testimony in this connection of the poets themselves (*e.g.* Mr. Albert D. Mackie's, quoted in a subsequent note) is highly significant. " There cannot be a Scottish poetry in the fullest sense unless there is in the fullest sense a Scottish speech ", says Mr. Speirs in his *The Scots Literary Tradition* ; " what survives of such a speech among what survives of the peasantry is in its last stages and is something its speakers have learned to be half-ashamed of." This is not the case. These Scots speakers have not only clung to their speech with the utmost tenacity, but there is ample evidence of their pride in it—evidence to be found in the Doric features of the local newspapers, in prizes for essays and poems in the vernacular in the schools and universities, in the fact that so much popular music-hall work, song and patter alike, is in Scots, in the enthusiasm for the old language in the Burns Clubs and other bodies, and above all in the speech of the common people amongst themselves. Mr. W. Cumming, for example, in the preface to the 1923 collection of *Swatches o' Hamespun* says : " The following are some phrases that have actually been spoken in my presence during the past few months :

' Ye keep a lot o' hens aboot ye, smith ! '
' Oh tye ; I keep a *mardel* o' a' kin' o' craiters.'

' Dyod ! Hen'erson's fowk hiv a *leeterty* o' *smytery* o'
    craiters.'
' I wis fair lair't in *tarrymickle* clay.'
' They've got sic a *smarrach* o' geets.'
' Did ye never taste *fleeten* brose ? '
' Aw saw him *stooin*' skellach wi' a scythe.'
' Shak up the cradle *cod* ' (*i.e.* bolster)."

These are Buchan dialect, but a like richness of
surviving dialect can be reported from practically
every district of Scotland, nor is there any less in
the cities and the mining towns and villages of the
" black belt " than in the rural areas, as the work
of dialect writers in Aberdeen, Dundee, Glasgow,
Edinburgh, and elsewhere during the past few years
amply attests.

P. xxviii. See the present editor's long essay,
" English Ascendancy in British Literature ", in
At the Sign of the Thistle (1934). In " Ireland's
Contribution to the English Language " (*Studies*,
vol. xxii, No. 88) Mr. P. J. Irwin points out the
surprising fact that, apart from familiar Anglo-
Irish dialect terms, the English language, as it is
now written and spoken, contains fewer than twenty
Irish loan-words. Scottish Gaelic and the Scots
vernacular have fared no better in this respect.

P. xxx. Apart from translations, Scottish litera-
ture, in keeping with its ancient traditions, and the
superior aptitude for foreign languages which has
always characterised the Scot compared with the
Englishman, is today far more internationalist than
English literature—healthily so, and not in the
febrile Bloomsbury fashion. It imports its foreign
influences direct, and not *via* the London clearing-
house. An examination of the Scottish output
during the past twenty years shows that the most
influential foreign poets have been Rainer Maria

Rilke, Paul Valéry, Alexander Blok, Vladimir Mayakovsky, Carl Spitteler, and the ancient Gaelic poets, while among the pronounced philosophical influences are Vladimir Soloviev, Leo Shestov, Heidegger, Jaspers, Kierkegaard, and Martin Buber. English influences are conspicuously absent. In addition to the works of translation mentioned, George Campbell Hay has a great many translations from the Irish and the Welsh, and Douglas Young effects translations into Latin, French, Attic Greek, Romaic Greek, German, and other tongues, and translates from the Greek, the Russian, and the Lithuanian into Scots or English. In the same way a scrutiny of foreign literary reviews shows that during the past few years far more critical attention has been concentrated on Carlyle and Byron than on English writers. In a brilliant essay, "Byron and the Colloquial Tradition in English Poetry" (published in *The Criterion*, January 1939), Mr. Ronald Bottrall says, with reference to a stanza of Byron's full of thieves' argot, that Mr. T. S. Eliot in comparing this stanza to Burns (*vide* Mr. Eliot's essay in *From Anne to Victoria*, edited by Bonamy Dobrée) is being most misleading. "Burns was using a vernacular which was his native speech, Byron was faking a brilliant *pastiche*. What Byron has in common with Burns is not his use of a vivid vernacular, or his homely turn of phrase, but his method of familiar, ironical address, his generous regard for the common people, and his large humanity. The language of Byron was aristocratic, and though it had a great tradition behind it, this language is charged with a lower poetic potentiality than the Scots of Burns. There is thus far less explosive force in Byron's phrasing than in that of Burns, but there is an equally powerful use of the rhythms of colloquial speech." Numerous references show the indebtedness of the new Scottish Literary Movement at its inception to Norwegian writers like Henrik Arnold Wergeland, Ivar Aasen, and Aasmund Vinge and the modern Icelandic poet Jonas Gudlangsson. Much of the best work on Gaelic literature and the older Scots poets has been done by German scholars ; English scholarship has always treated these fields in the scurviest fashion. Mr. James Colville in his *Studies in Lowland Scots* says : " It must surely be the familiarity which breeds contempt which tolerates an inexact and feeble standard of scholarship where the folk-speech is concerned. There is a better spirit abroad. A favourite thesis for a German doctorate is some obscure corner of Scottish literature. Before me is a learned and exhaustive academical dissertation on the Scots-English dialect, publicly defended before the Philosophical Faculty of Lund on March 5, 1862. Another and more recent is a curious philological analysis of verbal and nominal inflections in Burns. Yet in our own educational system there is no place for such distinctively national studies." In the same way today, the best pamphlets on the contemporary Scottish Literary Movement have been those of Professor Denis Saurat in French and Dr. Reinald Hoops in German, and recent Scots poetry has been the subject of lectures in Manchester, Toronto, and Cornell Universities, but not at home in the Scottish Universities.

P. xxxiii. With reference to Herr Bringmann's contention see *The Gaelic Commonwealth*, by Fr. William Ferris (Dublin, 1927).

P. xlii.   See for this poet *Huchown of the Awle Ryale, The Alliterative Poet ; a Historical Criticism of Fourteenth Century Poems ascribed to Sir Hugh of*

Eglinton, with facsimiles and other illustrations, by George Neilson, LL.D. (1902).

P. 2. 11. The earliest extant that is to say except in Gaelic—*e.g.* such pieces as " Deirdre's Farewell to Scotland " ; " The Deer's Cry ", ascribed to the Scottish-born St. Patrick, which, however, Professor Kuno Meyer says, " in the form in which it has come down to us cannot be earlier than the eighth century " ; the splendid " Arran " from the thirteenth-century prose tale called *Agallamh na Senorach* (" The Colloquy of the Ancients "),

> Arran of the many stags,
> The sea strikes against its shoulder,
> Isle where companies are fed,
> Ridge on which blue spears are reddened.
>
> .   .   .   .   .
>
> Seagulls answer each other round her white cliff.
> Delightful at all times is Arran.

the poems ascribed to St. Columba, most of them belonging probably to the twelfth century ; " Mairg Do'n Galar an Gràdh ", composed by Isabel, 1st Countess of Argyll (*fl.* 1459), a short lyric Messrs. MacKechnie and McGlynn in *The Owl Remembers* rather too enthusiastically declare to be " among the very finest love-songs in any language " ; and the " Song of the Sea ", ascribed to Rumann, who died in 748, with its great picture :

> Wind has come, white winter has slain us, around
> Cantire, around the land of Alba.

The oldest poem in the collection of thirty-eight of the poems by Scottish authors in *The Book of the Dean of Lismore*, edited with translations by Professor Watson in the first volume of the Scottish Gaelic Texts Society's series (1937), is a description of the fleet with which John MacSween unsuccessfully attempted to recover Castle Sween, in the English interest, from the Earl of Menteith in 1310. Other poems of historical interest in the same book are a lament for Angus, son of John of the Isles, who was assassinated at Inverness in 1490, composed by Gioffa Coluim Mac an Ollaimh, and a poem on the destruction of wolves in Scotland (which was ordered by the Scots Parliament of 1427–1428).

P. 3. III. George Buchanan has been rightly styled " the best Latin poet modern Europe has produced ". In 1523 he joined the auxiliaries brought over from France by Albany, and served as a private soldier in one campaign against the English. He had courted Mary's notice while resident in France by this " Epithalamium ", and in January 1561–1562 we find Randolph, the English ambassador, writing from Edinburgh : " There is with the Quene [Mary] one called George Bowhanan, a Scottish man very well learned ", and in a subsequent letter, dated from St. Andrews, he says, " the Quene readeth daylie after her dinner, instructed by a learned man, Mr. George Bowhanan, somewhat of Livy ". Mary spoke Scottish and French, was familiar with Italian and Spanish, and so much a master of Latin as to compose and pronounce in that language, before a splendid auditory, a declamation (which she afterwards translated into French) against the opinion of those who would debar her sex from the liberal pursuits of science and literature. In the epistle to his friend Peter Daniel, the learned editor of Virgil, prefixed to his *Elegiae Silvae Hendecasyllabi*, published in 1567 (in which year he was chosen Moderator of the General Assembly of the Church of Scotland), Buchanan says : " Between the occupations of a court, and the annoyance of disease, I have . . . been prevented . . . from collecting my poems which lie so widely dispersed. But as Pierre Montauré and some other friends demanded them with such earnestness I have employed some of my leisure hours in collecting a portion and placing it in a state of arrangement. With this specimen, which consists of one book of elegies, another of miscellanies, and a third of hendecasyllables, I in the meantime present you. . . . In a short time I propose sending a book of iambics, another of epigrams, another of odes, and perhaps some other pieces of a similar description." Buchanan's all too few writings in Scots vernacular are " of such excellence as to make it a matter of regret that he did not turn his attention oftener to the cultivation of his native tongue ". Buchanan's last production was his History of Scotland of which he wrote to a friend in August 1577 : " As for the present, I am occupiit in wryting of our historie, being assurit to content few and to displease mony tharthrow ". James Melville gives a most interesting account of a visit to Buchanan in September 1581, when the History was in course of being printed. Certain obscure passages being pointed out and further clarification urged, Buchanan said : " I may do na mair for thinking on another matter." " What is that ? " asked Mr. Andrew Melville. " To die," quoth he. And he cut short expressions of fear that the manner in which he had treated certain matters might, by offending the King, delay the issue of the work, by saying : " Tell me, man, if I have told the truth," and, being assured that he had, " I will bide his feide, and all his kin's, then," said he. As Dr. Irving observed in his biography of Buchanan (1817) : " Most of the ancient writers limited their aspiring hopes to one department of literature, and even to excel in one demanded the happy perseverance of a cultivated genius. Plato despaired of securing a reputation by his poetry. The poetical attempts of Cicero, though less contemptible perhaps than they are commonly represented, would not have been sufficient to transmit an illustrious name to future ages. Buchanan has not only attained to excellence in each species of composition, but in each species has displayed a variety of excellence. In philosophical dialogue and historical narrative, in lyric and didactic poetry, in elegy, epigram, and satire he has never been equalled in modern, and hardly surpassed in ancient, times. A few Roman poets of the purest age have excelled him in their several provinces, but none of them has evinced the same capability of universal attainment. . . . His diction uniformly displays a happy vein of elegant and masculine simplicity, and is distinguished by that propriety and perspicuity which can only be attained by a man perfectly master of his ideas and of the language in which he writes. The variety of his poetical measures is immense, and to each species he imparts its peculiar grace and harmony. The style of his prose exhibits correspondent beauties." Wordsworth said of Buchanan's *Calendae Maiae* that it is " equal in sentiment, if not in elegance, to anything in Horace ". Milton translated part of the *Baptistes*, Buchanan's Senecan tragedy on the death of John the Baptist. The best biography of Buchanan is that of P. Hume Brown (1890), though it needs supplementing and correction in the light of the Lisbon Records, which had not been discovered at that time. Excellent essays on various aspects of Buchanan's life and work, and translations of some of his poems, are to be found in *George Buchanan : Glasgow Quatercentenary Studies* (1906) and *George Buchanan : A Memorial, 1506–1906* (St. Andrews, 1907). As Dr. J. M. Aitken says in his book on Buchanan's trial before the Lisbon Inquisition, " Modern neglect has too much effaced the memory of Buchanan's widespread reputation in his own time and for long after, and today he is undoubtedly less well known (at least at first hand) than any Scotsman of equal standing ", and Dr. Aitken rightly desires " a revival of interest in the life and work of one who must always remain a mighty name in Scottish literature, but who is in danger of becoming for many merely *magni nominis umbra* ".

P. 6. III. Compare what Buchanan says here of Scotland's guardianship of the imperilled muses with the following passage from Henry Morley's *English Writers* : " When darkness gathered over all the rest of western Europe, the churches and monasteries of the British island, first among the Celts and afterwards among the English, supplied, says the Danish scholar [Professor Sophus Bugge], in and after the seventh century, the only shelter and home to the higher studies ". A recent writer in *The Voice of Scotland* has expressed the hope that history may repeat itself in this connection, now that European civilisation is worse imperilled than ever before, and that the Nine may again find refuge in the North (as, indeed, St. Columba prophesied would happen " before the end of the world "). Apart from his quality as a poet and his value as an early Scottish historian, George Buchanan attracts the special interest of younger Scottish writers today because of his place at the head of the long line described by Rudolph Rocker in his *Anarcho-Syndicalism, Theory and Practice*, when he writes of " that long evolution of the concepts of political and social radicalism in England which proceeds in a continuous line from George Buchanan through Richard Hooker, Gerard Winstanley, Algernon Sidney, John Locke, Robert Wallace, and

John Bellers to Jeremy Bentham, Joseph Priestley, Richard Price, and Thomas Paine ".

P. 6.   III. *The Latin fasces and Quirinus' robe :* *i.e.* the symbols of European hegemony.

P. 10.   V. For Henry the Minstrel, or Blind Harry, see *Sir William Wallace, a Critical Study of his Biographer, Blind Harry,* by James Moir (Aberdeen, 1888), and Mr. Moir's edition of *The Acts and Deeds of the most famous and valiant champion, Sir William Wallace, Knight of Ellerslie, issued by the Scottish Text Society* (1885–1889).

P. 12.   VII. See *John Barbour : Poet and Translator,* by George Neilson (1900), and *Barbours des Schottischen Nationaldichters Legendensammlung,* von C. Horstmann (Heilbronn, 1881).

P. 18.   XI. An account and appreciation of the personality and work of Donald Sinclair (Dómhnull Mac-na-Ceardaich), who was a personal friend of his, appears in the compiler's volume of essays, *At the Sign of the Thistle* (1934).   No collected edition of Sinclair's work has yet appeared.   He was (all in Gaelic, his only writings in English being a little political journalism in the interests of Scottish Independence) a poet, essayist, short-story writer, and author, also, of several successful plays, of which the best known is *Crois-Tàra* (The Fiery Cross), an English version of the first part of which, by the Hon. R. Erskine of Marr, was published in *Voices from the Hills (Guthan o na Beanntaibh),* published as a memento of the Gaelic Rally in 1927 by An Comunn Gaidhealach, while his beautiful play, *Long Nan Og,* interspersed with delightful lyrics, was published, with an introduction on Gaelic Drama by Aonghas MacEanruig and illustrations by Stiubhart MacGille-mhicheil, by Comunn litreachais na h'Alba (Duneideann, 1927).   Much of

Sinclair's poetry is difficult owing to his use of much obsolete or obsolescent Gaelic, and many localisms of the island of Barra, of which he was a native. The translation of " The Path of the Old Spells " has been specially made for this anthology.

P. 32. XVII. " This well-known Lochaber bard, called *Iain Lom*, or *bare* John (MacDonald), was of the Keppoch family ; lived in the reigns of Charles I and II ; and was a very old man about 1710 ", says Dr. Nigel MacNeill in *The Literature of the Highlanders* (2nd edition, 1929). ". . . Macdonald was politician, as well as poet, in his day. He was a keen Jacobite, and acted as laureate of the party in the Highlands. He was the means of bringing the armies of Montrose and Argyll together at Inverlochy, where, on Sunday, February 2nd, 1645, a bloody battle was fought, in which the flower of the Campbell clan were slain. He is a poet of great fire, vigour and satiric power." Dr. MacNeill, who in the book cited avails himself of Professor Blackie's English verse-translation of this poem, says of Blackie that his " literary deftness in translation and poetic genius have successfully transferred not only the sense of, but frequently improved on, the more artless of the productions of the Gaelic muse. If the versatile Professor is not always boldly and simply literal in his versions of Gaelic poetry, he never fails to seize and attractively exhibit the spirit of the bard." The present compiler has preferred here—as in most of the other translations from the Gaelic in this anthology—to give prose renderings which are truer to the originals than such improving jingles. A good deal of Gaelic poetry is to be found in English verse renderings by Rev. Thomas Pattison (*vide* his *The Gaelic Bards*, 1866), Professor J. S. Blackie and others, but these translations have been eschewed here simply because such mechanical English versification gives no true idea of the originals and most of these translations were made at a bad period, so that it is true of them, as of the earlier English verse-renderings of Irish Gaelic poetry made by Sir Samuel Ferguson and others, that they must be replaced by harder renderings like those more recent Irish ones of Professor Bergin, James Stephens, Frank O'Connor, and others, which have replaced the inept earlier renderings made under the falsifying influence of the " Celtic Twilight " school. This process of better translation has scarcely begun yet with regard to Scottish Gaelic poetry, however.

P. 38. XXI. Writing elsewhere of Mr. Murison's book on Sir David Lyndsay (1938), the present compiler regrets that it is mainly devoted to a work of supererogation—the justification of Lyndsay's attacks on the Roman Catholic Church of his day, and, while praising the book for its thorough scholarship and excellent analyses of Lyndsay's writings, wishes it had been devoted instead to answering the question of the cause of the sudden eclipse of the wide popularity of a poet whose work was for long regarded in Scottish homes as little less important than the Bible, and still had " charms " for Sir Walter Scott ; and insists that the vital thing about Lyndsay today is the fact that he opposed great established powers, spoke to (and for) the broad mass of the working people, and, in circumstances in many ways not dissimilar to those the latter are now facing, succeeded in discharging to tremendous effect and with great historical results something very like the task to which the satirical poets and poetic dramatists of the Left are today addressing themselves in this and other countries. " Once again ", he concluded, " there is an increasing realisation of the need for tackling in our poetry the real problems of our time and for addressing the people—and, with that, a need to make the political sympathies of our literature identical with our national interests. There is also a sharper apprehension of our still unsettled linguistic problems; and together with all these re-manifestations of the ancient difficulties of a Scottish national literature, there is the general crisis of civilisation and the incommunicability to the vast majority of our people of the great new scientific ideas which have so profoundly affected our entire intellectual background. The future of Scottish poetry lies in the success or unsuccess of its address to these great problems."

P. 43. XXIII. Duncan Ban MacIntyre, the famous hunter-bard of Glenorchy, as Dr. Nigel MacNeill says, " never learned to read or write. . . . Highly cultivated some of his mental powers must have been. His memory was phenomenal; and yet there have been at all times in the Highlands men trained like MacIntyre to remember and rehearse thousands of lines of poetry. Upwards of six thousand lines of poetry composed by himself have been published. All this he carried about with him for years, along with the poetry of others, an immense mass of which he knew and was able to repeat, until the Rev. Dr. Stuart of Luss was at the trouble of taking his poems down to the poet's own dictation some time before 1768, when they were first published in one 12mo volume of 162 pages." Along with Alexander MacDonald (*q.v.*), Duncan Ban MacIntyre ranks as one of the greatest of Scottish Gaelic poets—and, be it added, as one of the half-dozen greatest poets Scotland has produced in any tongue. MacIntyre was a poet of great range—" Coire-Cheathaich " (or " The Braes of the Mist ") is almost as famous as " Ben Dorain ", and to turn to work in a very different vein, " his Address to his wife—' Mairi Bhan Og '—may be read beside the sweetest and most expressive of the Lowland lyrics ". The translation of "Ben Dorain" given here was first published in *The Modern Scot* quarterly, and the compiler expresses his thanks to Mr. James H. Whyte, the editor and proprietor of that periodical, for allowing him to republish it in this anthology. *Siubhal, urlar,* and *crunn-luth* are the designations of different *tempi* in pipe music (*piobaireachd*).

P. 63. XXVI. William Livingston is a great Scottish Gaelic poet who has never been given his due, largely because (in addition to being violently anti-English) he reverted to classical Gaelic standards in the form and themes of his work when the vast majority of his countrymen were becoming increasingly incapable of comprehension of or sympathy with poetry of this sort under the increasing influence of Anglo-Scottish education. Livingston's work is at last beginning to attract a measure of the attention and respect it deserves. " Fionn MacColla " (Mr. T. Douglas MacDonald) devoted an interesting article to it in *The Free Man* in 1932 ; the young Gaelic poet, Somhairle MacGill-Eathain, has recently been lecturing on Livingston and his poetry ; and the present compiler, in his collection of essays *At the Sign of the Thistle* (1934), gives several pages to the " Duain agus Orain, le Uilleam MacDhuinleibhe ", and says : " He [Livingston] did not write ' love poetry '. He did not address himself to any of the infantile themes on which ninety per cent of versification depends. He stood clear of the tradition which insists that the substance of poetry must be silly vapourings, chocolate-box-lid pictures of nature, and trite moralisings ; that penny novelette

love is all right, but not politics, not religion, not
war, not anything that can appeal to an adult in-
telligence. He is a splendid masculine poet, who
' put away childish things '. The irresistible verve
of his utterance, the savagery of his satire, are
abhorrent to the spineless triflers who want pretty-
prettifyings, and not any devotion to matters of
life and death." In the poem translated here, *the
three Hughs* referred to are Hugh Roe O'Donnell
(1571 ?–1602), Lord of Tyrconnel ; Hugh O'Neill
(1540 ?–1616), Earl of Tyrone, and Hugh Macguire
(*d.* 1600), Lord of Fermanagh. *Foxes* (Gaelic, *bal-
gairean*) in the penultimate line is the term of
abuse, often used by Alexander MacDonald, John
Roy Stewart, and other Scottish Gaelic poets, for
the Hanoverians. It is usually given fully as
" *balgairean Shasuinn* " (foxes of Sassenachs).

P. 65. XXVII. An excellent account of Alexander
MacDonald, and of the state of his text, together
with bibliographical and philological notes and
translations of no fewer than fifteen of his Jacobite
songs, appears in Mr. John Lorne Campbell's
Highland Songs of the Forty-Five (1933). Accord-
ing to Mr. Campbell (deriving his authority for the
statement from a remark written upon the fly-leaf
of one of the few—about twelve in all—copies of
this rare book still known to be in existence),
MacDonald's volume of poems, the famous *Ais-
Eiridh na Sean Chánoin Albannaich* (" Albannaich "
is MacDonald's spelling), *i.e. The Resurrection of the
Ancient Scottish Language*, through " the invective
he heaped on the reigning House and its supporters
gained him the enthusiastic approval of friends and
the severe displeasure of the Government. Mac-
Donald himself escaped prosecution, but the unsold
copies were seized and burnt by the common
hangman in Edinburgh market-place in 1752." As

Mr. Campbell says, " the fire and passion of his [MacDonald's] language and the extensiveness of his vocabulary are unequalled by any of his contemporaries or successors ". Mr. Aodh de Blácam in *Gaelic Literature Surveyed* says MacDonald " fought under Charles Edward, from the raising of the standard to the dreadful day of Culloden. One of the best poems was made on the day after Culloden, when he and his brother were hiding in a cave : a poem of defiance and undaunted hope. . . Songs to incite the clans, and sonorous lines imploring Divine blessing on the Jacobite swords, spears, axes, and other weapons, exhibit MacDonald as the Homer that might have been of the last Jacobite campaign. He has love-songs too, and poems in description of scenery and of singing birds that recall the genius of Old Irish. He is the most individual, the boldest, of Scottish singers." The translation given here was first published in *The Modern Scot* quarterly and subsequently issued in a limited signed edition (1935) by Mr. J. H. Whyte at the Abbey Bookshop, St. Andrews. This edition was prefaced by a short essay on the metrics of the poem by the translator. *Himself* in verse 1, line 3, *i.e.* The Chief. *To keep the tack to her windward :* the tack (Gaelic, *cluas* =ear) is the lower foremost corner of a sail. *Pilot :* the Gaelic designation here, *Màirnealach*, is a pilot chiefly for observing the weather from the look of the skies. " *Dog's tooth* " *:* broken bit of rainbow. *Shower-breeze :* the Gaelic is *fuaradh-froise* =the breeze that precedes a shower. *Fise. Faise :* sounds of tearing.

Pp. 86, 87. XXIX and XXX. Fowler's poems have been edited for the Scottish Text Society by Dr. H. W. Meikle of the National Library of Scotland.

P. 88. XXXI. John Davidson wrote in his will

that no biography of him should be published.   His
wishes have been regarded.   This is unfortunate, as
the story of his life is essential to an understanding
of what has been called " the fiery, troubled move-
ment of his work ".   The most useful essays on
his work are H. Fineman's *John Davidson, a Study
of the Relation of his Ideas to his Poetry* (Phil-
adelphia, 1916), *John Davidson und sein geistiges
Werden unter dem Einfluss Nietzsches*, Gertrud von
Petzold (Leipzig, 1928), and the chapter on Davidson
in Professor B. Ifor Evans's *English Poetry in the
Later Nineteenth Century* (London, 1933).

P. 89.   XXXII.   The *Canadian Boat Song* has been
variously attributed to John Galt, " Christopher
North " (Professor John Wilson), and others, and
an alleged Gaelic original of which the version
given here is stated to be merely a translation has
also been published.   Several books have been
written on the question.   Readers may be referred
to " *The Lone Shieling, or Boatsong of Highland
Exiles* [author unknown], transcribed from *Black-
wood* of September 1829 by Walter G. F. Dewar,
with a Musical Setting by Alan Burr, and Render-
ings in Greek Verse by Harold A. Perry, and in
Latin by Lord Francis Hervey, and a Critical
Inquiry by the last-named into the Authorship of
the Poem " (London, 1925).

P. 94.   XXXVI.   Burns   called   " Tullochgorum "
" the first of Scottish songs ".   For this poet see
*John Skinner's Songs and Poems, with a Sketch of his
Life*, by Sir Hugh Gilzean Reid (Peterhead, 1859).

P. 99.   XXXIX.   The published poems of the dis-
tinguished artist, and King's Sculptor for Scotland,
James Pittendrigh Macgillivray, are contained in
two volumes printed for the author, viz. *Bog-myrtle
and Peat Reek* (Edinburgh, 1922) and *Pro Patria*

(Edinburgh, 1915). A very large body of additional verse has not yet been published in volume form, nor have Dr. Macgillivray's reminiscences of his associations with the artists of the famous Glasgow school and with Sir Patrick Geddes and his colleagues of the Outlook Tower, Edinburgh, which Dr. Macgillivray told the present editor a year or two prior to his death he had put in order for publication. No biography has yet appeared of Dr. Macgillivray, but a long essay on his poetry is to be found in C. M. Grieve's *Contemporary Scottish Studies* (1926).

P. 132. LIX. *There was nae reek i' the laverock's hoose:* it was a dark and stormy night.

P. 155. LXXIV. Of William Ross, who died of consumption at the age of twenty-eight, Dr. Nigel MacNeill says : " Ross is one of the best known and best beloved of all the Gaelic bards. Many of his songs are highly popular." In the third paragraph of this translation, *your journey oversea under a kerchief* refers to the sartorial sign that the lady was a married woman.

P. 167. LXXX. Dr. Agnes Mure Mackenzie in her *Historical Survey of Scottish Literature to 1714* calls this poem " the greatest and grimmest satire in our literature " and says that its " subject is one that has occupied writers from the Prophet Isaiah to Mr. Noel Coward. To use a phrase that is now become old-fashioned, it deals with the expensive Bright Young Person, and one could wish that our own contemporaries, who are so fond of writing about similar types, could do so with Dunbar's force and concision. It is one of the most flaying things in literature, and of uncommon technical interest, not merely because it is the last important piece in unrhymed alliterative verse, but because of the way in which its many-coloured brilliance of decoration is made an integral part of the satire itself, made to be ' burning instead of beauty ', though it is beauty and recognised for that. It begins with the splendour of a midsummer night in a palace garden, all green and coloured flowers and glittering lights, and three lovely delicate ladies as gay as the flowers, and as exquisite. . . . They chatter of the subject in which they take most interest. There are no men about ; it is strictly *inter augures*. They are of the type for whom harlotry is a hobby rather than a profession, but skilled amateurs who make a good thing out of it. And they discuss their methods as they might their service at tennis ; completely satisfied with their own outlook as a natural and adequate view of life. Then, when they have said enough to strip themselves naked, without a word of comment we are made to visualise them again, their delicate loveliness in the rich setting. . . . There is not a word of condemnation. We simply see both the inside and the out, *together*, and that is devastating. The thing is ghastly, but superb in its kind. It makes most modern work on the subject extraordinarily thin, diffuse, and flat.''

P. 191. LXXXI. Mr. James Colville in his *Studies in Lowland Scots* gives some appalling examples of wrong glossing of Scots texts by modern editors, and the present editor in a note in his *At the Sign of the Thistle* supplements these *gaffes* with others equally atrocious from recent American editings of the Scottish Ballads, Robert Henryson, etc. But probably none has ever been perpetrated more destructive of the whole intention and effect of a poem than Dr. W. Mackay Mackenzie's when, in his edition of *The Poems of William Dunbar* (1932), he glosses " like a caldrone cruke cler under kell " in the fourth line of this poem, "' clear ' in the sense of ' beautiful ' under her ' head-dress '" What it actually means, as the context and entire method of the poem make perfectly obvious, is black as soot, like a cauldron crook, a blackness of face emphasised by her head-dress as the blackness of the chimney-hook is emphasised by its white-washed setting ; in other words, " cler " is used sarcastically and means the very opposite of beautiful.

P. 217. LXXXV. Arthur Johnstone's Latin poetry abounds in felicitous references to Scottish places and matters. He writes of the Urie :

> Mille per ambages nitidis argenteus undis
> Hic trepidat laetos Urius inter agros,

and of Bennachie :

> Explicat hic seras ingens Bennachius umbras,
> Nox ubi libratur lance diesque pari
> (" Here, towering high, Bennachie spreads
> Around on all his evening shades
> When twilight grey comes on . . .").

In like fashion he has an epigram on the small burgh of Inverury, in the neighbourhood of his birthplace, Caskieben, in which he notes that the fuel of the inhabitants (*i.e.* the peats) comes from the land in which he was born. He took his degree of doctor of medicine at Padua, where he seems to have acquired some celebrity for the beauty of his earlier Latin poems, and afterwards travelled through Germany, Holland, and Denmark, finally taking up his abode in France, where, according to Sir Thomas Urquhart, he was laureated a poet in Paris at the age of twenty-three. He remained in France for twenty years (a period during which he was twice married, to ladies whose names are un-known, but who bore him thirteen children) and returned to Britain in 1632, becoming physician to Charles I. Johnstone died at Oxford in 1641. Comparing his Latin translation of the Psalms with George Buchanan's, one critic finds that " even after the luxuriant fervidness of Buchanan, there is much to admire in the calm tastefulness and religious feeling of Johnstone, and that the work of the latter is not only a more faithful translation, but given in a manner better suited to the strains of the holy minstrel than that followed by the fiery genius of Buchanan, when restricted to translation ". " He is not ", remarks this author, " tempted like Buchanan by his luxuriance of phraseology, and by the necessity of filling up, by some means or other, metrical stanzas of prescribed and inexorable length, to expatiate from the Psalmist's simplicity and weaken by circumlocution what he must needs beat out and expand. His diction is, therefore, more firm and nervous, and, though not absolutely Hebraean, makes a nearer approach to the unadorned energy of Jewry. Accordingly, all the sublime passages are read with more touching effect in his, than in Buchanan's, translation : he has many beautiful and even powerful lines, such as can scarce be matched by his more popular competitor, the style of Johnstone possessing somewhat of Ovidian ease, accompanied with strength and simplicity, while the tragic pomp and worldly parade of Seneca and Prudentius are more affected by Buchanan." Johnstone edited the *Delitiae Poetarum Scotorum*. It is to be hoped that the tercentenary of his death next year (1941) may see due recognition accorded to a great Scottish poet hitherto sadly neglected. His full and varied life and many interesting friendships, *e.g.* with Archbishop Laud, and with George Jameson, the painter, of whose house in Aberdeen Johnstone says in one of his epigrams :

Inde suburbanum Jamesone despicis hortum
Quem domini pictum suspicior esse manu)

call for a biographical study, and this might be
diversified with translations of many delightful
poems which, like " A Fisher's Apology " (the
translation of which was made specially for this
anthology and has not been previously published),
are scarcely known even to scholars and have never
been rendered into English. Students are referred
to *Musa Latina Aberdonensis*, edited by Sir William
Duguid Geddes, LL.D., vols. 1 and 2, New Spald-
ing Club (1892–1895). A third volume of *Musa
Latina Aberdonensis*, edited by William Keith
Leask, was published in 1910.

P. 254. c. William Soutar has published volumes
of poetry both in English and in Scots. His
vernacular work is to be found in *Poems in Scots*
(1935), *Seeds in the Wind* (Poems in Scots for Chil-
dren : 1933), and *Riddles in Scots* (1937). His other
volumes include *The Solitary Way* (1934), *Brief
Words (100 Epigrams)* (1935), *A Handful of Earth*
(1936), *Conflict* (1931), and *In the Time of Tyrants*
(1939). Mr. Soutar's essay, " Faith in the Ver-
nacular ", which appeared in *The Voice of Scotland*
quarterly, June–August 1938, is one of the important
manifestoes of the contemporary Scottish Literary
Movement.

P. 259. cv. Albert D. Mackie has only pub-
lished one volume of poetry, *Poems in Two Tongues*
(1928), in the preface to which he says : " The
poet was born in Edinburgh. Scots, as you have
it here, was not his mother tongue, but neither, for
the matter of that, was English. What he spoke
from earliest infancy was a bastard lingo, com-
pounded of rudimentary Scots on the one hand,
and mispronounced English on the other, and

developing, with the aid of the Scottish educational system, into a nameless language, English in vocabulary and Doric in idiom, which he speaks (God help him) to this very day. But for the purposes of poetry he early realised he must find a language—so he proceeded to teach himself English, as Scott and his contemporaries had attempted to do, by purging his tongue of the national elements called in England 'Scotticisms'. But this process only left him with a greater regard for the separated national elements, which he now realised to form at least the rudimentary frame of another language, which came, if anything, easier to his tongue. The kind of English in which he had learned to write was not spoken by any but the rarest, most casual acquaintances, whereas he could find in the hinterland, and indeed in the streets of his own town, a whole world of people who spoke this Scots with remarkable purity. Two living tongues! One spoken in its entirety some three hundred miles from where he lives; the other a matter of no miles worth considering! He acquired a greater facility at Scots, and not only because of this propinquity, but also because of its suitability for the expression of his own un-English moods and instincts. He learned the language, it is true, dialectally—he still speaks, and tries to write, with a Lothian pronunciation—but there have accreted round this main dialect terms originally outwith it, though never incompatible with the spirit of it. This is how a dialect may become a full-sized language, and how a Standard Scots may naturally come into being."

P. 304. CXXII. See Lachlan MacBean's *Dugald Buchanan, the Sacred Bard of the Scottish Highlands, his Confessions and his Spiritual Songs, rendered into English verse, with his Letters and a Sketch of his Life*

(London, 1919), and Dugald Buchanan, *Spiritual Songs*, edited with introduction, notes, and vocabulary, by Rev. Donald Maclean (Edinburgh, 1913).

P. 315. cxxvi. The most useful and informative essay on James Thomson's life and work for readers of English is probably that in Professor B. Ifor Evans's *English Poetry in the Later Nineteenth Century* (London, 1933), a valuable corrective to the knowledge of him as author only of *The City of Dreadful Night*. Readers may also be referred to *James Thomson*, H. S. Salt (1889) ; *James Thomson*, B. Dobell (1910) ; *James Thomson : sein Leben und seine Werke*, J. Weissel; *Wiener Beiträge zur englischen Philologie*, Bd. 24 (1906) ; and to the critical introduction by Edmund Blunden to *The City of Dreadful Night*, etc. (1932).

GLOSSARY

THE more familiar words slightly disguised in spelling are not included. It is impossible to give all varieties of spelling. Further, *i* and *y* are interchangeable. The same holds of *u* and *w*.

P. 2. *fiere* = comrade. *we'll tak a right gude-willy waught* = we'll take a drink with hearty good-will. *le* = tranquillity, shelter. *ramede* = redeem.

P. 10. *dissembill* = unarmed. *weid* = dress, covering. *pawmer* = palm-tree.

P. 11. *Bowand* = pliant, flexible. *aspre* = keen, sharp. *couth* = could, did. *hynt* = took. *ae fald* = single-hearted, trusty. *stour* = conflict, dust.

P. 12. *lawtie* = loyalty. *gentrice* = noble birth. *wauld* = wielding, guidance.

P. 13. *lypning* = trusting.

P. 14. *anerly* = only, alone. *Mais* = makes. *menis* = remember, have in mind.

P. 15. *trowis siccarly* = believe firmly. *succudry* = arrogance. *covatise* = covetousness. *senyory* = mastery.

P. 21. *heill* = health. *plesance* = pleasure. *brukle* = brittle. *sle* = cunning. *sary* = sorry. *dansand* = dancing. *erd* = earth. *sickir* = sure. *wickir* = willow. *Potestatis* = powers. *Anarmit* = armed.

P. 22. *mellie* = mellay. *moderis* = mother's. *sowkand* = sucking. *piscence* = power. *strak* = stroke.

P

practicianis =skilful. *Lechis* =healers. *makaris* =
poets. *laif* =rest.

P. 23. *eik* =also. *balat* =ballad. *Anteris* =ad-
ventures. *endit* =writing, literature. *lifly* =lively.

P. 24. *quham* =whom. *wichtis* =men. *pete* =
pity. *On forse* =perforce. *remeid* =remedy. *dede*
= death. *dispone* =prepare.

P. 53. *goog* =flabby or ill-conditioned flesh.
oop =curve over or go round.

P. 91. *Archin'* =flowing smoothly. *arrachin'* =
tumultuous. *Allevolie* =volatile. *areird* =trouble-
some. *louch* =downcast. *auchimuty* =reduced to a
mere thread. *aspate* =in full flood.

P. 92. *averins* =heather - stems. *bightsom* =
ample. *aftergait* =outcome. *barmybrained* =wan-
ton. *barritchfu'* =troublesome. *attercap* =spider.
Atchison =old Scots coin. *blawp* =dull, yawning
look. *steeks* =shuts. *Fiddleton Bar* =place in
Ewesdale, Dumfriesshire. *Callister Ha'* =place in
Wauchope, Dumfriesshire. *swaw* =ripple. *Brent
on* =straightforward. *boutgate* =roundabout. *be-
schacht* =crooked. *Bellwaverin'* =uncertain. *borne-
heid* =headlong. *Brade up* =with address. *sclaffer-
in'* =slovenly. *rouchled* =ruffled. *Abstraklous* =
outrageous. *austerne* =austere. *belths* =whirlpools.
brae-hags =wooded cliffs. *bebbles* =tiny beads.
amplefeysts =idiosyncrasies. *toves* =moods. *aiglets*
= points. *gowl* =glen. *goves* =comes angrily. *Lint* =
flax. *amows* =disturbs. *abradit* =abraded. *linns* =
rocky stairway. *gowd* =gold. *begane* =decked. *jows*
= rocks along.

P. 93. *Cougher, blocher, boich,* and *croichle* =
onomatopoetic terms. *Fraise in ane anither's
witters* =run through each other. *births* =currents.
burnet =brown. *holine* =holly green. *watchet* =
dark green. *chauve* =black and white. *coinyelled* =

pitted. *aiker* =motion. *Toukin'* =distorted. *turn-gree* =winding stair. *dishielogie* =tussilago. *partan's tae* (literally crab's toe) =cutty pipe. *creel* =influence. *bauch* =dull. *Corrieneuchin'* =murmuring.

P. 94. *sumph* =stupid fool. *fraise* =commotion.

P. 95. *dowf* =empty. *dowie* =spiritless.

P. 97. *He rid at the ring* =tilted at the tournament.

P. 101. *hoysed* =hoisted.

P. 102. *lap* =leapt.

P. 103. *wap* =wind or wrap. *lang or* =long before.

P. 104. *kaims* =combs. *win their hay* =get in their hay.

P. 107. *dight* =wipe (here, wipe out). *swat* =sweated.

P. 109. *swapped* =exchanged.

P. 113. *reaving* =tearing. *bigg* =build.

P. 114. *crammasy* =crimson. *goun* =gown. *a wheen o' blethers* =a pack of nonsense. *broukit* =neglected. *bairn* =child. *greet* =weep. *haill* =whole. *clanjamfrie* =collection.

P. 115. *betrasit* =betrayed. *lift* =sky. *kye* =kine. *Whatrack* =what does it matter? *fang* =seize. *anis* =once.

P. 116. *fellon* =deadly. *rippat* =predicament. *widdefow* =fit for the gallows. *nowdir* =neither. *wallaway* =willy-nilly. *mon* =must.

P. 117. *Falset* =falsehood. *ding* =hammering sound. *the Word* =Holy Scripture. *keek* =peep, dawn.

P. 118. *paraphrases* =passages of Scripture done into metre for singing by congregations.

P. 128. *For-tiret* =wearied out. *hye* =haste.

P. 129. *knet* =twined. *bewis* =boughs. *suete* =
sweet. *jenepere* =juniper. *twistis* =twigs. *rong* =
rung. *Ryght of thair song* =rightly with their song.
copill =verse, stanza.

P. 130. *a littil thrawe* =a little time. *stent* =
stopped. *a-lawe* =down. *hippit* =hopped. *fret
thame* =adorned themselves. *makis* =mates. *playne*
= play. *abate* =halted. *astert* =rushed. *abaisit* =
abased. *takyn* =token.

P. 131. *louse* =loosen. *astert* =escape. *that
dooth me sike* =that causes me to sigh. *Why lest
God* =why pleased God. *That lufis you all* =that
loves you wholly. *So ferre I fallyng* =so far I fallen
was.

P. 132. *ingenrit* =engendered. *dauphin* =dol-
phin. *teachit* =taught. *weet* =wet. *forenicht* =
early evening. *watergaw* =indistinct rainbow. *chit-
terin'* =shivering. *on-ding* =downpour. *laverock* =
lark.

P. 135. *effeir* =bearing, ways, manners. *attour*
= above.

P. 136. *luely* =quietly. *caller* =cold. *waukrife*
= alert. *smool'd* =stole away. *daw* =dawn.

P. 141. *skaillis* =clear away. *pairtie* =partner,
mate. *Hie tursis their tyndis* =high toss their
antlers.

P. 142. *hurchonis* = hedgehogs. *fone* = foes.
freikis =men, persons. *wight* =strong. *wapins* =
weapons. *trone* =throne.

P. 143. *groomis* =young men, boys.

P. 144. *fowmart* =polecat.

P. 145. *heuch* =a rugged steep or cliff. *knop-
ping* =budding. *schill* =shrill. *roches* =rocks.

P. 146. *ingine* =wit. *Devalling* =descending.

P. 147. *fe* =sheep. *till* =to. *thou rue on me* = have pity on me. *loud and still* =openly and secretly. *My dule in dern bot gif thou dill* =my secret woe unless thou share. *raik on raw* =range in row.

P. 148. *leir* =learn. *lair* =lore. *feir* =good bearing. *do thee deir* =daunt thee. *Press* =exert. *wanrufe* =uneasy. *hale abufe* =healthy on the uplands. *tak tent* =take heed. *rede* =advise. *bute for bale* =salve for sorrow.

P. 149. *liggit* =lain. *maugre haif I, an I bide* = ill-will have I if I tarry. *steir* =stir. *reivis my roiff and rest* =robbest me of peace and quiet. *sic a styll* = such a state. *sich* =sigh. *braid attour the bent* = strode across the brake. *shent* =lost.

P. 150. *Full weary eftir couth weep* =very weary and like to weep. *till her tuk gude keep* =to her gave good heed. *Withouttin depairting* =without dividing. *whill* =until. *gestis* =romances. *Mot eke* =might add to. *firth* =enclosed land. *fauld* = open pastures.

P. 151. *janglour* =tattler. *perfay* =by my faith. *wend* =expected. *heal* =health. *as otheris feill* =as others fail. *aneuch* =enough. *Attour the holtis hair* =over the grey hills. *leuch* =laughed. *wo and wreuch* =woeful and wretched.

P. 152. *Na deeming suld her deir* =no censure should hurt her. *leesome* =lawful. *mailyeis* =eyeholes. *continuance* =continence. *fassoun* =fashion. *thôle* =endure.

P. 153. *tepat* =cape. *Her patelet of gudepansing* =her ruff of good thought. *hals-ribbon* = throat ribbon. *seill* =happiness, salvation.

P. 159. *bough - hough'd* =with crooked thighs.

hem-shinn'd =crook-shinned. *baudrons* =the cat
loof =palm of hand. *dights* =wipes. *grunzie* =
snout. *hushion* =stocking leg. *walie* =large. *nieves*
= fists. *fyle* =dirty.

P. 160. *beikand* = warming. *pleuch* = plough.
hussif-skep =housewifery.

P. 161. *but and ben* =outer and inner room of
small cottage. *snodly* =comfortably. *cled* =clad.
gaislingis =goslings. *gled* =kite. *kirn* =churn.
scum'd =skimmed. *bledoch* =buttermilk. *disjeune*
= breakfast. *hynt* =lifted up, carried. *gadstaff* =
cudgel. *soukit* =sucked. *kye* =cows.

P. 162. *loan* =lane. *rung* =stick. *red* =restore
order. *Than by their comis* =then past there comes.
brodit =pierced. *rock of tow* =distaff of wool.
loutit =stooped. *lowe* =flame. *The sorrow crap* =
devil the yield. *cummerit* =cumbered, troubled.
yirn =coagulate. *cun'd* =had experience of. *little
thank* =scant gratitude. *rout* =a heavy blow. *straik*
= stroke. *harnis* =brains. *kindling* =firewood. *mow*
= mouth.

P. 163. *knowe-heid* =hillock. *stottis* =oxen.
wraik =wreck. *mot* =might. *bruik* =enjoy. *seill* =
happiness.

P. 167. *Hegeit* =hedged.

P. 168. *in derne* =in secret. *to dirkin efter
mirthis* =to lie in wait for anything amusing.
donkit =dampened. *dynnit the feulis* =the birds
made a din. *holyn* =holly. *hewit* =of hue. *heynd* =
gracious, gentle. *pykis* =prickles. *plet* =plaited.
grathit in to =busy making ready. *schyre* =sheer.
curches =kerchiefs. *kirsp* =a delicate textile fabric.
fairheid =beauty. *spynist* =opened out. *vardour* =
verdure. *annamalit* =enamelled.

P. 169. *wlonkes* =fair ones. *ying* =young. *rewit*

= have rued, have regretted. *rakles* =reckless.
belyf =at once. *barrat* =trouble. *speir* =inquire.
chaip =escape.

P. 170. *merrens* (obscure). *fylueit* =exhausted.
feiris =mates. *larbaris* =impotent persons. *Gymp*
= neat, graceful. *gent* =beautiful. *makdome* =
form, figure. *ganest* =most suitable. *Yaip* =eager,
active. *ying* =young.

P. 171. *perfurneis* =accomplish. *forky* =force-
ful. *fure* =person. *furthwart* =forward, ready.
forsy in draucht =sound in wind. *wallidrag* =sloven.
wobat =caterpillar. *wolroun* =(probably) mon-
grel. *bumbart* =drone. *flewme* =phlegm. *skabbit* =
scabby. *skarth* =cormorant. *scutarde* =evacuator.
scart =scratch. *scunner* =disgust. *carybald* =mon-
ster. *brym bair* =fierce bear. *als* =as. *sary* =sorry.
lume =tool. *sakles* =innocent, impotent. *goreis* =
filth. *gladderrit* =besmeared. *gorgeit* =stuffed.
gutaris =gutters. *glar* =mud. *hiddowus* =hideous.
Mahowne =Mahomet, i.e. the devil.

P. 172. *sanyne* =blessing. *schaiffyne* =shaving.
schalk =churl. *schevill* =wry. *schedis* =forces apart.
hurcheone =hedgehog. *heklis* =rubs as with a
heckle. *chaftis* =jaws. *stound* =sudden sharp pain.
schore =threatening. *bogill* =ghost. *blent* =looked.
spreit =spirit. *smy* =wretch. *smake* =wretched.
smolet (obscure). *fepillis* =fidgets. *farcy* =one
suffering from that disease. *flyrit* =looks lustfully.
gillot =mare. *noy* =annoyance. *cummerans* =en-
cumbrance. *mangit* =bewildered, silly. *eldnyng* =
jealousy. *thewis* =habits. *gib* =tom-cat. *engyne* =
spirit, imagination. *trawe* =trick. *knaip* =lad. *cop*
=cup.

P. 173. *yeild* =impotent. *yuke* =itch. *daine* =
haughty. *dour* =stubborn. *pene* =penis. *purly* =
poorly. *rede wod* =furious. *buddis* =bribes. *baid*
=enduring. *bawch* =feeble.

P. 174.   *raucht the cop* =passed the cup.   *wlonk*
= fair   one.   *menskit* =honoured.   *farne* =fared.
leill spousage =loyal wifehood.   *south* =sooth, truth.
traist =trust.   *ragment* =tale.   *roust* =disturbance.
rankild =rankled.   *brist* =burst.   *beild* =festered.

P. 175.   *swalme* =swelling.   *hur maister* =whore-
master.   *hugeast in erd* =biggest   in   the   world.
lychour =lecher.   *sugeorne* =delay.   *oulkis* =weeks.
brankand =showing off, swaggering.   *curtly* =smart.
damys =makes water.

P. 176.   *fruster* =barren.   *syde* =at large.   *sege* =
talk.   *war* =worse.   *josit* =enjoyed.   *berdis one
bewch* =birds on the bough.

P. 177 =*freke* =fellow,   man.   *walteris* =tosses.
craudoune =coward.   *kenrik* =kingdom.   *tume* =
empty.   *yoldin* =yielded,   relaxed.   *hache* =ache.
swerf =faint.   *beswik* =strike forcibly.   *crabit* =cross.
tene =anger.

P. 178.   *bourd* =jest.   *swapit* =exchanged.   *pert-
lyar* =more pertly.   *plane* =complaint.

P. 179.   *schene* =beautiful.   *dispitous* =contempt-
ible.   *lyth* =listen.   *losingeris* =deceivers.   *terne*
= fierce.   *tretable* =tractable.   *turtoris* =turtle-
doves.   *dowis* =pigeons.   *stangand* =stinging.   *edderis*
= adders.

P. 180.   *hair* =hoary.   *hogeart* =obscure.   *hostit*
= coughed.   *fone* =foolish.   *cowit* =cropped.   *crynd*
= shrunk.   *slokyn* =assuage.   *goif* =gaze.   *chuf* =
churl.   *girnand* =girning.   *chymys* =mansion.   *chevist*
= assigned by deed.   *wod* =mad.   *na* =than.

P. 181.   *tuichandly* =touchingly.   *grene* =graven.

P. 182.   *lichtlyit* =belittled. *hatrent* =hatred. *wosp*
= stopper.

P. 183.   *stew* =fury.   *stoppell* =stopper.   *hals* =

throat. *wrokin* =avenged. *flyte* =rail. *fenyeit* =
feigned. *bowdyn* =swollen. *billis and bauchles*
= title-deeds and documents. *molet* =bridle-bit.
moy =mild. *renyeis* =reins. *rak* =stretch. *rif* =
tear. *sondir* =sunder. *mensk* =manliness, dignity.
cumaris =gossips. *cabeld* =haltered. *cout* =colt.
cappill =horse. *crelis* =wicker baskets. *kest* =cast.
skeich =shy. *sker* =scared. *nothir* =neither. *ganyt*
= suited. *lumbart* =banker.

P. 184. *feill* =many. *drupe* =feeble. *chalmir* =
chamber. *daynte* =esteem. *dink* =smartly. *heryit*
= harried (i.e. ruined). *pako* =peacock. *forleit* =
abandoned. *herle* =heron. *bowrd* =jest. *breif* =tell.

P. 185. *hanyt* =spared, unspent. *loppin* =leapt.
lob =clumsy. *avoir* =cart-horse or old horse.
geldit =robbed. *spulyeit* =despoiled. *feid* =enmity.
langit =belonged.

P. 186. *dyvour* =bankrupt. *dollin* =buried. *dolly*
= dreary. *blynis* =cease.

P. 187. *Kythis* =appears, shows. *yone pane dre* =
such agony suffer. *leit* =pretend. *crabit* =irascible.

P. 188. *dogonis* =worthless fellows. *Hutit* =
hooted (?). *halok* =foolish. *haldin a haly wif* =
reckoned to be a pious wife.

P. 189. *lugeing* =lodgings. *persewis* =frequents.
rownis =whisper. *ralyeis* =jest. *raiffis furght* =
break forth. *kerffis* =carves. *blenkis* =glances. *lyre*
= body, skin. *lig* =lie.

P. 190. *schaw* =copse.

P. 191. *rakit* =went. *rise* =branches. *pastance*
= pastime. *quhilk* =which. *waill* =choose. *threpit*
= insisted. *dreidles* =without fear. *elriche* =fairy.

P. 192. *Ourtane* =overtaken. *herbry* =lodging.
ailhous =alehouse. *yettis* =gates. *clour* =blow.

P. 193. *pycharis* =pitchers.

P. 194. *doolie* = mournful. *dyte* = writing, poem. *oratur* = oratory. *brast* = burst. *hecht* = promised.

P. 195. *lattit* = hindered. *beikit* = warmed.

P. 196. *ganecome* = return. *quair* = book. *lybell of repudie* = a legal document containing a written repudiation. *A per se* = paragon. *maculait* = defiled. *air and lait* = early and late. *giglotlike* = like a wanton.

P. 197. *brukkilnes* = frailty. *neist* = next.

P. 198. *hy* = haste. *responsaill* = responsibility. *outwaill* = outcast. *wyte* = blame. *forlane* = forsaken.

P. 199. *generabill* = created. *reull and steir* = govern and guide. *auster* = stern. *lyre* = skin. *cheverit* = shivered. *lyart* = hoary. *Felterit* = matted. *gyis* = dress. *flasche of felloun flanis* = sheaf of deadly arrows.

P. 200. *listis* = borders. *gair* = gore (of robe). *weir* = to ward off. *hewmound* = helmet. *habirgeoun* = armour to defend neck and breast. *bullar* = bubble. *tuilyeour* = like a man of strife. *weir* = warning.

P. 201. *Bot bait or tyring* = without halt or weariness. *feird* = fourth.

P. 203. *facound* = fecund.

P. 205. *penuritie* = poverty. *fraward* = impetuous. *belyve* = quickly. *heile* = health. *hoir* = harsh. *hace* = hoarse.

P. 206. *lazarous* = beggar. *areir* = behind. *tyde* = happening. *on grouf* = on belly.

P. 207. *lipper* = leper. *weird* = doom. *spittail hous* = hospital. *almous* = alms.

P. 208. *But meit or drink* = without meat or drink. *blaiknit* = darkened. *baill* = sorrow. *on breird* = growing springing up. *gravin* = buried.

burely =handsome. *browderit* =embroidered. *bene* =pleasantly. *prene* =pin.

P. 209. *ludge* =lodging. *waillit* =choice. *mowlit* = mouldy. *peirrie and ceder* =perry and cider. *rawk* =harsh. *ruik* =smoke. *Sowpit* =water-laden.

P. 211. *stevin* =stem or prow of boat. *plye* = condition.

P. 212. *swak* =fling. *can roun* =can whisper. *feill* =knowledge.

P. 213. *stad* =beset. *Preif* =prove. *widdercock* = weathercock.

P. 214. *taidis* =toads. *drowrie* =love, love-token. *swelt* =swooned.

P. 215. *boun* =bound, compelled. *monische* = admonish. *Ming* =mix.

P. 235. *corbies* =crows.

P. 236. *hause-bane* =neck bone. *theek* =thatch, line.

P. 256. *A daimen-icker in a thrave* =occasional ear of corn in two shocks of grain.

P. 257. *snell* =bitterly cold. *coulter* =plough-share. *cranreuch* =hoar-frost. *agley* =askew.

P. 258. *hotts* =small heaps. *truffs* =turves. *fier-cie, fleuk, wheezloch, wanton yeuk* =ailments of horses. *douce* =gentle. *canny* =kindly.

P. 259. *mowdie-worps* =moles. *Yirked* =jerked. *yirdy* =earthy. *tramorts* =corpses. *Binnae* =except.

P. 265. *rodden-tree* =ash. *teuchat* =lapwing. *craggit* =long-necked. *nabbin'* =catching. *puddocks* = frogs. *seggs* =sedges.

P. 266. *closs* =passage, entry. *kitlins* =kittens. *boss* =empty. *clawed the caup* =had to scrape the pot or bowl (i.e. gone short). *hott'rin'* =simmering.

travise =stall ; anything laid across by way of bar or partition. *baillie* =enclosure.

P. 267. *halflin* =adolescent. *futt'rat* =weasel. *bawd* =hare. *youkie* =itchy. *sough the Catechis* = blow the Catechism on his pipe. *lickit* =punished. *loons* =lads.

P. 268. *brunt* =burned. *gaberlunzie* =wallet that hangs on the loins. *gaberlunzie man* =man who carried such a wallet, i.e. packman or pedlar.

P. 270. *whang* =portion. *priving* =tasting. *minny* = mother. *Ill-fardly* =in an ugly way. *cauk and keel* =chalk and ruddle.

P. 271. *eild* =old age. *graithit* =dressed. *reiling* = bustle, turmoil. *garray* =uproar. *glew* =glee.

P. 272. *guckit* =silly. *Hopcalyo, Cardronow* = names of Scottish villages.

P. 273 *birken* =birch. *smolt* =calm. *half of the gate* =half-way. *winklot* =wench.

P. 274. *olyprance* = display. *crouse* = elated. *wauch* =wall. *lauch* =lawing, amount due. *auch* = owe.

P. 275. *heydin* =scorn. *dunt* =blow. *broggit* = spiked. *wood* =mad.

P. 276. *ourhye* = overtake. *styme* = glimpse. *girdin* =girth. *culroun* =rascal.

P. 277. *nocks* =notches, grooves. *lever* =rather.

P. 278. *stekill* =latch.

P. 279. *fippilit* =fidgeted.

P. 280. *nappy* =âle. *skellum* =rascal. *blellum* = babbler, blusterer.

P. 281. *melder* =a grinding of corn. *fou* = drunk. *swats* =ale.

P. 282. *skelpit* =slapped.

P. 283. *bogles* =hobgoblins. *houlets* =owls. *bore* = hole, chink. *usquabae* =whisky. *boddle* =a small coin (2 pennies Scots).

P. 284. *winnock-bunker* =window-seat.

P. 285. *cleekit* =linked. *carlin* =old woman. *coost* =discarded. *sarks* =shirts. *creeshie* =greasy. *hurdies* =hams, buttocks. *Rigwoodie* =bony, lean. *spean* =wean. *crummock* =staff. *waulie* =jolly. *cutty* = short. *harn* =coarse cloth. *coft* =bought.

P. 286. *hotch'd* =jerked. *fyke* =bustle. *byke* = hive.

P. 287. *fient a* =not a. *ettle* =intention. *claught* = clutched.

P. 288. *doxies* =dears. *callets* =trulls.

P. 290. *nolt* =black cattle. *herreit* =ransacked.

P. 291. *stouth* =theft. *tursis* =carry away. *spuilye* = despoil. *rock* =distaff. *Ripes* =breaks open. *kist* = chest. *ark* =box, coffer.

P. 292. *reivis* =snatches away. *wob* =web. *forfare* =perishes.

P. 294. *causay* =street. *soup* =sweep. *claggokis* = wenches. *raploch* =coarse cotton. *clekkit* = hatched. *Claggit* =mired. *howis* =houghs.

P. 295. *flypit* =turned inside out. *borrowstounis* =royal burghs, or grounds belonging to these.

P. 296. *jorum* =jar.

P. 297. *hoast* =cough. *buskit* =dressed. *cockernony* =snood.

P. 298. *cuits* =ankles. *cootie* =small pail. *Spairges* =sprays. *scaud* =scald.

P. 299. *blate* =bashful. *scaur* =timid. *Tirlin'* = stripping. *boortrees* =elder-trees. *sklentin* =slanting, oblique. *rash-buss* =clump of rushes.

P. 300. *howkit* =dug. *hawkie* =cow. *yell* =dry, without milk. *wark-lume* =tool.

P. 301. *Spunkies* =will-o'-wisps. *snick-drawing* = latch-opening. *brogue* =trick. *reestit* =smoked. *gizz* =wig. *smoutie* =smutty.

P. 302. *men'* =improve.

P. 305. *solsequium* =marigold.

P. 306. *empesh* =injure.

P. 311. *schrewis* =accursed persons. *schrevin* = confessed. *Fasternis evin* =the eve of Lent. *gallandis ga graith a gyis* =gallants prepare a play. *gamountis* =gambols. *waistie wanis* =empty dwelling. *rumpillis* =disordered folds. *kethat* =cassock. *nanis* =nonce. *trumpour* =deceiver. *gyrnd* = grinned. *Heilie* =proud. *hawtane* =haughty.

P. 312. *luche* =laughed. *Quhill* =till. *gekkis* = gestures of derision. *Blak Belly and Bawsy Brown* = popular names of certain spirits. *sturt* =disturbance. *barganeris* =quarrellers. *bodin in feir of weir* =arrayed in feature of war. *jakkis* =jackets of mail. *chenyeit* =covered with chain-mail. *Frawart wes thair affeir* =rude was their bearing. *beft* = buffeted. *jaggit* =pricked. *feid and fellony* =feud and fierceness. *lay* =lie. *rownaris of fals lesingis* = whisperers of false news.

P. 313. *ockeraris* =usurers. *Hud-pykis, hurdaris, and gadderaris* =misers, hoarders, and gatherers. *warlo* =wizard. *a fudder* =great quantity (properly 128 lb. weight). *fyreflawcht* =wildfire. *tomit* = emptied. *allkin prent* =all kinds of coinage. *grunyie* =grunting mouth. *bumbard-belly huddroun* = tun-bellied gluttons. *slute daw* =slothful idler. *duddroun* =drab. *sounyie* =solicitude. *lunyie* =loins. *counyie* =apprehension. *berand* =snorting. *tramort* = dead bodies.

P. 314. *turkas* =torture-pincers. *wame* =belly. *dres* =address. *collep* =drinking vessel. *wallydrag* = (literally) the weakest bird in a nest. *lovery* = desire, reward. *but dowt* =without doubt. *glemen* = musicians. *padyane* =pageant. *Be he the cor-renoch had done schout* =by the time that he had cried the dirge. *tarmegantis* =heathenish crew (a play here on the word ptarmigan).

P. 315. *rowp lyk revin and ruke* =croak like raven and rook. *smorit* =smothered.

P. 332. *distene* =sully, deprive of splendour. *burell* =strong, handsome.

P. 333. *forthy* =because.

P. 335. *alanerlie* =only.

P. 337. *pow* =head. *bear the gree* =carry off the pre-eminence. *bienly* =comfortably. *Waesuck* = alas. *feck* =plenty.

P. 338. *gawsy* =jolly. *sturrah* =fellow. *green* = long.

P. 339. *heese* =uplift (literally, hoist).

INDEX OF AUTHORS AND
TITLES OF POEMS

[1] Dr. H. W. Meikle, of the National Library of Scotland, fixes 1582 and 1603 as the dates between which Fowler's poems were probably written.

INDEX OF FIRST LINES

THE END